DAILY LIFE IN

THE 1960s
COUNTERCULTURE

Recent Titles in
The Greenwood Press Daily Life Through History Series

DAILY LIFE IN

THE 1960s COUNTERCULTURE

JIM WILLIS

The Greenwood Press Daily Life Through History Series

GREENWOOD

An Imprint of ABC-CLIO, LLC
Santa Barbara, California • Denver, Colorado

Library of Congress Cataloging-in-Publication Data

Names: Willis, Jim, 1946 March 19– author.
Title: Daily life in the 1960s counterculture / Jim Willis.
Description: Santa Barbara : Greenwood, an Imprint
    of ABC-CLIO, LLC, [2019] | Series: Greenwood Press daily life
    through history series | Includes bibliographical references and index.
Identifiers: LCCN 2019014138 (print) | LCCN 2019016983 (ebook) |
    ISBN 9781440859014 (ebook) | ISBN 9781440859007 (alk. paper)
Subjects: LCSH: United States—Social conditions—1960–1980. |
    Counterculture—United States—History—20th century. | Protest
    movements—United States—History—20th century. | United
    States—Politics and government—1963–1969. | United
    States—History—1961–1969. | Popular culture—United
    States—History—20th century. | United States—Civilization—1945– |
    Nineteen sixties.
Classification: LCC HN59 (ebook) | LCC HN59 .W5253 2019 (print) |
    DDC 306.0973—dc23
LC record available at https://lccn.loc.gov/2019014138

ISBN: 978-1-4408-5900-7 (print)
      978-1-4408-5901-4 (ebook)

23 22 21 20 19   1 2 3 4 5

This book is also available as an eBook.

Greenwood
An Imprint of ABC-CLIO, LLC

ABC-CLIO, LLC
147 Castilian Drive
Santa Barbara, California 93117
www.abc-clio.com

This book is printed on acid-free paper ∞

Manufactured in the United States of America

This book is dedicated to 22 fellow *Bombers*
from Midwest City (Oklahoma) High School who
died fighting the Vietnam War.

You will always be remembered.

CONTENTS

PREFACE AND ACKNOWLEDGMENTS

The longtime NBC newsman Bob Dotson often reminds us that, when you get to know someone's stories as told through his or her own articulated memories, you get to know the similarities between you and that storyteller. In a larger sense, as you see conditions that person faced and hurdles the person cleared in the iconic 1960s, you may well find parts of a road map to help you in your own challenges, inspirations, and successes in the current era. For his part, Dotson articulated hundreds of such memories in his *American Story* feature over his four-decade career at NBC. Others have noted that life amounts to a very small percentage of what happens to you and a very large percentage of how you respond to it. *Daily Life in the Counterculture 1960s* depicts conditions that Americans faced in that decade, but it also depicts how many people responded to those conditions. A lot of those stories are told through the eyes of the individuals—mostly young people at the time—who lived them. You will find many of those anecdotes (both published and unpublished) in italics, while shorter memories are often told in standard quote format.

This is the second book in the *Daily Life* series that I've written for Greenwood Press, but it's the first that examines an experience that I was a part of myself. I came of age in the 1960s, a time that historians rightly call this counterculture era in America, and it actually extended on to 1975, which the Vietnam War ended for America.

I graduated from high school in 1964 and from the University of Oklahoma in 1968. Those four years probably saw more changes take place on college campuses than ever before in the 20th century. First, in my freshman year at OU, the Reserve Officer Training Corps (ROTC) was mandatory for most male students. But by the end of my sophomore year, it was made optional. Second, in 1964, women and men students had to be locked in their dorms by 9:00 and 9:15 p.m., respectively, but men could get back out for the night at 11:00 p.m. after a mandatory study hall time. But by 1968, all dorm students were given keys to come and go as they pleased, and the first co-ed dorms were going up. Third, in 1964, dorms were managed by "counselors," and they had the right to ground students for the weekend for various offenses, including refusing to clean up their rooms satisfactorily. But a couple years later, in the wake of the federal court case *Dixon v. Alabama*, the university could no longer legally "act as parents," and counselors became "resident advisors" without authority to ground them for messy rooms. Fourth, in 1964 the university imposed public display of affection (PDA) rules on campus, meaning displays of affection were to be kept to a minimum. But by 1967, students began holding "Gentle Thursday Love-ins" on the South Oval of the campus.

I was very aware of all the dissension on campus, but I was not involved in any of the student protests, siding instead with the conservative elements at OU. I pledged a fraternity and was in the Navy ROTC all four years. Our brigade would form up at the campus armory every Tuesday afternoon and march to the drill fields, with orders to step over any war protesters who would occasionally lie down on the campus sidewalks, trying to prevent us from conducting our drills. I was conditioned by my conservative, patriotic Oklahoma culture to believe in what government leaders and the military were saying and saw no reason to change. It would be another decade before I would start seeing things differently.

With my navy chapter cut short by a hearing loss, I attended seminary for two years, thinking I would become a pastor. I had been introduced to the Christian faith by way of a campus evangelical movement called Campus Crusade for Christ, which was growing in popularity around the country in the 1960s. Deciding that a ministerial career was not a good fit, however, I deferred to my college major of journalism and began a lifelong journey as a journalist (and then journalism educator) in 1970 and covered several stories related to the protests of the Vietnam War. I began work on a newspaper in a college town near Oklahoma City and, even in that red state, there were enough student protests to keep me hopping. They mostly came in the form of staged demonstrations designed to draw out the news media at which young men might stand up and burn their draft cards while denouncing the presidential administration and the values that got us mired in a war that few people understood. I remember that often when I left the newsroom to cover one of those events, my editor would caution me "Be careful out there!" as if somehow students upset at the Vietnam War would pose a physical threat to me or other reporters. Such threats never materialized, but I appreciated my editor's concern anyway.

I was always into music and became a fan of folk music in the late 1950s and early 1960s. It was largely through hearing this music and listening to the lyrics sung by Peter, Paul, and Mary; Pete Seeger; Joan Baez; Judy Collins; and others that I tapped into the social issues of the day, including the civil rights struggle and the controversy surrounding the Vietnam War. In looking back over the decades, I believe music was more central to young people's identities in the 1960s than in any other decade since. That's the reason that an entire chapter is devoted to it in this book.

The same is true for the way in which movies reflected the tumult of the decade. The 1960s was a decade of experimentation, on both a societal and individual level, and the films of that era mirrored these experiments and pushed the boundaries forward even beyond what society was doing at the time. Early in the decade, screen depictions of racial tensions were surfacing and forming the context of *West Side Story*. Race would be at the center of other key films of the decade like *In the Heat of the Night* and *Guess Who's Coming to Dinner*. The preoccupation with drugs would appear in several films, most notably *Easy Rider*. The "free love" movement would be depicted in films like *Bob & Carol & Ted & Alice* and *The Graduate*, the film that would help define young people in the 1960s. Another chapter in this book looks at the role these and other movies played.

Like these chapters, others in the book are focused around the issues that made the decade what it was: protest movements, politics, drugs, military life (especially since every eligible young man 18 and above was subject to a military draft), religion, intellectualism, economics, and how individuals and families tried to live ordinary domestic lives in the midst of all this upheaval and change.

I would like to thank those who contributed their own memories of the decade, because the intent of the book is to present much of the story of the 1960s through the memories of people who lived through these years as young people. I will drop in my own memories of a particular slice of 1960s life. But the key memories are provided by others, and they include the following veterans of the counterculture decade: Richard Cheek, Roger Brady, Margaret Palmer Hellwege, Marti Watson Garlett, David Esselstrom, Ray McCormick, Otis Sanford, A. David Landsperger, John Shutkin, John Unger Zussman, Patricia Zussman, Charles Degelman, Suzy Underwood, Steve England, Mary Kay Havens, Mary Clem Good Morris, Judy Chrisope Porter, Lydia Lee, Ginger Bate, Tom Nenon, Joseph Bogan, Jene Cheek, Alan Rifkin, Betty Briggs, Kathleen Woodruff Wickham, Judy Chrisope Porter, Carol King and Diana Glyer. The 1960s was such an iconic decade that many people are still reminiscing in print, on TV, and in the social media about their experiences, and some of those are also included in the chapters.

Of special note are the website Myretrospect.com and its cofounders John and Patricia Zussman and Susan Hansen. Some of the longer anecdotes in this book come from seven contributors to that site, and their names are included in those just listed. I am grateful for both their permissions to use their stories as well as to John and Patricia Zussman for their concurrence. Retrospect is a wonderful repository of stories from some gifted writers about what the 1960s, 1970s, and 1980s meant to them, and I encourage everyone to check it out and to contribute their own memories.

A word about the formatting in these chapters: as noted earlier, I have chosen to put many of the anecdotes—especially the longer ones—in italics, without open or closed quotes, to help them stand out from the background narrative about the decade and to make them a little more free-flowing and easier to read. Shorter anecdotes and memories are put into normal direct quote style. In most cases, persons offering their memories are identified, but, in some cases, they have requested anonymity.

Finally, as always, I would like to thank my wife Anne for her everlasting patience and guidance at times when I've gotten stuck in a particular passage or piece of time of this tumultuous decade. As a scholar herself, her advice is always sound. And as a gifted musician, she has sometimes provided a pleasing soundtrack at the piano for me as I have secluded myself in my study. She is the kind of spouse every writer wishes they could have, and I'm grateful for her every day.

INTRODUCTION

THE ROOTS OF THE COUNTERCULTURE MOVEMENT

If you were growing up in the late 1950s and early 1960s, a must-see comedy series with a telling undertow was *The Many Loves of Dobie Gillis*. Created by the gifted author and screenwriter Max Shulman who often wrote satirical comedies that addressed societal trends, *Dobie Gillis* was an important introduction to the so-called counterculture era of the later 1960s and early 1970s. Not only was it the first major-network series featuring a teenage cast, but it also dealt with the counterculture movement of the 1950s known as the Beat generation or, more simply, the beatniks.

The tongue-in-cheek series took place in a small midwestern city and centered around a trio of different characters who would all represent elements of the counterculture movement to follow. Dobie Gillis himself was a white middle-class teenager, somewhat bored with his suburban lifestyle, who was looking for something more meaningful and finding it in teenage girls. In the midst of his many affairs, however, he always seemed in search of something more as each week's episode would find him sitting in the city park beneath Rodin's statue of *The Thinker*. He struck the same hunched-over pose, chin resting on his fist, pondering the meaning of his life. The motif was somewhat ironic, given that Dobie was not a good student in high school and lived more for weekend life. His sidekick was Maynard G. Krebs, a fellow student at Central High with a different take on life. Maynard was a confirmed bongo drum-playing beatnik with a Van Dyke beard sans the moustache. Krebs loved jazz music, avoided girls—whom he found too mysterious—and also avoided work at all costs. His thoughts of what the "good life" constituted were summed up by whatever the status quo was not. Always clad in a short-sleeved sweatshirt, Maynard rejoiced in being different.

Added to this male duo was the female lead, Zelda Gilroy, who was the true intellectual of the trio and usually smarter about life than either Dobie or Maynard. Despite not being blessed with the good looks of Dobie's many loves, Zelda became a confidant and near-constant companion, and these three characters would become as close as Jerry, Elaine, George, and Kramer on the series *Seinfeld*, three decades later.

Dobie Gillis aired for 147 episodes between 1959 and 1963 and opened the door to a new television perspective on America's younger generation. It came on the heels of other popular family sitcoms like *Father Knows Best*, *Make Room for Daddy*, and *The Adventures of Ozzie & Harriet*, all of which viewed the teenage years through the portal of their parents and which seldom—if ever—questioned or poked fun at traditional values in society. *The Many Loves of Dobie Gillis* was not afraid to do just that, and Maynard G. Krebs became the most popular of the lead characters on the show, rising from what was originally intended as a supporting role. Clearly his counterculture perspective resonated with many young people in America, several years before the protesters of the following decade took center stage.

It is important to remember what came before the counterculture era of the 1960s, which, most historians believe, started about 1965 and carried on until 1975. Up until the mid-1960s, the country seemed to live in a period characterized more by post–World War II normalcy. There were obvious exceptions to a worry-free life, however. There was the concern over Russia and the Soviet Union and the specter of a nuclear war. Schools were holding "duck-and-cover" drills for students, and people were building below-ground fallout shelters they mistakenly thought would protect them from nuclear waste. And, in November 1963, the country was jarred awake by the assassination of popular president John F. Kennedy in the streets of Dallas, Texas. Also by that year, America was becoming more concerned about a place called Vietnam and American military "advisors" who had been going there to help South Vietnam defend itself from communist North Vietnam.

Then, starting on November 14, 1965, those American fighters in Vietnam became more than advisors and became full-fledged soldiers in combat as 1,000 soldiers of the Seventh Calvary Unit faced off against 2,500 battle-hardened North Vietnamese soldiers in the Ia Drang Valley. Hundreds of U.S. soldiers lost their lives during the four days of fighting. America was now involved, big-time, in Vietnam, and the numbers of American troops there would grow geometrically in the coming months and years.

After that, the Vietnam War became the main flash point of the era and the main (but not the only) target of counterculture protest and wrath. The latter-day version of the beatniks was the hippies, and those who identified with that movement did so because of their own Maynard G. Krebs-like distrust of society's norms.

Adding to the intense passions shown by those young men in the counterculture movement was the fact that all those between the ages of 18 and 35 who had not already served in the military were facing the threat of the mandatory draft that was then in effect. The specter of taking two years out of one's life to join the military and serve half of it fighting in Vietnam was more than enough incentive to get your attention. Added to that was the heartfelt belief by many young people that this was the wrong war for America to be involved in. The reasons for involvement made no sense to them.

But many historians feel you need to turn the dial back much further in American history to see how the counterculture movement has always been a part of the country's profile. How far to turn that dial back? Try the days of Ralph Waldo Emerson and Henry David Thoreau. Back to the time when both men began speaking and writing about the peace that comes from shunning worldly possessions and instead embracing the simple things in life and nature. For these were the same thoughts permeating the hippies of the 1960s and 1970s. Yet they were written a century earlier, still to be found in writings like Emerson or Thoreau.

Emerson wrote:

- "We are always getting ready to live, but never living."
- "Money often costs too much."
- "To be yourself in a world that is constantly trying to make you into something else is the greatest accomplishment."

Thoreau wrote in *Walden*:

- "A man is rich in proportion to the number of things which he can afford to let alone."
- "For my greatest skill has been to want but little."
- "I went to the woods because I wished to live deliberately, to front only the essential facts of life, and see if I could not learn what it had to teach, and not, when I came to die, discover that I had not lived."
- "The mass of men lead lives of quiet desperation."

Any or all of these thoughts were probably uttered, either verbatim or in paraphrased form, by followers of the counterculture movement of the 1960s. And surely as hippie communes were springing up around America, they drew inspiration from the 19th-century farming commune visited by transcendentalists like Emerson and famed New York newspaper editor Arthur Brisbane. The commune was founded by Unitarian minister George Ripley and his wife Sophia Dana Ripley. They called it Brook Farm, and it covered 175 acres just outside of Boston, in West Roxbury. This experiment in communal living, where intellectual introspection was matched with manual farm labor in a socialist environment of sharing among its members, lasted from 1841 through 1847.

When I think of each of the final quotes noted earlier from Emerson and Thoreau, however, I picture Ben Braddock, the leading character from the 1967 classic film, *The Graduate*, which was the signature film for the baby boomer generation as they were finishing college just as the counterculture movement got under way. When Ben was suffering through the college graduation party his upper-class parents were throwing for him at the start of the film, he personified both Emerson and Thoreau in his exasperation. When he was chafing at the suggestion by his dad's business friend, Mr. Robinson, that he would find success by entering the field of *plastics*, surely we could hear Thoreau whispering in Ben's ear, "To be yourself in a world that is constantly trying to make you into something else is the greatest accomplishment." That one line from the script also made *plastic* the embodiment of the establishment world to the counterculture revolutionaries of the 1960s. And when Ben donned his new scuba gear and used it to dive to the bottom of the backyard pool and escape the throngs of his parents' friends high above, we could hear Thoreau whispering, "The mass of men lead lives of quiet desperation."

The point is that the young people who became the leaders and followers of the counterculture decade of 1965–1975 did not simply just appear on the scene one day, ready to do battle with traditional American society, its norms, and values. The stage had been set for them, not only in the previous decade but also in the previous century by others who chose to blaze new trails because they found the old ones were leading them into denser thickets. And yet there was something special and different about this decade-long protest that came to embrace so much of America and infuse an identity into a generation like few—if any other—decades have done in American history. Virtually every aspect of life was touched by this counterculture decade: from politics to music, from war to peace, from authority to equality, from discrimination to civil rights, from literature to film, from business to pleasure, from love to hate. All these and other aspects of American life went under the microscope between 1965 and 1975. And the legacy of these years has left a lasting imprint on America.

There has never been another decade like it.

TIMELINE OF EVENTS

It is hard to imagine a decade that had so much packed into it as did the 1960s. From the first man in space to a presidential assassination, to the start of a 10-year war to the birth of the counterculture and hippie movements to nationwide protests over that war and civil rights, to the passage of national civil rights and voting rights legislation, to the assassination of the country's preeminent civil rights leader to the first man from Earth landing on the moon, the 1960s had it all. This timeline lays out the most significant of these events.

1960   A group of students stages a sit-in against segregation at the Woolworths lunch counter in Greensboro, North Carolina, on February 1. The event triggers national interest in the evolving civil rights movement.

An American U2 spy plane, piloted by Francis Gary Powers, is shot down over Russia on May 1 by the Soviet Union, and Powers is detained for what would be two years. Cold War tensions increase.

The September 26 debate between presidential candidates Richard M. Nixon and John F. Kennedy becomes the first televised presidential debate in history.

John F. Kennedy wins the November 8 presidential election, becoming the first Roman Catholic to hold the office, in the tightest vote count since 1884.

A joint fighting force of insurgents and communists arises in South Vietnam in December, and the United States takes notice and calls this force the Viet Cong.

The first birth control pill is developed in December, enabling the sexual revolution of sex without babies to take shape over the decade.

1961   Bob Dylan stages his first billed appearance on April 11 and will go on to become one of the leading protest singers of the decade.

A CIA-led invasion in April in the Cuban Bay of Pigs fails to overthrow the communist leader Fidel Castro, and it proves an international embarrassment for the United States.

A group of "Freedom Riders" leaves Washington, D.C., on May 4 on buses to make various stops in the South to speak out for the civil rights movement.

Astronaut Alan Shepard becomes the first American to venture into space, with his suborbital mission launched successfully on May 5. The race to the moon is on.

Federal Communications Commission chair Newton Minow criticizes television executives in his "Vast Wasteland" speech on May 9 for a failure to use TV to serve the public interest.

1962   Astronaut John Glenn becomes the first American to orbit Earth on February 22.

Author Rachel Carson publishes *Silent Spring*, the first modern-day book to make the case for protecting the environment. Many date the start of the "green movement" to Carson's book.

The first national convention of the Students for a Democratic Society (SDS) is held in June, wherein the SDS issues its manifesto that came to be known as the *Port Huron Statement*.

In October, African American student James Meredith registers at the University of Mississippi, breaking that school's color barrier.

In October, President John F. Kennedy faces down the Soviet Union in the Cuban Missile Crisis, as the world sits perched on the edge of nuclear war precipitated by a U.S.-Soviet confrontation in the waters off Cuba.

1963   Betty Friedan authors *The Feminine Mystique* and ushers in the modern-day women's rights movement with her critique of women's roles in society.

Rev. Martin Luther King delivers his stirring "I Have a Dream" speech in Washington, D.C., on August 28 to a crowd estimated at 250,000 people. It becomes a landmark event in the civil rights movement.

Vatican II begins on October 11, called by Pope John XXIII. Its council sessions will cover two years and will change the Catholic Church, bringing it more in line with the modern era.

President John F. Kennedy is assassinated in Dallas on November 22, leaving the nation stunned and ushering in Vice President Lyndon Baines Johnson to the Oval Office.

1964   On June 22, three civil rights workers go missing while volunteering in Mississippi and are found murdered. It was to be the start of the "Summer of Freedom," proclaimed and organized by the Student Nonviolent Coordinating Committee (SNCC).

The Civil Rights Act is passed on July 2 by Congress and becomes the law of the land.

Congress passes the Gulf of Tonkin Resolution on August 2, allowing President Lyndon Johnson to wage war against North Vietnam without a formal declaration of war. It signals the start of a decade-long war for the United States.

Martin Luther King is awarded the Nobel Peace Prize on October 14.

On November 3, Lyndon Johnson easily defeats GOP challenger Barry Goldwater in the presidential race, winning 60 percent of the popular vote.

The new British singing group, The Beatles, make two appearances on the popular Ed Sullivan variety show on television, garnering 70 million viewers, on February 9 and 16. The group will change popular music history.

1965   On February 21, the black nationalist leader Malcolm X is assassinated while speaking at an event in New York City.

President Johnson signs the new Medicare Bill into law on July 30, establishing government health care for the elderly.

The Voting Rights Act is signed into law on August 6, aimed at eliminating discrimination in polling places around the country.

Between August 11 and 16, the Watts section of Los Angeles erupts in riots leaving 34 people dead and $200 million in property damages.

The word "hippie" is coined by a *San Francisco Examiner* writer, Michael Fallen, on September 5. He uses it in a series of stories describing the beatniks who migrated into the Haight-Ashbury district of San Francisco in search of a communal lifestyle with like-minded counterculture young people.

The battle of Ia Drang takes place in Vietnam in November, the first engagement of an American ground brigade against North Vietnamese regular soldiers. Hundreds of U.S. troops die over four days, inflicting three times the number of casualties on North Vietnamese troops. The Vietnam War is in full swing for the United States.

1966   Black militant Stokely Carmichael assumes leadership of the SNCC on June 16, turning it away from its nonviolence philosophy and replacing it with the slogan of "Black Power."

The National Organization for Women begins on June 30 with the goal of bringing equality to women in the United States.

On September 8, the long-running TV series *Star Trek*, which would spawn several movies and TV sequels, premieres.

On October 15, the Black Panther Party is founded in Oakland, CA, by Bobby Seale and Huey Newton, promoting the use of violence to achieve civil rights for blacks.

On November 8, Edward Brook, a Republican from Massachusetts, is elected the first African American U.S. senator in 85 years.

1967   The first Super Bowl is played on January 15 when the Green Bay Packers meet and win the game over the Kansas City Chiefs.

The American troop total in Vietnam rises to nearly 400,000 as the war escalates and causes more dissension and tension back home.

Thurgood Marshall is confirmed for the U.S. Supreme Court in August and becomes the first African American to take a seat on the high court.

The "Summer of Love" takes place in and around San Francisco as thousands of hippies and young people identifying with the movement gather, with the epicenter being the Haight-Ashbury district.

On November 9, *Rolling Stone* magazine is launched by Jann Wenner. It will become the first significant magazine uniting music, politics, and culture in the United States.

1968   The Tet Offensive takes place on January 30–31 in Vietnam as a resurgent enemy strikes at several targets in the country, and some 2,500 American troops are killed. The offensive belies the official statements from the military and White House that America was winning the war, and it causes anti-war protesters to increase their activities and divides the nation even more.

After returning from Vietnam, CBS news anchor Walter Cronkite—"the most trusted man in America"—pronounces the Vietnam War "unwinnable" on national TV, and it becomes a key reason President Johnson decides not to seek reelection to a second term.

On June 6, Democratic presidential candidate Robert F. Kennedy is assassinated in Los Angeles, just after winning the California primaries.

The Democratic National Convention erupts in anger and violence in Chicago from August 25 through 29.

On November 5, Shirley Chisholm becomes the first African American woman elected to Congress.

Richard M. Nixon wins the White House on November 5, narrowly defeating Democratic challenger Hubert H. Humphrey.

1969   The Gay Liberation Movement is launched when a June 27 riot breaks out at the Stonewall Tavern in New York City as police clash with gays who are at the tavern to mourn the death of entertainer Judy Garland.

On July 20, a half-billion viewers watch as Neil Armstrong and Buzz Aldrin walk on the moon, the first humans to ever set foot on it. To many, it is the crowning moment of the space race that began with President Kennedy's announcement at the start of the decade.

A nationwide Peace Moratorium draws some two million protestors on October 15 and becomes the largest such demonstration in American history as Americans gather to protest the war in Vietnam. In Washington, D.C., alone, some 250,000 demonstrators turn out.

The Strategic Arms Limitation Talks begin on November 17 between the United States and Russia in efforts to limit the spread of nuclear warheads between the two nations.

More than 400,000 people gather and party in upstate New York on a farm near Woodstock between August 15 and 17 to hold what many believe was the most important pop music festival in history.

The first e-mail message is transmitted over a computer on October 29, via ARPANET. It is sent from a UCLA computer to a Stanford computer.

Sesame Street, the children's educational program that will become an important influence in the lives of generations to come, is first aired on November 10 on the PBS predecessor, NET.

1

PROTEST MOVEMENTS

I don't keep much. Yes, stuff clutters my life but not from way back. Family
things went into diaspora after my father died. My mother wisely refused
to become the widow Degelman in our little New England town. She sold
the house and left for New York University to begin a new life. My personal
stuff fell prey to gypsy days and a metaphoric compulsion to shed my skin by
giving stuff away or throwing it out.

This is how San Francisco writer Charles Degelman, who reached
adulthood in the 1960s, begins his narrative of his life in which he
has discarded many of life's trivial things, choosing instead to cling
to his principles and beliefs. The essay appears in Myretrospect.
com, the fascinating website for baby boomers to tell their stories.
Degelman is typical of young people in the 1960s, who refused to
just go with the cultural flow as the docile 1950s came to an end
and serious national threats like Vietnam and racial discrimination
caused him and many others to question tradition and the values it
was built on. Degelman was a young intellectual at Harvard during
the 1960s and used his writing talents to formulate his opposition
to a culture that seemed to discount values like peace and equality
for all. He continues:

I kept a few things. Chinese pewter candlesticks my grandparents brought
back from China before WWII. An oak table, crafted by my father's Japanese

friend, built before I was born. He crafted the table out of tight-grained oak, hand-planed and perfectly proportioned. . .

I kept three guitars: a Martin D-28 dreadnought, now battered by use, eroded from flatpicking, but lovingly cared for. A Dobro steel guitar, enameled a screaming cobalt blue with a chrome soundpan. I played both guitars on the streets in the 1970s.

My third guitar was built in LA's Boyle Heights by the Delgado Brothers' fourth generation of guitar makers. I was ushered into the Delgados' fragrant, dusty shop by my friend Hirth, LA's own Doctor John. A remarkable songwriter and stellar guitarist, Hirth was born in Boyle Heights to a Chicano father, a labor organizer, and a Jewish mother, back when the neighborhood was half Jewish, half Chicano. In back room of the Delgado Brothers' shop, Hirth and I played guitars at each other to hear the full-frontal voice of each instrument. Hirth died last year but he visits me in the guitar. He says he enjoys the vibrations of my sofa-bound noodling and tells me jokes while I play.

Moving from the few cherished material belongings he has kept from the 1960s, Degelman discusses the fire that has always propelled him to protest against societal and government conditions and policies that he feels are discriminatory or just flat-out wrong. Such was the spirit of those in that decade who dared take a stand against their prevailing culture and risk—or possibly revel in the idea of—being an outcast from that society. Such a fiery spirit was not unusual among young people in the 1960s, especially on college campuses, as they looked around and saw what they perceived to be hypocrisy dominating American institutions of government and big business. And, as these men and women grew older, their symbols of protest from the era became symbols of pride that they had at least tried to shine lights on the wrongs of the day.

I've also kept my resistance. I'm not a fighter but I've resisted forever. As a kid, I avoided playground fisticuffs and barroom punchouts. As a resistor, I cast my share of stones but I didn't get off on street fighting with cops. They're big, they're scared, they can be mean. Besides, they got the guns and you don't.

A DECADE OF PROTEST

The 1960s was a decade-long protest against conditions as they were in a country that was torn apart by the Vietnam War, the push for civil rights, and the Free Speech Movement (FSM) that was centered on college campuses around the country. A full cataloguing of all the various protest movements of the 1960s is beyond the scope of this book, because there were so many regional and local groups—some more loosely organized than others—that operated alongside the nationally organized movements. Nevertheless, a handful of large movements left big footprints in the sands of the 1960s, and those groups are profiled in this chapter.

In his essay on the 1960s, Degelman talks about resistance and why he engaged in it, despite the fact he also feared it and knew he was putting himself at risk.

Resistance can be more terrifying than exhilarating, but I resisted anyway. I loved resistance and I feared it, but when new and revolting developments threatened my resistance, I held it all the more dearly to my heart. For example, once upon a time, a revolutionary group called Weatherman splintered off from its parent organization, Students for a Democratic Society. The Weather People declared war against the government of the United States and learned to build bombs. Everyone involved stood at a crossroads.

I understood Weatherman's motivations, we had all been driven mad by the injustice of racism and the war. But did their hasty declaration of war represent a viable resistance strategy? Or did it signal the birth of an incubator baby in a premature revolution? What was to be done? We discussed the differences arduously but had to choose our crossroads alone.

Here Degelman provides an explanation of why some nonmilitant protest movements divided into separate groups, with the splinter group favoring militant tactics to make their message heard. These groups like the Weatherman became frustrated when rhetoric and marches didn't move the needle of change quickly enough for them. They felt violence would bring more widespread recognition of their complaints and demands. Although they were understood by their nonviolent counterpart members, crossing the line to violence was a move that many young revolutionaries were not ready to make.

Weatherman became the Weather Underground under pressure from women in the movement. I was impressed by the Weather Underground's ability to destroy malevolent federal property (draft board offices, draft induction centers, FBI and COINTELPRO facilities) but the Weather people never became a revolutionary army. . . .

The "we" became "they." They made mistakes. They blew up three of their own while building a bomb in a West Greenwich Village townhouse.

Those were dark days but I kept my resistance. Resistance is resilient, not born or smothered. The System will beat, distort, and trivialize any power that threatens it, but for the lucky few who "dare to struggle, dare to win," resistance can be full of hope as well as darkness.

We recruited our sense of humor, all our intelligence and guile to keep resistance for the future. Rather than selling out, we adjusted our expectations, changed our strategies, and kept resistance alive. It was difficult not to; resistance carries its own momentum.

We developed alternatives to capital consumerism—land-based utopias and food co-ops, free presses and clinics. A broader view of the world began to emerge. Instead of fighting for the here and now, environmentalism and the health of Mother Earth became the focus. The political turned personal as feminism gathered strength. Ethnic studies programs came to fruition on campuses. We hadn't lost and we hadn't stopped. We kept our resistance.

It is interesting to see how the expectations and tactics of young protesters evolved into pushing for broader and more long-term changes like the environment, feminism, and championing ethnic diversity. These young people, many of whom were intellectuals, could see beyond the here and now to see the importance of changing hearts and minds about larger threats and inequities in American society. Degelman (2016) continues:

Now we have a same old new world. Sometimes I think I know too much to entertain any more notions of fundamental change. I know who the presidential candidates are—and aren't. I know that we do not live in a prerevolutionary climate, not yet. I know the limits of the Presidency; it does not offer a pulpit for broad social change. . . .

I keep my art. I keep my resistance. My resistance and my art keep each other. I've also kept the pewter candlesticks, the oak table, the three guitars and—with luck and meditation—I'll manage to keep my friend Hirth.

THE FREE SPEECH MOVEMENT

If there was a single movement that served as the ignition for what would become known as the counterculture decade, especially for young people, it was the FSM, ushered in at the University of California at Berkeley in 1964. That was a significant year in many ways because it was the year the Civil Rights Act passed Congress, was the threshold year for the coming Voting Rights Act of 1965, and was the first year that America's military footprint in Vietnam grew unmistakably large and committed. By the end of the year, some 23,000 American troops were on the ground there and, within the next 12 months, there would be more than 184,000. Protest was growing among Mexican American farm laborers in California and elsewhere that would soon erupt into the farm labor movement. All the pieces for protest were in place, voices were growing louder, and the students at Berkeley, Michigan, Wisconsin, and other campuses didn't like it when those protest voices were silenced by administrators or the government. At Berkeley, students abhorred the idea of censorship and took it on themselves to make a stand in December 1964. Therefore, on that one evening, some 1,000 students marched into the campus administration building, Sproul Hall, took a seat wherever they could find a vacant spot on the floor, and refused to leave until their demands were met by administrators. Chief among those demands was that the university cease its practice of banning speakers on campus because of their political views, no matter how radical those views might seem. The FSM was born.

At that sit-in, Berkeley students would sing, discuss the objects of their protest, plan how to make their statements, and even do a little studying for class until after 3:00 a.m. when the university chancellor issued a demand for them to vacate Sproul Hall. When most of them refused to leave, police were called in to clear them out, and violent confrontations ensued.

The Associated Press reported that "an army of law enforcement officers broke up a massive sit-in occupation" and described the student protestors as "limply defiant" as they were "dragged" down the stairs on their backs and shoved into police vans. "Cries of police brutality rose from demonstration supporters watching outside" (Cox, 2017). Undeterred, Berkeley president Clark Kerr refused to end the police action and said the FSM had become "an instrument of anarchy." When it was all over later in the morning, police had arrested nearly 800 students for their part in the sit-in.

In the coming weeks, University of California, Berkeley, administrators decided to give in to public pressure and ease restrictions on campus speech and political activity. Sproul Hall—and especially its steps outside—would become a center for protest speeches in the months and years to follow. The FSM quickly grew beyond Berkeley and onto other campuses nationwide, and the Sproul Hall sit-in would be one of several such demonstrations between 1964 and 1965 across the country.

I was just beginning my own college experience as a freshman at the University of Oklahoma in 1964 and, while California was always ahead of us in cultural shifts by at least a year or two, it wasn't long before I began seeing FSM-style events popping up on our own campus. Our student newspaper began covering these events and gave them wider exposure and appeal to the young idealists and to those who were simply frightened about the prospects of being drafted to fight a war they didn't understand and yet could end their lives. Speaking one's own mind started becoming popular as the months and years progressed, and what students were saying was usually critical of government actions.

STUDENTS FOR A DEMOCRATIC SOCIETY

In the spring of 1965, Jim McCorkel Jr., a student at the University of North Carolina at Chapel Hill (UNC), was upset about the way things were going in America, and he felt the time was right for saying so. He and other students and faculty were moved by the FSM under way on West Coast schools like the University of California at Berkeley and felt campus administrations were too reluctant to invite speakers from the "new left" to campus. Therefore, McCorkel submitted an application to UNC to have a chapter of a student organization called Students for a Democratic Society (SDS) to be officially recognized by the administration. That application was accepted and approved, and a new avenue of protest was opened at this venerable university, often called one of the "public Ivies."

As for SDS, it had been in existence for five years since its founding at the University of Michigan in 1960.

The SDS was probably the most recognizable student protest group of the 1960s. The constitution of this North Carolina chapter indicates that free speech was a central motivator in getting this chapter started. Debates had been occurring on campus about banning controversial speakers, and many students and faculty felt the controversial issues needed to be addressed as openly as possible. The UNC chapter's constitution noted: "We maintain a vision of a democratic society where, at all levels, people have control of the decisions which affect them and the resources on which they are dependent" (Students for a Democratic Society, n.d.).

As an official student organization, the UNC chapter of SDS needed faculty advisors, so two stepped forward in the form of physics professor Joe Straley and campus YMCA co-director Norm Gustaveson. On the student leadership side, McCorkel and his friends Gary Waller, Jerry Carr, and Stuart Matthews took the initiative to invite activists like Fran Wilkinson, who had been an outspoken proponent of the First Amendment and just as outspoken in his criticism of Sen. Joseph McCarthy in the 1950s and of FBI director J. Edgar Hoover's illegal wiretapping of government critics. The SDS chapter also invited Herbert Aptheker, a noted Marxist historian and political activist. But, as was the case on other campuses around the country with SDS chapters, the members of the UNC chapter were the object of scrutiny by the FBI as well as campus police and administrators. According to exhibits at UNC, the chief of campus police made little attempt to hide the fact he was trying to get as much information as he could on people who frequented the SDS meetings, going so far as to attend meetings himself and jotting down who was there. The SDS was a relatively new organization, and university administrators did not know what exactly they had with the group, whether they were trouble or posed a danger to the campus. In the case of UNC, the dean of student affairs wrote to both Hoover and the head of the House on Un-American Activities (HUAC), Edwin Willis, for guidance in what to make of SDS or how to treat it. To the dean's query, Willis responded, "[SDS] has not been cited as subversive by this Committee. . . . This, however, should not be construed as either a clearance or an unfavorable finding of this Committee regarding the organization." In many ways, this response shows the paranoia still gripping what had been an extremely controversial congressional committee in the 1950s, responsible for ruining the reputations of many innocent Americans, especially around the time of McCarthyism. But many conservatives in the country still put stock in the HUAC.

Clearly, however, Hoover and Willis's response to the UNC dean's request left the administration with no guidance from Washington on what to do with its SDS chapter (Students for a Democratic Society, n.d.).

THE *PORT HURON STATEMENT*

The first chapter of SDS held its inaugural meeting in Ann Arbor, Michigan, on the campus of the University of Michigan in 1960. The first SDS convention came two years later where the organization's manifesto, the *Port Huron Statement*, was approved after it was originally written by a staff member named Tom Hayden. He would become an influential leader in the anti-war movement and later become a state senator in California. The *Port Huron Statement* was a sweeping critique of America's politically driven failures to secure global peace and to keep the country safe from many threats including nuclear war and the race with the Soviet Union to build missiles that could deliver nuclear warheads. On the home front, its targets were government failures in income equality, racial equality, corporations, political parties, and labor unions.

But the SDS manifesto went beyond criticizing the government. It called for reforms, urging more power to the people through citizen lobbying groups, more consideration of workers' voices in management decisions, more welfare projects, and an anti-poverty program. In striving to achieve these goals, SDS called for nonviolent civil disobedience of the kind being preached by Rev. Dr. Martin Luther King. The idea was that young people—particularly college students and faculty—would be at the vanguard of this protest movement but that the rest of the country would catch the spirit of the young and it would eventually permeate all levels of society.

The SDS was also active at America's oldest university, Harvard, and one incident showed how members of that chapter found a large venue to issue their demands: in this case, to protest the Reserve Officer Training Corps (ROTC) at Harvard. The event was the June commencement on the Cambridge campus, and the *Harvard Crimson* newspaper described the SDS activity this way:

> *Normal Commencement proceedings were disrupted this morning after President [Nathan] Pusey let an SDS member speak at the ceremony. Bruce C. Allen '69 who said he was one of the seniors suspended for occupying University Hall, spoke for nearly ten minutes until six Class Committee members and Class Marshals came to the stage and led him away.*
>
> *About 150 students—between 50 and 60 of them seniors—then marched out of the Tercentenary Theater, chanting "Smash ROTC; No Expansion."*
>
> *Allen had been allowed to speak by Pusey after he had been approached several times by SDS members asking that their voice be heard at the commencement. . . . He began by "thanking the administration for its gracious concession" . . . in the context of throwing out 17 people for fighting against ROTC and expansion, letting one person talk is a hollow joke. I think they were afraid of our militancy.*
>
> *The audience responded with a mix of boos and cheers, and Allen launched into a list of SDS demands including that the ROTC be "smashed." (Harvard Crimson, 1969)*

DR. MARTIN LUTHER KING JR.

In 1960, a Baptist minister named Martin Luther King Jr., named for the great Protestant Reformation leader, moved his family to his native city of Atlanta. There he would co-pastor the Ebenezer Baptist Church alongside his father. The younger King had already made a name for himself in the African American community through his work in the Southern Christian Leadership Conference (SCLC), which had been formed three years earlier to combat racial discrimination and inequality in the South. But what came forth from the church pulpit was much more than Sunday sermons on equality; what came forth was a man who led most of the impactful civil rights battles of the decade.

Following in the tradition of global civil rights leaders like India's Mahatma Gandhi, King's contribution to the greater civil rights movement in America was his emphasis on nonviolent civil disobedience. This would distinguish him from other civil rights groups of the decade, most notably the Black Panther Movement. And, of course, the other distinguishing mark of Dr. King was his rhetoric, which was both poetic and inspirational. His 1962 "I Have a Dream" speech stands today as one of the finest public addresses ever uttered. As revered as he would become, King's nonviolent philosophy would be tested time and again in confrontations with opposition groups and law enforcement officers in the South and at confrontations arising from marches, sit-ins, and boycotts. Dr. King himself would be arrested on more than one occasion, with the most notable coming on April 12, 1960, when he was arrested in Birmingham for leading a protest. What was envisioned as a way to get him off the streets, however, turned out to be a venue providing him to write his famed "Letter from a Birmingham Jail." This treatise would become one of the most visible essays of the civil rights movement. It offered a superb rationale for the philosophy of civil disobedience and, although originally written to a collection of white pastors who had been critical of his methods, wound up—in the present-day vernacular—"going viral" to the whole country.

For many white Americans, it was Dr. King's passion and rhetoric that made them look at America from the black person's viewpoint and not from their own privileged vantage point. For them, the urgency that black Americans were feeling became their urgency as well, and this was true especially for young people and those on college campuses. For many whites, the first time they even came close to blacks was in the college classroom and dorm. The discussions over pizza and beer about cultural issues—discussions that may have only been white-only or black-only moments before— became an exchange of ideas between white and black students, and each got to hear the other's frustrations and fears as well as joys of accomplishment. It gave many college students a chance to view America through each other's eyes, and some saw American differently as a result. Many young whites joined in the protest marches for civil rights; some experienced violent reactions from whites, as they stood shoulder to shoulder with blacks. And some were murdered, like Andrew Goodman and Michael Schwerner who were killed in the 1964 Freedom Summer in Neshoba County, Mississippi. They died alongside their black friend, James Earl Chaney, all killed by Ku Klux Klan members.

Certainly not all whites were in agreement with Dr. King's agenda and vision, however. Many whites resisted elevating blacks to a position of true equality in America, fearing changes that would upset the culture they were used to. And many felt that passing a civil rights act would not change the thinking or attitude of whites toward blacks. A popular mantra among whites, which I personally heard many times in discussions on race, was "You just can't legislate morality." I grew up in Oklahoma which was—and still is—a very conservative state. In my hometown there were very few blacks and none at all in the schools I attended, all through high school. The black students in the Oklahoma City area mostly went to Douglass High School, which was an all-black school. In my all-white suburb of Midwest City, we knew nothing about black students, and we often feared the worst as a result. We bought into the negative stereotypes, and when we did come in contact with Douglass students on the athletic field or basketball court, those student athletes were sometimes the brunt of harsh white jokes. Looking back, it's difficult to believe people behaved like this, but such attitudes and behavior were fruits of the tree called segregation.

Unless a white person were to move from the segregated area he or she lived in to a more integrated one, that fear and those stereotypes were likely going to stay with him or her as a truism. However, as young white people went to college and came in contact with black students, the segregated thinking was replaced—or at least supplemented—by a more inclusive and enlightened view. Their fears of the "other" began to dissipate as they saw it was possible for blacks and whites to understand and respect each other.

Dr. Thomas J. Nenon, dean of the College of Arts & Sciences at the University of Memphis and a philosophy professor, recalls the influence that Dr. King had on him as a longtime Memphian and civil rights advocate:

Martin Luther King was the main thing here in Memphis. The sanitation strike and King's assassination. Those were just central to your life. We had institutional racism but we also worked hard to improve things, and Dr. King's legacy helped. Here in Memphis all that showed up in the music and in recording labels like Stax records. (Thomas J. Nenon, interview on December 24, 2018)

Indeed, the city's love of blues and rock and roll was a key thing that brought—and still brings—the races together, often right down on the famed Beale Street on Friday and Saturday nights.

THE MARCH ON WASHINGTON

A few months later, King helped organize the March on Washington for Jobs and Freedom. This was a high-profile event, covered nationally by the news media, that came off as designed: a very peaceful rally that focused on the inequities black Americans were facing. It was held on August 28 and drew more than 300,000 African American and white supporters to the capitol mall. Included in the program were popular folk singers such as the group Peter, Paul, and Mary, who carried the message of equality in song. The centerpiece of the event, however, was King's famous "I Have a Dream" speech that still resonates today and that is considered one of the finest addresses ever given on civil rights. The March on Washington is credited with being one of the most significant influences leading to congressional approval of the Civil Rights Act of 1964. And, for Dr. King and his movement, this Washington demonstration solidified his reputation as the face of civil rights in America. Later that year, *Time* magazine made him its "Man of the Year," and he was awarded the Nobel Peace Prize.

In 1965, Dr. King would lead the civil rights march, focused on voter registration for blacks, from Selma to Montgomery, Alabama. King was aided by President Lyndon Johnson, who sent federal troops to help maintain peace during that event. And, again, a King-led march spurred on Congress to pass another significant civil rights law: the Voting Rights Act that meant African Americans had equal rights to cast their ballots at the polls.

Dr. King would continue fighting for civil rights until he was assassinated in Memphis on April 4, 1968, while supporting a strike by the city's sanitation workers. James Earl Ray was arrested and convicted for killing King as he stood outside his room at the Lorraine Motel.

SIT-INS AND BUS RIDES

In 1960, a group of four African American college students decided enough was enough when it came to segregating dining rooms and restaurants. They walked into a Woolworth's department store in Greensboro, North Carolina, on February 1, sat down at the segregated lunch counter where only whites were to be served, and politely asked for service. When they were denied that service, they decided not to leave. The passive resistance they showed helped fuel a civil rights protest movement that would sweep across the South. The four students were joined by hundreds of other protestors over the next six months, and the result was the desegregation of that lunch counter in July that year. The four students who would go down in history were Ezell A. Blair Jr. (who now is Jibreel Khazan), Joseph A. McNeil, Franklin E. McCain, and David L. Richmond.

The next year, hundreds of black and white civil rights volunteers loaded up buses in Washington, D.C., and began the famous "Freedom Riders" tour of southern towns and cities, stopping and promoting their message of racial equality. They were met with resistance—sometimes violent—and arrests at some of the stops but continued on and made the national news in doing so, spreading the message of civil rights. The group was led by an interracial activist group known as the Congress of Racial Equality. The Freedom Rides took place between May and December 1961 and involved 60 different rides and 436 participants.

SOUTHERN CHRISTIAN LEADERSHIP CONFERENCE

Three years before the 1960s began, the SCLC was founded in Montgomery, Alabama, to promote the cause of civil rights and do it using nonviolent means. The Montgomery Bus Boycott had just occurred, and it seemed to SCLC founders that the time was right for an organized civil rights movement that could draw together the various individual strands of the push for equality for African Americans. The organization named Martin Luther King its president, a post he would retain until his assassination in 1968.

Because the church played a key role in the lives of southern black communities, it was natural that it would provide the impetus for bettering the lives of the families and individuals living in those neighborhoods. Hence, the SCLC was founded on the cornerstone of the black churches. Dr. King was a Baptist minister at Dexter Avenue Baptist Church in Montgomery, took on key roles in boycotts and demonstrations, and seemed the natural leader for the SCLC, which was originally named the Southern Negro Leaders Conference on Transportation and Non-violent Integration. After changing its name to the Southern Christian Leadership Conference, the organization developed a mission statement around three key "wants." These were the following:

1. White Americans should not stand and meekly watch while wrongs were being committed against the black community. It was important to the SCLC that it not depict all whites as racists, and it helped to bring whites into the movement to help fight for civil rights. It is also one of the key reasons that the organization dropped the word "Negro" from its original name, wanting to show it welcomed supporters from all races.
2. Black Americans were urged by the SCLC to actively search for justice and to stand up against injustices.
3. Everyone who joined or worked in support of the SCLC had to adopt the stance of nonviolence, no matter what was being done to them by whites. In fact, the motto the SCLC adopted was "Not one hair of one head of one white person shall be harmed."

From its beginnings in Montgomery, the SCLC fanned out to neighboring states until it became active in every southern state. Although various local civil rights groups were already at work, the SCLC leadership believed that a coordinated approach to fighting injustice and inequality was needed, and it believed the organization could provide that coordination. Among its many activities was a central one of helping African Americans register to vote in upcoming elections and to promote the cause of civil rights in America as a moral necessity. But the SCLC realized through some of its protests and demonstrations that nonviolent confrontation did not draw much media coverage, and the leaders also knew such coverage was needed to get their message out to the larger country. Therefore, the organization got some unexpected help in obtaining media coverage as white-led southern law enforcement groups turned violent against the nonviolent civil rights marchers. The most widely covered of these confrontations came in Birmingham in 1963. As civil rights marchers demonstrated in the streets, city police under the leadership of Bull Connor turned to violence to disperse the demonstrators. As television cameras rolled, police turned high-pressure fire hoses on the marchers and, when that didn't produce the wanted results, the police unleashed their dogs who attacked defenseless marchers. The marchers refused to fight back, and the whole tableau seemed to visualize white southern racism, depicted on television screens around the country.

Looking back on the bloody confrontation five decades later, the *New York Daily News* wrote in 2012:

> *They were eight days that tore at America's conscience. From May 2 to May 10, 1963, the nation bore witness as police in Birmingham, Ala., aimed high-powered hoses and unleashed snarling dogs on black men, women and even children who wanted just one thing: to be treated the same as white Americans. . . . "A Negro woman was bitten on the leg by a police dog," United Press International reported. "A Negro man had four or five deep gashes on his leg where he had been bitten by a dog. A sobbing Negro woman said she had been kicked in the stomach by a policeman." (Siemaszko, 2012)*

The images of the Birmingham confrontations led the newscasts over and over again on NBC, CBS, and ABC, which were the only television news options available for national news. Everyone in America who was watching TV news was watching the same images, and the video of anguish and bloodshed resonated emotionally with viewers and gave the civil rights movement the launching pad it needed to attract attention and support.

The picture was too much for Birmingham leaders to live with, so, before long, the city was moving toward desegregating its facilities. And, on the national scale, it prompted President John F. Kennedy to move into a higher gear in pushing for national civil rights legislation. In 1964, the year after Kennedy's assassination, the Civil Rights Act was approved by Congress.

The SCLC survived Dr. King's assassination, and it is still active today and still promoting civil rights and equality for all races. Its mission and focus, as stated on the SCLC website, declares: "In the spirit of Dr. Martin Luther King, Jr., the Southern Christian Leadership Conference (SCLC) is renewing its commitment to bring about the promise of 'one nation, under God, indivisible' together with the commitment to activate the 'strength to love' within the community of humankind" (Southern Christian Leadership Conference, 2015).

AN EDITOR'S EXPERIENCE

To Otis Sanford, the 1960s were all about the struggle for civil rights. Although he understood the importance of Vietnam and the Cold War threat, the day-to-day threat faced by racist whites in the South was the more pressing issue to be overcome.

> *"The white person with the gun rack in his pick up was our threat," said Sanford. The youngest of seven children who grew up in Mississippi in the*

'50s and '60s, he added, "Our concern was about segregation; mistreatment of African Americans wherever we went. The closed society of Mississippi; the outright defiance of Supreme Court rulings. Brown vs. the Board of Education *was not recognized in Mississippi until the mid-1960s. And a lot of people were getting killed for no reason."*

Sanford was 15 when Dr. Martin Luther King was killed in Memphis, and he marks that as the most significant event of the whole civil rights movement.

"That's when things began to change. The eyes of the world were trained on what was going on in the south," he said. "The national media began covering civil rights big time. People saw water hoses and dogs being turned on black folks. People were just incredulous to this. Dr. King's death was the last straw. LBJ finally saw that this was not right and began efforts to change things."

Although only a teen in the 1960s, Sanford said he was aware of what was going on in the country and the world. "I did what teenagers did, but I was paying attention pretty closely back then. I was plugged in and tuned in and had been a news junkie all my life."

It was that interest in the world, coupled with the fact his parents were both civil rights activists, that caused Sanford to press for change and to eventually become a journalist. In fact, he was the first black reporter hired by the traditionally segregationist newspaper, *The Clarion Ledger*, in Jackson, Mississippi. He worked hard and, two years later, was hired as a reporter by the *Commercial Appeal* in Memphis, Tennessee, eventually rising to become editorial page editor and managing editor of that newspaper. Today Sanford holds the prestigious Hardin Chair of Excellence in Journalism at the University of Memphis.

Speaking of being hired at the *Commercial Appeal*, Sanford said, "That was my Golden moment. If it hadn't been for the (1960s) era, I don't think things would have changed."

Sanford sees the counterculture era of the 1960s and early 1970s as a hinge of history, the point after which everything changed, at least for blacks.

"I do think it was a watershed," he said. "A lot of things started to change. We finally got out of the (Vietnam) war and, where the civil rights movement was concerned, more things started to change. African Americans were not passed over for jobs. Schools were desegregating. You saw tremendous change."

Sanford sees a clear difference between his American experience and that of his parents, who were born in 1910. "My parents did not even have an opportunity to vote in Mississippi until they were 55," he said. "African Americans had to take tests on the Constitution that whites did not. When my mother took her test, she knew more about the Constitution than the guy giving her the test did."

And his experience was even different from that of his six older brothers and sisters.

My older brothers and sisters were under no illusion that they could go to a white school like Ole Miss. But I went to Ole Miss. The first four of them had to go to all-black schools in Mississippi, and the other two went to community college. I started at a community college in 1971, then transferred to Ole Miss. There were about 300–400 African Americans there by then, about ten years after James Meredith. For me it was enlightening just to be around smart students. It was great to be with other African Americans who were qualified just to get into a place like that.

Sanford said he didn't feel the academic standards were any different for blacks than whites, but he said it was harder to excel on the extracurricular side. He pointed to a time when he was in line to be editor of his community college newspaper, only to lose it to a less-qualified white student, and he attributed that decision to racism.

The Vietnam War ranks were populated with a high percentage of blacks who had less opportunity to attend college (and thus get a student deferment) than whites. Therefore, did blacks join in the anti-war movement at Ole Miss?

Black Americans had more reason to protest the war, but I did not see that many blacks out there protesting it. Because we were out there marching for civil rights here at home. The Vietnam protests were more of a white person's protest. "Down with the establishment" was the same theme but the objects of protest were different.

The black protests that Sanford witnessed and participated in were not aligned with radical groups like the Black Panthers, which he perceived as more of a West Coast movement. The civil rights protests Sanford sees as most effective were ones carried out within the legal system.

You had African American lawyers like Benjamin Hooks and A.W. Willis who took up the charge here and started filing lawsuits. Thurgood Marshall came here once to desegregate the schools. The African American legal community made the waves and started to change things.

Finally, in 1969 and '70 where I live, people said we can no longer sustain the separate but equal mentality. Let's not divide our public amenities any more. People started slowly but sure to come to their senses.

Sanford sees the counterculture era as driven by youth who didn't worry about the risks they took at the time. And "thank God for that," he said. "If it hadn't been for those young people, the changes might not have ever come."

Again, however, for Sanford and his family and friends, the 1960s was mostly about the march toward greater civil rights.

All African Americans had injustices we had to overcome, to get somewhere. Especially the ambitious ones. And I was ambitious. (Otis Sanford, telephone interview with Jim Willis, September 8, 2017)

THE BLACK PANTHERS

While equal rights and justice for African Americans were goals shared by all civil rights proponents in the 1960s, not everyone agreed on how those goals should be reached. While Dr. King was building his movement on nonviolent confrontations, the Black Panther Party was taking a more militant stance in fighting the government. Founded in 1966 by activists Huey Newton and Bobby Seale, the original focus of the Panthers was to fight police brutality against African Americans. In fact, the original name of the group was Black Panthers for Self-Defense, and members engaged in armed citizen patrols in Oakland and other cities across the country. True to the name of the movement, its leaders and members—which numbered between 2,000 and 5,000 at its peak—wore black leather jackets and black berets and carried firearms.

The story of these armed patrols was told in 2012 by a former Black Panther Party captain who belonged to the Seattle chapter of the Panthers. His name is Aaron Dixon, and he recalled telling a high school principal, "If you don't protect these Black kids, then we will do it, understand?" The confrontation came about following the pleadings of a black mother who had contacted the Seattle chapter of the Black Panther Party, asking for help in keeping her son safe at the Rainer Beach High School where he was the frequent target of bullies. She said the school's administration was doing nothing to help. According to Dixon's account, the school principal responded to his statement by saying, "I promise I will make sure nothing happens again."

The Seattle chapter was the first Panther group outside of California, and Seale recruited Dixon, who was only 19 at the time, to be its captain. Although hesitant at first, Dixon finally agreed. "I felt deeply about the movement that was rapidly gaining steam, coming on the horizon, but I was not yet a true, committed revolutionary," he writes in his book, *My People Are Rising: Memoirs of a Black Panther Captain.* As time went on and he observed what was happening in his chapter and others in the country, Dixon notes, "We had many recruits yet we lacked a clear understanding or model of exactly what we were supposed to be doing on a daily basis and also in the long term." In other words, he said, Black Panther recruits had a lot of energy and desire to protect other blacks but not much in the way of actual operating guidelines. Nevertheless, the Seattle chapter grew quickly. Within its first two months of existence, the chapter was processing more than 300 applications for people who wanted to join and contribute to the revolution. Says Dixon, "Events were occurring at high speed. . . . It wasn't long before our little sleepy Madrona neighborhood was transformed into a Black Panther Party fortress."

Contrary to popular belief, several of the Black Panther chapters, like Seattle, were multiracial in membership, not just composed of African Americans. And they were young. Wrote Dixon, "It was not unusual that a handful of the new recruits were Asian—like fifteen year-old Guy Kurose, who was Japanese; seventeen-year-old Mike Gillespie a Filipino trumpet player, and Mike Tagawa a Japanese Vietnam vet. These guys had grown up in our neighborhood and identified with young Blacks in many ways."

The rhetoric, activities, and perceived threats the Panthers posed did not go unchecked by the government. The federal government's Counter Intelligence Program (COINTELPRO) called the Black Panther Party the "greatest threat to the internal security of the United States." With that came greater scrutiny and surveillance and what the party called the false conviction and jailing of Huey P. Newton and the "New York 21," to the "assassinations" of Bunchy Carty, Fred Hampton, and George Jackson (Hagopian, n.d.).

The Black Panther Party's goals grew beyond protection of African Americans from police harassment. Organizers Newton and Seale borrowed from Marxism in drawing up the platform of the party. In a "Ten-Point Program," the thinking of the Black Panther Party was outlined. Those points demanded the end to police brutality and for greater equality and justice for African Americans. It demanded more employment opportunities and equal access to housing as well. Through it all ran the thread of Black Power and the need for African Americans to take control of their communities to protect their rights and their safety. More than just a gang of militants, the Panthers envisioned a political organization whereby they could get their members elected to the legislature and to Congress and work through established channels to bring about their goals. These plans, however, failed to materialize, as internal disagreements among Black Panther members and chapters, as well as counterintelligence measures by the FBI and other law enforcement groups, sapped any political strength the party might have otherwise gained. Nevertheless, at local urban levels, the Panthers did manage to start up some needed social programs—including free health-care and breakfast programs for children—in some 13 of their chapters across the country.

The end of the Black Panther Party came with its dissolution in 1982. Seven years later, the New Black Panther Party emerged in Dallas, but original Panther members claim no connection between the two groups, and the new party has been labeled a hate group by the Southern Poverty Law Center (Black Panthers, n.d.).

THE KENT STATE SHOOTINGS

Protests on college campuses in the 1960s were routine, although some campuses were more active than others. Four months after the decade ended, one such protest by college students claimed the lives of four students. The site was Kent State University, and the students were protesting what had been the secret bombing of neutral Cambodia during the war in Vietnam. The deaths occurred when soldiers of the Ohio National Guard fired their weapons into a crowd of university demonstrators, killing four and wounding nine. All were students of the university, located in northeast Ohio. The Kent State students began protesting on May 1 and, as police and National Guard presence increased on campus, some students started throwing rocks and bottles at them and received tear gas in return. The situation grew more tense through the weekend.

Ohio's governor Jim Rhodes ordered an estimated 1,000 National Guard troops to the Kent State campus on May 3, anticipating an increase in tensions. But Rhodes did more than that: He lashed out at the Kent State students for being unpatriotic in denouncing a war that American soldiers were fighting. He called the protestors "the worst type of people that we harbor in America" and called them the "strongest, well-trained, militant, revolutionary group that has ever assembled in America" (Kent State Shootings, n.d.). In so doing, many felt Rhodes exacerbated the situation, brought tensions to a boiling point, and eventually the lid blew off. More confrontations ensued, only this time the students were facing drawn bayonets of the National Guard troops. Although classes would resume the following day, protestors would not be denied, and open conflict broke out between students and soldiers. Tear gas canisters were thrown at students who threw them back to the troops, along with rocks. Many students taunted the soldiers and yelled, "Pigs off campus!"

The Ohio Central History Project picked up the narrative there, when the soldiers started shooting their rifles:

> *Eventually seventy-seven guardsmen advanced on the protesters with armed rifles and bayonets. Protesters continued to throw things at the soldiers. Twenty-nine of the soldiers, purportedly fearing for their lives, eventually opened fire. The gunfire lasted just thirteen seconds, although some witnesses contended that it lasted more than one minute. The troops fired a total of sixty-seven shots. When the firing ended, nine students lay wounded, and four other students had been killed. Two of the students who died actually had not participated in the protests.* (Kent State Shootings, n.d.)

The impact of the confrontation and resulting tragedy made immediate news, and it fueled a nationwide strike by students. In the wake of that, hundreds of universities and colleges closed down temporarily around the country. But the impact of the tragedy went beyond college campuses and into politics. President Nixon was in office at the time, and his chief of staff H. R. Haldeman would write a few years later in his memoirs that the Kent State shootings and aftermath increased Nixon's level of paranoia about protesters and the Democratic Party. This, in turn, set the stage for the kinds of "dirty tricks" by his Committee to Re-Elect that culminated in the break-in and attempted cover-up of the Democratic National Headquarters in the Watergate office complex in 1972. Beyond politics, the Kent State shootings—often dubbed "massacre"—showed vividly how divided the country was over the ongoing Vietnam War. It also showed Americans that the war protesters were not just hippies but also serious college students who came from middle- and upper-class homes across the country.

THE STONEWALL RIOTS

In the early morning hours of June 28, 1969, police in New York City staged a raid on a gay nightclub in Greenwich Village called the Stonewall Inn. A large crowd of patrons was gathered there, in part to pay respects to the entertainer Judy Garland who died earlier that week. The raid touched off violent clashes between police and protestors who were making a stand for gay rights, and the confrontation turned bloody over the next six days. Two people would die in the violence. Homosexual relationships were illegal in New York then, and police were allowed to make arrests of individuals who were not wearing clothing deemed appropriate to their gender.

The surprise raid caught patrons off guard and angered many who were supporting equal rights for gay and lesbian individuals. The Stonewall raid and resulting violent protests would be the beginning of a gay rights movement that would grow nationally and around the world.

One man who was there, Michael Fader, said the Stonewall raid was the last straw for him and his friends:

> We all had a collective feeling like we'd had enough of this kind of shit. It wasn't anything tangible anybody said to anyone else, it was just kind of like everything over the years had come to a head on that one particular night in the one particular place, and it was not an organized demonstration. . . . Everyone in the crowd felt that we were never going to go back. It was like the last straw. It was time to reclaim something that had always been taken from us. . . . All kinds of people, all different reasons, but mostly it was total outrage, anger, sorrow, everything combined, and everything just kind of ran its course. It was the police who were doing most of the destruction. We were really trying to get back in and break free. And we felt that we had freedom at last, or freedom to at least show that we demanded freedom. (Carter, 2010)

Looking back, it is interesting to note that much of America either lost track of the Stonewall riots or never heard about them, until the real push for LGBQT rights began in the 1990s. Once that movement started making headlines and progress, however, the Stonewall story began circulating to a wider audience and "Stonewall" became a rallying cry for many supporters of the gay rights movement. The Stonewall riots fulfilled much of the same function for the LGBQT movement that the Birmingham confrontation had done for the civil rights movement. It brought a mostly hidden issue into public view, in a very dramatic and violent way, and made it hard to ignore.

BIBLIOGRAPHY

"Black Panthers," History.Com, n.d., as accessed on March 11, 2018, at https://www.history.com/topics/black-panthers

Carter, David. *Stonewall: The Riots That Sparked the Gay Revolution*, New York: St. Martin's, 2010, p. 160.

Cox, John Woodrow. "Berkeley Gave Birth to the Free Speech Movement of the 1960s," *The Washington Post*, April 20, 2017, as accessed on May 15, 2019, at https://www.washingtonpost.com/news/retropolis/wp/2017/04/20/berkeley-gave-birth-to-the-free-speech-movement-in-the-1960s-now-conservatives-are-demanding-it-include-them/?utm_term=.684e256bec68

Degelman, Charles. "Rosewood, Petwer, Oak, Resistance, and a Friend," *Retrospect*, May 15, 2016, as accessed on April 16, 2018, at https://www.myretrospect.com/?s=rosewood+pewter

Hagopian, Jesse. "Memoirs of a Seattle Black Panther," *International Socialist Review*, n.d., as accessed on March 9, 2018, at https://isreview.org/issue/85/memoirs-seattle-black-panther

"Kent State Shootings," Ohio History Central, n.d., as accessed on April 16, 2018, at http://www.ohiohistorycentral.org/w/Kent_State_Shootings

"SDS Member Talks at Ceremonies," *Harvard Crimson*, June 12, 1969, as accessed on March 15, 2018, at http://www.thecrimson.com/article/1969/6/12/sds-member-talks-at-ceremonies-pnormal/

Siemaszko, Corky. "Birmingham Erupted into Chaos in 1963 as Battle for Civil Rights Exploded in the South," *New York Daily News*, May 5, 2012, as accessed on March 12, 2018, at http://www.nydailynews.com/news/national/birmingham-erupted-chaos-1963-battle-civil-rights-exploded-south-article-1.1071793

"Southern Christian Leadership Conference," The History Learning Site, March 27, 2015, as accessed on March 12, 2018, at http://www.historylearningsite.co.uk/the-civil-rights-movement-in-america-1945-to-1968/southern-christian-leadership-conference/

"Southern Christian Leadership Conference: Our Story," n.d., as accessed on March 12, 2018, at https://nationalsclc.org/about/

"Students for a Democratic Society," n.d., as accessed on March 1, 2018, at https://exhibits.lib.unc.edu/exhibits/show/protest/biographies/students-for-a-democratic-soci

2

POLITICS

In thinking about politics in the 1960s, picture this: the decade begins with the country being governed by a handsome, young, charismatic, and idealistic president. He has an equally attractive wife who is the symbol of sophistication and class that would set a new standard in America. The new president promises the nation that he will defend them from the expansionist threats posed by the Soviet Union, while advancing America further into space than ever before thought possible. His destination is a lunar landing.

The president is able to stare down Russia during a major missile crisis in Cuba that brought the two countries to the brink of nuclear war, but he is unable to stop the encroaching "Americanization" of a civil war in Vietnam. Later, after his shocking assassination in 1963, the country would plunge headlong into that war. Along with that plunge comes the realization among the American public that foreign policy is no longer an abstract issue they can ignore. That policy now means young American men are likely to be drafted when they reach the age of 18, and they will probably go lay their lives on the line in a confusing war in Vietnam. Meanwhile, the civil rights movement has gained steam across the country, so domestic policy is not just an abstract political issue either.

POLITICS HITS HOME TO INDIVIDUALS

The result of all this is that voting and political involvement by the people is perceived as a civic duty and also as an issue of survival for many young people in the country. The baby boomers, who came into existence in 1946, were hitting the age of 18, and they were angry and worried enough that they willingly jumped into the political fray and let their voices—and often demands—be known. The military draft—controversial as it was—provided great impetus for anti-war activism, and racial harassment, discrimination, and violence provided the motivation for civil rights activists. This then was the environment that political parties, candidates, and elected officials had to navigate in the 1960s.

DRAMA AND HEARTACHE

As a decade, the 1960s brought America a political arena that included probably more drama, heartache, and turbulence than any decade in history. Among the signature moments were the following:

- The election in 1960 of John F. Kennedy, a young charismatic Massachusetts senator, to the White House over a more senior establishment candidate
- The continued battle for states' rights in the South and the fight in Washington, D.C., for the Civil Rights Act
- America's involvement in Vietnam that began with the dispatch of a small number of military advisors to South Vietnam
- The assassination of President Kennedy in 1963, a moment that shocked the nation and sent it into a period of collective grief
- The ascension to the presidency of Vice President Lyndon Baines Johnson from Texas and the beginning of his "Great Society" program
- The passage of the Civil Rights Act in 1964 and the attempts to enforce its provisions in states that didn't want it
- The growing "Americanization" of the Vietnam War to the point where some 550,000 American troops were fighting there at any one time by the decade's end
- The loss of confidence in Johnson and his stepping down after one term, the widening "credibility gap" between Washington and American citizens
- The most contentious and violent political party convention, taking place in the summer of 1968 in Chicago
- The 1968 election of Richard M. Nixon, the man who had lost the election to Kennedy at the start of the decade
- The government's attempts, sometimes involving violent force, in dealing with an ongoing string of demonstrations against the Vietnam War and unequal treatment of races in America

Much of this drama spilled over from Washington, D.C., and spilled out into the campuses of universities and colleges and onto the streets of American cities. Nevertheless, much of America tried to carry on as usual without becoming involved in the protests. For many, as always, there was more than enough to do with trying to graduate from school, make a living for the family, enjoy life, get married, have babies, and plan for the future. But it was all done against a national backdrop of demonstrations and divisiveness.

KENNEDY ENTERS THE WHITE HOUSE

President Dwight David Eisenhower was finishing his second term in office as the national party conventions produced their nominees for the 1960 election. The Republicans chose Vice President Richard M. Nixon, 47, while the Democrats selected a 43-year-old senator from Massachusetts, John Fitzgerald Kennedy. Eisenhower was the first president to be denied a possible third term because of the recently passed Twenty-Second Amendment limiting presidents to two terms. The popular election turned out to be one of the closest in history, with Kennedy winning that vote by a slim 112,827 votes. That count would later be suspect because of alleged voting irregularities in Alabama, but his electoral college margin was wider at 303–219, even though Kennedy carried fewer states than Nixon (22 to 26, with 2 states going to Sen. Robert Byrd, an independent). This was also the first election that Hawaii and Alaska could participate in since they had just become states in 1959.

The differences between Nixon and Kennedy were never in sharper focus than on television, which became a significant factor in this election for the first time in history. This was the first presidential campaign that used live televised debates, and the more rested, poised, and charismatic Kennedy finished way ahead of the more uptight, nervous, and even sweating Nixon on camera. The country had also just been through an economic recession and, since a Republican had been president, many voters blamed it on that party and were looking for change. Much like the young Barack Obama decades later, Kennedy had change written all over him. He was also the first Roman Catholic to become president, and that worked to his advantage as he was able to mobilize more voters from the Catholic Church than Nixon did from protestant churches. This was despite the fact that Kennedy downplayed his religious heritage as a Catholic and, in so doing, irritated some Roman Catholic leaders.

Possibly most important was that Kennedy exuded a charisma and idealism that resonated well, especially with younger voters.

Although the voting age at the time was 21 and not 18 as it is today, Kennedy managed to appeal to a large number of 20- and 30-somethings in America. Assessing his popularity, writer Dylan Matthews of the *Washington Post* wrote the following on the 50th anniversary of Kennedy's assassination:

> "It tells us a great deal about the meaning of John F. Kennedy in our history that liberals and conservatives alike are eager to pronounce him as one of their own," [writer E. J.] Dionne notes. "A Gallup poll last week found that Americans rate him more highly than any of the other 11 presidents since Eisenhower. A 2011 Gallup poll found that he came in fourth when Americans were asked to name the greatest president of all time, behind Ronald Reagan, Abraham Lincoln, and Bill Clinton, but ahead of George Washington, Franklin Roosevelt, and Thomas Jefferson.
>
> Some of that reputation is hard to argue with. Kennedy was a brilliant rhetorician who inspired a generation of young Americans, and his death left a lingering scar on the American psyche." (Matthews, 1963)

One baby boomer described his reaction to Kennedy's presidency as follows:

> *I was in high school when Kennedy and Nixon battled each other for the White House. Although I was young and didn't know too much about the issues, I connected with the idealism of this young, energetic, and handsome man. Many of my friends felt the same way. High schoolers tend to be some of the most idealistic people on the planet, believing all things are possible and latching onto ideas that later might seem simplistic but which make sense when you're 17. I remember some of Kennedy's sayings to this day like, "Ask not what your country can do for you, but what you can do for your country." That kind of selfless attitude was one a lot of us aspired to, although we found it very hard to practice in our daily lives. But this is probably when I first began realizing—maybe without consciously doing so—the charisma and idealism are important aspects of leadership. Those ideals can serve as guiding principles, even though they may get compromised in order to reach worthy goals. You at least have to have the guiding light, and John Kennedy was that for so many in my generation.*

THE BATTLE OVER CIVIL RIGHTS

When John Kennedy entered the White House, his idealism and a vision for a better America included the cessation of racial discrimination and greater equality for all Americans. The push toward a national civil rights act gained steam under Kennedy, especially after the sometimes-violent confrontations between blacks and whites in the South during the 1950s. A high-profile standoff between nine African American students and Arkansas governor Orval Faubus took place at Little Rock Central High School in 1957 and brought the country's attention to the debate over civil rights. The students were eventually allowed to attend, but it took the intervention of President Dwight D. Eisenhower to make it happen. The die had been cast, and the modern-day precedent was set for a president to start enforcing constitutional guarantees of equality for all. Kennedy was next in line to move that ball forward, and passage of a national civil rights act seemed the way to do it. Kennedy and his advisors knew it was a risky move and might not pass Congress, but the movement had gained enough steam—and there was more than enough violence in black white confrontations in southern states—to make it a risk worth taking.

Notes from the Smithsonian Institution's Civil Rights History Project show how young people were drawn into the civil rights movement:

> At its height in the 1960s, the Civil Rights Movement drew children, teen-agers, and young adults into a maelstrom of meetings, marches, violence, and in some cases, imprisonment. Why did so many young people decide to become activists for social justice? Joyce Ladner answers this question in her interview with the Civil Rights History Project, pointing to the strong support of her elders in shaping her future path:
>
> > "The Movement was the most exciting thing that one could engage in. I often say that, in fact, I coined the term, the 'Emmett Till generation.' I said that there was no more exciting time to have been born at the time and the place and to the parents that movement, young movement, people were born to. . . . I remember so clearly Uncle Archie who was in World War I, went to France, and he always told us, 'Your generation is going to change things.'"
>
> Several activists interviewed for the Civil Rights History Project were in elementary school when they joined the movement. Freeman Hrabowski was 12 years old when he was inspired to march in the Birmingham Children's Crusade of 1963. While sitting in the back of church one Sunday, his ears perked up when he heard a man speak about a march for integrated schools. A math geek, Hrabowski was excited about the possibility of competing aca-demically with white children. While spending many days in prison after he was arrested at the march, photographs of police and dogs attacking the chil-dren drew nationwide attention. Hrabowski remembers that at the prison, Dr. King told him and the other children, "What you do this day will have an impact on children yet unborn." He continues, "I'll never forget that.

I didn't even understand it, but I knew it was powerful, powerful, very powerful." Hrabowski went on to become president of the University of Maryland, Baltimore County, where he has made extraordinary strides to support African American students who pursue math and science degrees.

As a child, Clara Luper attended many meetings of the NAACP Youth Council in Oklahoma City because her mother, Marilyn, was the leader of this group. She remembers, "We were having an NAACP Youth Council meeting, and I was eight years old at that time. That's how I can remember that I was not ten years old. And I—we were talking about our experiences and our negotiation—and I suggested, made a motion that we would go down to Katz Drug Store and just sit, just sit and sit until they served us." This protest led to the desegregation of the drug store's lunch counter in Oklahoma City. Luper relates more stores about what it was like to grow up in a family that was constantly involved in the movement.

While some young people came into the movement by way of their parents' activism and their explicit encouragement, others had to make an abrupt and hard break in order to do so, with some even severing familial ties. Joan Trumpauer Mulholland was a young white girl from Arlington, Virginia, when she came to realize the hypocrisy of her segregated church in which she learned songs such as "Jesus loves the little children, red and yellow, black and white." When she left Duke University to join the movement, her mother, who had been raised in Georgia, "thought I had been sort of sucked up into a cult . . . it went against everything she had grown up and believed in. I can say that a little more generously now than I could have then." Phil Hutchings' father was a lifetime member of the NAACP, but couldn't support his son when he moved toward radicalism and Black Power in the late 1960s. Hutchings reflects on the way their different approaches to the struggle divided the two men, a common generational divide for many families who lived through those times: "He just couldn't go beyond a certain point. And we had gone beyond that . . . and the fact that his son was doing it . . . the first person in the family who had a chance to complete a college education. I dropped out of school for eleven years. . . . He thought I was wasting my life. He said, 'Are you . . . happy working for Mr. Castro?'" (Youth in the Civil Rights Movement, n.d.)

THE STAGE IS SET

The stage for a major change in America had been set by an organized series of nonviolent protests against racial discrimination in southern cities like Greensboro, North Carolina, and Montgomery, Selma, and Birmingham, Alabama. Some of those protests turned violent as white segregationists engaged the demonstrators in bloody confrontations while law enforcement officials did little to stop the violence. Leading the nonviolent movement was Dr. Martin

Luther King, who, 14 months prior to the passage of the 1964 Civil Rights Act, penned his famous letter from a Birmingham jail while being held for his part in promoting nonviolent demonstrations.

The fight for civil rights reached the boiling point on June 11, 1963, when a pair of black teens attempted to register for classes at the University of Alabama in Tuscaloosa. Despite the national push for desegregation, Alabama remained the lone state where segregation was the norm for its schools. Just as Governor Faubus had done six years earlier in Arkansas, Alabama governor George Wallace stood in the way of these students with the intent of keeping the University of Alabama an all-white institution. He was flanked by state troopers on the steps of the university administration building to prevent the students from registering. This was despite President Kennedy's attempts to change Wallace's mind. When it became obvious that the governor was not going to back down willingly, Kennedy signed Presidential Proclamation 3542 ordering him to do so and allow the black students to enroll in the university. Had that failed, the president was ready to use Executive Order 11111 that would have called up and federalized the Alabama National Guard to come to Tuscaloosa and arrest Governor Wallace. The order was not needed, however, as the governor stood aside and let the students enroll, thereby desegregating the University of Alabama (JFK Faces Down Defiant Governor, n.d.).

The Alabama standoff was covered by the national media and was the lead story that night on network newscasts. Sensing he had the attention of the country on the issue of civil rights, Kennedy decided to go live that night on national television to make his case for bringing racial discrimination to an end in the United States. The speech, drafted by presidential speechwriter Ted Sorensen that afternoon, was delivered that night on prime-time television, although the final draft was not completed until 7:55 p.m. That draft was combined with a more extemporaneous draft written simultaneously by the president and brother Robert F. Kennedy, and President Kennedy made his case to the American people on time. The speech became known as the "Moral Crisis" speech because that's how Kennedy framed the racial discrimination issue in America. But the president didn't just talk about the problem; he called for a solution, and that was a charge to Congress to pass a national civil rights act.

In the ensuing year, racial tensions continued to rise in the South, and in June 1964, three young civil rights workers—James Chaney, Andrew Goodman, and Michael Schwerner—were found murdered in Neshoba County, Mississippi, as they worked in the "Freedom Summer" campaign to register blacks to vote in the state of Mississippi.

Three weeks later, Congress passed the Civil Rights Act of 1964, outlawing discrimination on the basis of race, color, religion, sex, or national origin. President Kennedy immediately signed it into law.

In many ways, however, the fight had just begun to enforce the measures of the act, and others would die in the fight before it was over. One of those victims would be Dr. King himself, who was gunned down at the Lorraine Motel in Memphis on April 4, 1968. He was in town to support black sanitation workers who were on strike against the city, protesting bad working conditions and unequal pay.

PRESIDENT KENNEDY IS KILLED

I remember the day President Kennedy died at the beginning:

It was a normal November day in 1963 at Midwest City High School, in a suburb of Oklahoma City. Students and teachers were finishing up the morning activities and getting ready for lunch break. And then a television or two in the school broke into regular programming with alarming news. President John Kennedy had just been shot while visiting Dallas. More news would follow. . . . Word spread like an Oklahoma prairie fire throughout the large school. Students broke into small huddles to talk about the news. Mostly, however, the sound that was most audible in the building was the sound of silence as everyone waited to see whether their president would survive the attack.

The impact of Kennedy's abrupt death was felt around the world. British historian and writer Lisa Jardine remembers what that day meant for her.

Like almost everyone else of my generation, I can remember exactly where I was when I heard that John F Kennedy had been assassinated in Dallas, Texas, on 22 November 1963. I was cycling down King's Parade on my way to an early evening seminar, when I was flagged down by a fellow student whom I had never really liked. At first I simply refused to believe him. Once I had been convinced that the devastating news was true, my own private version of "shooting the messenger" meant that I could never bear to be in that particular student's company thereafter. . . .

Left-leaning young people all around the globe experienced the death of Kennedy as an almost personal loss, a cruel blow to their idealistic vision of a better, fairer world led by a charismatic, dynamic and progressive US president. As an active member of the Cambridge University Labour Club in those days, I was a sympathetic bystander to the increasingly violent civil rights protests in the US during the mid-Sixties, and deeply involved with fellow Cambridge students in the growing international opposition to the Vietnam War. Over those years, I was involved in numerous anti-war meetings and protests. (Jardine, 2009)

Anytime the nation faces a change in presidents, there is always a period adjustment. But when the president is a popular one, is in his first term, and is cut down by an assassin's bullet, the change is even more traumatic and anxiety ridden. Such was the case when John Kennedy was visiting Dallas on November 23, 1963, as part of a western states campaign trip, and was shot and killed as his open-air car paraded past Dealey Plaza. The story of the assassination, and the subsequent arrest of Lee Harvey Oswald and his own slaying a few days later, has been told many times. What hasn't been told so much is the effect that all this had on the people of the United States. When a nation faces such an abrupt and violent end to its president, people must confront some very unsettling questions. Among them are the following:

- What happened and why?
- Who did it and why?
- How could this have happened?
- What do we do now?
- Are we safe?

THE WORLD TUNES IN

Since television news was now a dominant means of information in American homes, Americans flocked to their television sets that day and night to find answers to those questions and hopefully to relieve some anxieties and to begin the grieving process for the man who may have been the most charismatic president America had known to that point. Here is how a special edition *TV Guide* magazine, published just two months after the JFK assassination, described that afternoon and the role that television played in it:

"From Dallas . . . a flash . . . The President died at 2 o'clock Eastern Standard Time . . . The President is dead. . . "

On a New York street NBC focuses its cameras on a chicly dressed, middle-aged woman wearing dark glasses and a tailored hat at the moment the news comes over an auto's loudspeaker. The woman starts, lets out a cry and falls back into the crowd.

At that moment there began something which could only happen in the age of TV. As a Nation we were able to live out our grief in concert and at the same time begin the arduous business of picking up the pieces. Moreover, we were able to prepare ourselves for the new order of things. At the end of the Four Days we were to know the new President intimately, who he was, where he came from and, most important of all, how he behaved in a time of extreme stress. As [CBS News anchor Walter] Cronkite was later to comment: "We saw before our very eyes a smooth transition of government. No confusion. Only a man in command moving ahead to the problems at hand." And [ABC newsman Ron] Cochran was to add: "Television had actually become the window of the world so many had hoped it might be one day." (TV Guide, 1964)

In the early 1960s, there were only three commercial television networks; cable television had not yet begun, so there were only three places on TV where Americans could get their news: ABC, NBC, and CBS. The most popular newscasts at the time were offered by CBS, and the most trusted man in America was its chief news anchor, Walter Cronkite. It is not surprising that so many Americans turned to him to get their answers on the Kennedy tragedy. Looking back, it was as if 180 million Americans were gathered in the family room to hear our favorite "Uncle Walter" announce that one of our most beloved relatives had just died. The family may have had different opinions about JFK's policies, but the man himself was loved. So full of ideals, so charismatic, so young to die.

Mary Kay Havens, an Oklahoma high school student when Kennedy was shot, described her reaction on that day this way:

I was in English class, just after lunch on Friday, November 22, 1963. The teacher was attempting to bring order to the class when the intercom came on unexpectedly. A lot of static was on the announcement and the rowdy boys in class made the message even harder to hear. Then we heard: President Kennedy . . . shot . . . Dallas. A pall came over the room as we listened. We thought surely a president could not be killed in the United States in 1963. That was something that happened only in far off, uncivilized countries.

Soon after, school was dismissed and I don't remember how I got home. I do remember walking in the door and seeing my Dad in tears staring at the television. We were all in disbelief. We had been to Dallas, and even in Parkland Hospital. We had gone to downtown Oklahoma City to see Kennedy in a campaign parade. My family had been Democrats forever, and still blamed Herbert Hoover for the Dust Bowl and the depression. President Kennedy was young, enthusiastic, handsome, had a beautiful family. Surely, no one would have wanted to kill him.

We prayed he would not die. We didn't know if this was the beginning of something even worse, but could not imagine what could be worse than

President Kennedy being shot. We were glued to the television for two days, trying to process this terrible event and wondering what was happening to our country and our freedom.

Sunday morning was the first time we left the house. We went to church and then to the Monroney Junior High Pancake Breakfast, which had been previously scheduled. Everyone needed some diversion, but televisions were on in the cafeteria where the pancakes were served. The televisions were very small by today's standards, black and white, and on rolling AV carts. Everyone was sad, but knew we had to go on. Again there was a commotion as the television showed the killing of Lee Harvey Oswald. Newscasters tried to explain how many questions about President Kennedy's assassination would never be answered because the man arrested for his killing was now dead.

LBJ SWORN IN

On the same day that Kennedy was shot and killed, Vice President Lyndon B. Johnson was sworn in as the 36th president of the United States. He would finish out Kennedy's first term and then be elected president in 1964 in a lopsided race against Republican Barry Goldwater, senator from Arizona. Johnson would inherit four years of tumult and declining popularity and then decide not to run for a second term. Ironically, one of his signature accomplishments would be presiding over the country when the Civil Rights Act was passed in July 1964, eight months after the death of the president who had championed it.

Taking over for a president as popular and charismatic as John F. Kennedy would have been an immense challenge for any vice president in 1963. But for a man who had very little charisma himself and do it as an unpopular war was claiming more and more American lives, the challenge might seem impossible. Such was the challenge facing Lyndon Baines Johnson, a former senator from Texas who had been tapped by Kennedy as a running mate largely to help win the southern vote.

Lisa Jardine captures some of the irony that existed in the man known as LBJ.

Lyndon Baines Johnson was a man of many contradictions. Personally rude, overbearing and at times politically unscrupulous, he was nevertheless capable of immense personal charm, particularly when he was lobbying and brokering backstage in the Washington corridors of power. A fiercely proud Texan, who in the course of his rise to power openly backed reactionary and retrograde legislation on race, union labour and protectionism, he was eventually responsible for establishing some of the most important cornerstones of liberal American legislation, the most significant of which was groundbreaking anti-poverty and civil rights legislation, whose effects can still be felt in the United States today. (Jardine, 2009)

It took awhile for Americans to get used to this abrupt change in personas from Kennedy to Johnson. Whereas Kennedy was an urbane sophisticate from Massachusetts who spoke with a Brahmin accent and seemed poised and charismatic in front of a camera, Johnson was a rough-and-tumble Texan with a thick Lone Star accent who seemed more crude and more comfortable astride a horse on his ranch than in Washington, D.C. But Johnson's ability to get things done, aided immensely by his time in the Senate and his forceful methods in getting others to sign on to his agenda, resulted in his election to his first full term as president in 1964. He ran against the arch-conservative senator from Arizona, Barry Goldwater, in a campaign that made many Americans think Goldwater would push America into a nuclear war. Once installed in his own presidency, LBJ was able to secure passage of such landmark legislation as the Civil Rights Act of 1964. Had it not been for the Vietnam War and the quagmire it produced for America, LBJ might have gone easily into a second term. Instead, his deepening commitment to that war and the increase in troop strength he authorized during his presidency cost him a chance at reelection. After famed CBS news anchor Walter Cronkite made his historic television pronouncement that the Vietnam War was "unwinnable," Johnson decided not to seek reelection, fearing he had lost the support of middle America. His presidency came to an end in 1968 following his first full term in office.

NIXON REAPPEARS

Richard M. Nixon had spent years licking his wounds from his narrow defeat for the presidency in 1960 at the hands of John F. Kennedy. In the meantime, he had run another unsuccessful race—for governor of California in 1962—and was waiting for his chance to return to the political arena in Washington. Lyndon Johnson's decision to not seek reelection in 1968 gave him that chance, and Nixon made the best of it, staging a campaign that won him the Republican nomination and pitted him against the liberal and popular Democratic senator from Minnesota, Hubert H. Humphrey. But at what was to be a glittering and inspiring national showcase for Humphrey—the 1968 Democratic National Convention in Chicago—a nightmare instead ensued.

THE 1968 DEMOCRATIC NATIONAL CONVENTION

To set the context, the convention occurred in August, just two months after the assassination of popular Democratic presidential contender Robert F. Kennedy and four months after the assassination of Martin Luther King. A series of protests in 100 American cities followed King's assassination, and this year of violence was the reason Mayor Daley took such security precautions in Chicago.

It may seem ironic that anti-war protesters chose the Democratic convention, instead of the Republican, to protest. But it showed how counterculture America was not just targeting political parties but the entire political system that, in their view, had failed the country and was costing it thousands of lost lives in a war America should not be in at all. The staged protests were also meant to serve as an urgent call to the party protesters believed had the better chance of rescuing America. Whatever the motivations, the protests and the violence that Chicago police used against it wound up pouring salt into the wounds of an America divided over the Vietnam War and over the spirit of peaceful protest. And it wound up costing the Democrats dearly in terms of popular belief that Humphrey could heal those wounds. The 1968 Democratic National Convention became the bloodiest and most violent convention ever staged in America.

Here is how a writer for *The Smithsonian* described the preparation for the convention, planned by Chicago mayor Richard J. Daley to be a fortress against any efforts to take attention away from Humphrey on his way to the nomination:

> He [Daley] had ordered new redwood fences installed to screen the squalid lots of the aromatic stockyards adjoining the convention site. At the International Amphitheatre, conventioneers found that the main doors, modeled after a White House portico, had been bulletproofed. The hall itself was surrounded by a steel fence topped with barbed wire. Inside the fence, clusters of armed and helmeted police mingled with security guards and dark-suited agents of the Secret Service. At the apex of the stone gates through which all had to enter was a huge sign bearing the unintentionally ironic words, "HELLO DEMOCRATS! WELCOME TO CHICAGO."
>
> The National Guard had been mobilized and ordered to shoot to kill, if necessary.
>
> Even as delegates began entering this encampment, an army of protesters from across the country flowed into the city, camping in parks and filling churches, coffee shops, homes and storefront offices. They were a hybrid group—radicals, hippies, yippies, moderates—representing myriad

issues and a wide range of philosophies, but they were united behind an encompassing cause: ending the long war in Vietnam and challenging Democratic Party leaders and their delegates to break with the past, create change—yes, that was the term then on every protester's lips—and remake the battered U.S. political system.

What followed was worse than even the most dire pessimist could have envisioned. The 1968 Chicago convention became a lacerating event, a distillation of a year of heartbreak, assassinations, riots and a breakdown in law and order that made it seem as if the country were coming apart. In its psychic impact, and its long-term political consequences, it eclipsed any other such convention in American history, destroying faith in politicians, in the political system, in the country and in its institutions. (Johnson, 2008)

Some 10,000 protesters had gathered in nearby Grant Park on August 28 to demonstrate against the failing attempts of the U.S. government to stop the war in Vietnam and heal other wounds in America. They were met by 23,000 Chicago police and National Guardsmen, and the heat of the confrontation rose quickly as a young protester began lowering the American flag. Police and Guardsmen stepped in and began beating the protester and others who were in the vicinity. The violence, including the use of police dogs that attacked protesters, ensued and was caught on camera by the myriad of national and local news agencies on the scene. The melee lasted for some time and provided far more drama for TV than did the staid proceedings going on inside the convention center. Looking back on the confrontation and the police response, the government-commissioned Walker Report said the police response to the protesters was characterized by

unrestrained and indiscriminate police violence on many occasions, particularly at night. That violence was made all the more shocking by the fact that it was often inflicted upon persons who had broken no law, disobeyed no order, made no threat. These included peaceful demonstrators, onlookers, and large numbers of residents who were simply passing through, or happened to live in, the areas where confrontations were occurring. (Walker, 1968)

Here is how one attorney and writer, Suzy Underwood, describes her memories of the convention from the decade in which she was an activist herself:

Sometimes it seems that my life has moved, is moving, in a pretty straight line, but this prompt has made me examine that trajectory and think about the times that my path was dramatically altered. Certainly the birth of each of my three children changed my life in ways that I could not have imagined before it happened. But that is an experience shared by almost everyone who has ever had children, so I don't want to write about that. Trying to pick the one event that dramatically turned my life in a new direction inevitably takes me back to the 1968 Democratic Convention in Chicago.

I had spent the summer working for the McCarthy campaign in Washington D.C., and in mid-August drove out to Chicago with three other young women only slightly older than I. The week before the convention we were put up in the homes of Chicago-area McCarthy volunteers. My friend Ellen and I shared a room in a beautiful house owned by a U of Chicago professor. Every day we went to the Amphitheatre where the convention was to be held, getting the McCarthy area ready for the delegates who would be there the following week. The week of the convention itself we were not allowed in the ampitheatre because we did not have credentials. So that week we worked and slept in the Hilton Hotel, where the McCarthy campaign had two entire floors. It was hectic and exciting, and at that point I was still naive enough to believe that McCarthy might be nominated for President.

All week there had been demonstrations going on in the streets, organized by the Yippies (including my beloved Phil Ochs), but we had stayed upstairs in the Hilton because we were still being "Clean for Gene." We heard stories about clashes with the police and the National Guard, but had not seen any of it. However, when the news came that the delegates had nominated Hubert Humphrey, who had not participated in a single primary, as the Democratic candidate for President, we were outraged, and we were out of there. We went down to the street to join the protests and fight the pigs. Grant Park was right across the street from the hotel, and it was mobbed with demonstrators. At first it was very cathartic being out there, yelling at the cops and feeling the energy of all the other demonstrators, but then they started firing tear gas into the crowd. Suddenly I couldn't breathe, I couldn't see, and I couldn't stop coughing.

Somebody grabbed my hand and said "RUN," pulling me along. I ran blindly, following this unknown person who was holding my hand. We ran down to the end of the block and then turned the corner, so that we would be out of the path that the wind was blowing the tear gas. We stopped, leaning against the side of a building along with many others. Somebody had a bag of grapes and was passing them out, saying "here, eat some grapes, it will make your throat feel better." When he offered me a bunch of grapes, my immediate response was "Are they union grapes?" (I was a strong supporter of Cesar Chavez and the UFW even then.) He said, "I don't know, just eat them!" So I did. I figured under the circumstances Cesar would approve.

I went back to the Hilton, and was regrouping in the lobby, when the cops came in and said that everyone was under arrest. They kept us there for the longest time, and even when we told them we were staying there in the hotel, they wouldn't let us go upstairs. Finally, after what seemed like hours, Senator McCarthy came to the lobby and vouched for us and convinced the cops to release us. I don't think all of the people in the lobby were actually McCarthy staff, but they all came upstairs with us anyway, and just hung out wherever there was room. The next day (which was actually my birthday), the Senator took all of us who were on his staff back to New York or Washington in his private plane. The Convention was over and he wanted to get us safely out of there.

Even in high school I was pretty far left in my political beliefs, so the Convention didn't change my positions on the issues—except to make me hate and distrust the police—but it made me cynical about working within the system, and expecting change to occur because it was right. I now saw that nothing would be accomplished without organizing and fighting every step of the way. At college I joined SDS. I occupied a building to demand that ROTC be removed from the Harvard campus. I went on numerous marches and demonstrations, in Boston, in New Haven, in Washington. For a while I truly believed that there was going to be a revolution, and that I would be out on the barricades killing pigs (the derisive term used by activists in the 1960s).

Eventually I realized that the revolution was not going to happen, and I was not going to kill any pigs. I don't know if that was another turning point, or just coming to terms with reality as a result of growing older. I'm certainly glad now that I never killed anybody. But it's a little disappointing to see that we haven't come as far as we should have in 48 years. Maybe I, or we, got too complacent once we grew up. Or maybe there is another turning point still to come. (Underwood, 2016)

The Democrats were unable to recover from the public's perception of them with the concepts of disunity and disarray, and Richard Nixon won the presidency with 301 electoral college votes to 191 for Humphrey and 46 for Alabama governor George Wallace. The country was now to embark on a new chapter with a president who would take them deeper into Vietnam, widen the credibility gap, and eventually be driven from office by the infamous episode known as Watergate.

THE NIXON YEARS

When Richard Nixon entered the White House as the 37th president in January 1969, America was reeling from a confusing and unpopular war in Vietnam. It had been four years since the first major battle of that war, Ia Trang, and some 37,000 American troops had already been killed. The protests over that war had spread across the country, focused mainly on college campuses and in major urban areas, but there were also the protests—often violent—over the push for greater civil rights. The newly minted president inherited that divided America. He adopted a theme of "Peace with Honor" for Vietnam, but that peace would not come until the year after he would leave office. The paranoia that Nixon brought with him into the presidency caused him to see those who protested and disagreed with him as enemies, hence the creation of his infamous "enemies list" and of his "plumber's unit" in the White House to try and identify those who were leaking information to the press and whose agendas were different than his. Included in his enemies list were several well-known news correspondents, because President Nixon did not like the news media at all and felt they were trying to subvert him at every turn.

Although the term "credibility gap" was not coined first to refer to Nixon—it first was used to describe LBJ's alleged duplicity in claims about Vietnam—Nixon's own lack of transparency widened the gap even further. The "gap" referred to the lack of distrust that much of America had developed toward the White House on issues related to Vietnam and civil rights. The release of the classified and infamous "Pentagon Papers" by the *New York Times* and *Washington Post* in 1971 stretched that gap to the ripping point. The voluminous report, never meant for public eyes, chronicled the history of America's involvement in the Vietnam War, which showed motivations that differed from presidential rhetoric and also revealed the existence of a "secret war" by America in neutral Cambodia and Laos. The documents were released to the *Times*, and then the *Post*, by Daniel Ellsberg, who had worked on the Defense Department team that had prepared the report. The *Times* published its first installments of the Pentagon Papers verbatim in 1971. They were met with objections from Nixon, who secured an injunction against further publication until the Supreme Court struck it down. While the injunction was in force, however, the *Washington Post* began publishing them too. Even though the Supreme Court overruled the White House, it was the first time in modern history that a U.S. court had restrained a news organization from publishing a story. The Supreme Court decision resulted in an underscoring of the "no prior restraint" meaning of the First Amendment.

The Supreme Court heard arguments on that case, officially known as the *The New York Times Company v. The United States*, on June 26, 1971, and issued its decision four days later. Ironically, it would be June 1972, when the beginning of the end occurred for the Nixon administration. It was on June 17 that year when the break-in at the Democratic National Headquarters occurred in the Watergate office complex. That led to a protracted series of investigative stories by the *Washington Post* and the *New York Times*, which ultimately connected the dots of that break-in to the Oval Office. President Nixon faced impeachment, and he resigned his presidency halfway through his second term effective August 9, 1974.

THE ROLE OF THE NEWS MEDIA

Throughout the 1960s, the nation's news media played a key role in political developments, doing what it was designed to do: serve as a "fourth estate" that kept watch over the three official branches of government. As it was doing so, it was evolving and learning how to do its watchdog role better. In the case of television, that was especially so. Two years before the 1960s began, Edward R. Murrow of CBS News made his famous speech before the Radio and Television News Directors Association in Chicago, in which he trumpeted a warning that television news was being overtaken by the entertainment wing of broadcasting, and he called for network news divisions to resist and to instead inform and educate the public on vital issues of the day. The portion of his speech most remembered went like this:

> *Our history will be what we make it. And if there are any historians about fifty or a hundred years from now, and there should be preserved the kinescopes for one week of all three networks, they will there find recorded in black and white, or color, evidence of decadence, escapism and insulation from the realities of the world in which we live.*
> *. . . This instrument can teach, it can illuminate; yes, and it can even inspire. But it can do so only to the extent that humans are determined to use it to those ends. Otherwise it's nothing but wires and lights in a box.*
> (Murrow, 1958)

In many ways, network television news took Murrow's warning and pleading to heart and built several hours a day of evening news programming and public affairs. Network newscasts were expanded from a half-hour to an hour; those anchoring those newscasts were among the best professional journalists themselves. Names like Walter Cronkite, David Brinkley, and Chet Huntley were chief among them. Future news anchors, earning their stripes as reporters in the 1960s, included Dan Rather, Tom Brokaw, John Chancellor, Barbara Walters, Harry Reasoner, Frank Reynolds, Howard K. Smith, Peter Arnett, and Peter Jennings.

Beyond the technological developments that would usher in videotape as a replacement to film (thereby cutting out processing time and getting video on-air much faster), there was the introduction of weekly news magazines. The first was *60 Minutes*, the famed CBS show that has run continuously since that start more than 50 years ago. It set the standard for other news magazine shows to meet, yet none has never attained the consistent quality and impact of *60 Minutes*.

As these newscasts and news magazine shows gained in importance and viewership, they served as a watchdog that politicians could not take lightly. Knowing there were these beacons surveying the waters was enough to limit the amount of government corruption that existed and help expose that which did exist. Earlier in this chapter, one such example was discussed when the *New York Times* and the *Washington Post* obtained and published the so-called Pentagon Papers, exposing the real reasons for America's involvement in the Vietnam War and its secret bombing of neutral Cambodia. The classic example was only a couple years away as the decade ended, when those same two newspapers spearheaded the exposé of the Watergate scandal that led to the forced resignation of President Richard M. Nixon.

As for newspapers, the 1960s was a high-water decade for circulation figures, and newspapers around the country took advantage of the good revenue stream to beef up newsrooms and create investigative reporting units that did not fear digging into controversial subjects and issues. As the 1960s drew to a close, daily weekday newspaper circulation stood at 62 million. The coming decades would be less kind as television matured and the Internet and social media came on the scene. By 2015, that same newspaper circulation figure would drop to just fewer than 38 million (Newspaper Fact Sheet, 2017).

The biggest impact of the news media on political issues in the 1960s, however, came in press coverage of the Vietnam War and of the struggle for civil rights, especially in the South. Vietnam was America's first "living room war," because it was the first one that network television news was able to cover and to do that on a nightly basis, week after week, month after month, year after year. It was this intensive coverage and the public opinion arising out of the images that were shown that put enormous pressure on Washington to try and hasten the end to American involvement in Vietnam. The same kind of effect arose from the extensive media coverage of violent civil rights clashes in the South. Much of America had seemed uninformed about the degrees of discrimination and oppression that African Americans had been confronting in the

South. But the cameras and correspondents of network television brought all of it into the nation's living rooms. Feeling pressure, Washington reacted with both the civil rights act and the voting rights act by mid-decade.

BIBLIOGRAPHY

"America's Long Vigil," *TV Guide*, January 25, 1964, as accessed on December 7, 2017, at http://jeff560.tripod.com/tvgjfk.html

Jardine, Lisa. "Lyndon Johnson, the Uncivil Rights Reformer," *Independent*, January 1, 2009, as accessed on December 28, 2017, at http://www.independent.co.uk/news/presidents/lyndon-b-johnson-the-uncivil-rights-reformer-1451816.html

"JFK Faces Down Defiant Governor," History.com, n.d., as accessed on May 1, 2014, at http://www.history.com/this-day-in-history/jfk-faces-down-defiant-governor

Johnson, Haynes. "1968 Democratic National Convention: The Bosses Strike Back," *Smithsonian*, August 2008, as accessed on January 1, 2018, at https://www.smithsonianmag.com/history/1968-democratic-convention-931079/#RYTP69dk2qMFsFeW.99

Matthews, Dylan. "Americans Think John F. Kennedy Was One of Our Greatest Presidents. He Wasn't," *Washington Post*, November 22, 1963, as accessed on November 24, 2017, at https://www.washingtonpost.com/news/wonk/wp/2013/11/22/americans-think-john-f-kennedy-was-one-of-our-greatest-presidents-he-wasnt/

Murrow, Edward R. Speech to Radio and Television News Directors Association, Chicago, Illinois, 1958, as accessed on May 13, 2018, at https://www.poynter.org/news/today-media-history-edward-r-murrow-challenged-broadcast-industry-his-1958-rtnda-speech

"Newspaper Fact Sheet," Pew Research Center, June 1, 2017, as accessed on May 13, 2018, at http://www.journalism.org/fact-sheet/newspapers/

Underwood, Suzy. "The Universe Is Ablaze with Changes," *Retrospect*, August 10, 2016, as accessed on May 9, 2018, at https://www.myretrospect.com/stories/universe-ablaze-with-changes/

Walker, Daniel. "Rights in Conflict," Report to the National Commission on the Causes and Prevention of Violence, December 1, 1968, as accessed on January 1, 2018, at http://chicago68.com/ricsumm.html

"Youth in the Civil Rights Movement," Civil Rights History Project, n.d., as accessed on May 4, 2018, at https://www.loc.gov/collections/civil-rights-history-project/articles-and-essays/youth-in-the-civil-rights-movement/

3

INTELLECTUAL LIFE

Along with all the soul-searching of the 1960s counterculture decade, came some significant thinking about society and humankind's role in—and responsibility to—that society. Some of this thinking was expressed in films, music, and television programs noted elsewhere in this book. But much of it also came in the writings of many who were concerned about the threats America faced in the 1960s, writings that inspired endless late-night conversations across the country from coffee shops to living rooms to dorm rooms and university lecture halls. The turbulence of the decade leant itself well to such discussions about high-stakes aspects of life and how the country was changing.

THE CENTER WAS NOT HOLDING

Many intellectuals uttered statements during the 1960s that could be used to sum up the thinking of large chunks of American society and culture. One of the most remembered, however, came from California author Joan Didion in her book, *Slouching towards Bethlehem*, a phrase that comes from a William Butler Yeats poem, "The Second Coming." The phrase seems to anchor Didion's commentary on America in the 1960s. She writes:

> *The center was not holding. It was a country of bankruptcy notices and public-auction announcements and commonplace reports of casual killings*

*and misplaced children and abandoned homes and vandals who misplaced
even the four-letter words they scrawled.* (Didion, 1968)

Didion and her writer husband John Gregory Dunne had moved
to Southern California in the early 1960s from New York City and
then soon migrated up to the Bay Area. In so doing, she moved
into the epicenter of the counterculture movement that would soon
sweep across all of America, especially its universities and intellectual centers. It was not surprising that what she encountered in
the Haight-Ashbury district of San Francisco and on the campus
of the University of California at Berkeley informed her thinking
about a changing America. Originally working on an article about
hippies for the traditional *Saturday Evening Post*, the 32-year-old
Didion wound up writing a book that radicalized the thinking of
many Americans who read it. The writer engaged in what journalists today would call immersive or even participatory journalism,
hanging out with drug users and young people who had fled their
traditional middle-class homes looking for answers to deep questions they were having or looking just to escape what they perceived as the trap and threats of the "establishment."

Writing about Didion's "radicalization," the *New Yorker* said
in 2015:

*In the summer of 1967, the Haight was a magnet for people looking to do
drugs. Didion hung out mainly with runaways and acidheads. She met people like Deadeye, a dealer, and his old lady Gerry, who wrote mainly poetry
but gave it up after her guitar was stolen. . . . She meets Jeff and his fifteen-
year-old girlfriend, Debbie, who has run away from home. Didion asks them
about their plans. "We're just gonna let it happen," Jeff says. She meets
Steve who says, "I found love on acid. But I lost it. Now I'm finding it again.
With nothing but grass." She meets Vicki, who dropped out of Laguna High,
"because I had mono," and followed the Grateful Dead to San Francisco. . . .
Didion got plenty of material, but she had no idea how to make a story out
of it.* (Menand, 2015)

Latching on to Yeats's poem as a theme, however, she finished
the story for the magazine, and her book came out of that. She put
the collection of images she found into the vernacular of the societal
dropouts she lived with and covered. In some ways, she became
one of them, and all journalists know about the dangers that pose
to one's objective reporting. In some of her writing, there was a
sense that Didion herself worried at times that she was personally
being drawn too far into the world of the hippies, too far for her

own good. She also drew some criticism by traditional journalists for mixing in too much subjective imagery, while too much of her work was based on actual interviewing and note-taking of what was said. Others—especially those on the counterculture left—worried that she was using the mainstream media to denigrate the counterculture world. There were disturbing—yet accurate—images in *Slouching towards Bethlehem* about young people doing some dangerous things. She wrote a lot about the use of LSD and how it influenced young girls to commit suicide and about parents on acid who left their toddlers unsupervised to do dangerous things, in one case, setting the living room on fire.

Reviewing her work, Louis Menand wrote:

> Didion presented her article as an investigation into what she called "social hemorrhaging." She suggested that what was going on in Haight-Ashbury was the symptom of some sort of national unraveling. But she knew that, at the level of "getting the story," her piece was a failure. She could see, with the X-ray clarity she appears to have been born with, what was happening on the street; she could make her readers see it; but she couldn't explain it. (Menand, 2015)

Regardless of the debate journalists may have over Didion's reporting methods, the fact remains that *Slouching towards Bethlehem* remains one of the most often cited commentaries of counterculture life in the 1960s.

BAKING DIGGER BREAD

San Francisco writer Charles Degelman found an inviting home in the late 1960s among the counterculture theater radicals in the city by the bay. Trading Boston, Cambridge, and the East Coast for California and the epicenter of counterculturalism, Degelman illustrates what life was like living and working among these young radicals who called themselves *Diggers*. Among the followers were intellectuals who translated their thinking into action by helping others in a kind of modern-day commune.

The first Digger bakery began in the basement of a church on Waller Street. To make Digger bread for free, you need to scavenge free but healthy ingredients and tools. Baking bread for free took ingenuity and the Diggers were long on ingenuity. The church lent its ovens to the endeavor and Digger bakers hustled free whole wheat flour from a Hunters Point wholesaler who gave them damaged sacks. . . . The most ingenious characteristic of Digger Bread

*was its shape. With no money to buy large baking pans—bakery brothers
and sisters collected one-and two-pound coffee cans. . . . They'd add sugar,
honey, molasses, anything sweet, even dried fruit that they collected on their
early-morning runs to the city's sprawling produce market. The wholesalers
looked forward to visits from the Digger scavengers. They began to applaud
the one-percent-free Digger mission. After all, the wholesale workers shared
common purpose with the colorful diplomats from the Haight-Ashbury—to
feed the hungry. The market workers set aside fruits, vegetables, and grains
that quietly dropped off the market's loading docks and found themselves
joining bubbling soups and stews in the cauldrons that Digger cooks brewed,
lading out a bowl to anybody hungry, daily in the parks. . . .*

*Gradually, the Digger bakers improved their technique and Digger bak-
eries opened up, six or seven of them around Northern California. Anyone
could become a Digger baker. The only stipulation? You had to give it away.*

*In the spirit of their ingenious determination to create a free society, Dig-
gers brought food to the Americas, those who had been spit from the belly
of the beast and those who chose to walk away from the American Dream.
Digger bread was tough, nourishing, went down warm, smelled of molasses,
and it was one hundred percent free.* (Degelman, 2015)

This excerpt from Degelman's essay shows the spirit and motivation behind the actions of young people in the 1960s who chose to
make statements with their lives, eschewing the normal career path
a college graduate might embark on. The path these people took
was one of bonding with like-minded individuals who wanted to
serve the marginalized and outcasts instead of pursuing a personal
profit motive. The enclaves in San Francisco and other cities these
revolutionaries forged and inhabited were also centers of intellectualism and free thinking where college students and young graduates could come and exchange ideas about societal corruption and
talk about how to improve those conditions. Protest music, drugs,
and "free love" often were apart of these enclaves. Some were
attracted by these aspects, but the hard-core protesters were there
because of their idealism, fueled by their frustration with societal
conditions of war and inequality.

THE SECULAR CITY

In the middle of the decade, another writer burst onto the intellectual and literary scene in the form of Harvey Cox, who had been
a Baptist pastor and chaplain at Oberlin College. Cox had gone
through something of a personal awakening as he observed what
was happening in America, and out of his thinking came a signature

book for the decade called *The Secular City*. Many who read it began perceiving Cox as a modern-day prophet, and the book became a million-seller and jumped onto the best-seller lists. The main argument of the book was that Christianity needed to be desacralized or, in other words, needed to have the sacred removed from it to have it make more sense for people in the then modern world of the 1960s. In place of the sacred, he urged a move to the "technopolis" or the "place of human control, of rational planning, of bureaucratic organization." It all may sound strange, but Cox made his philosophy fit well into the turbulence and questioning nature of the decade. He asserted that 20th-century religion and spirituality needed to distance itself from "all supernatural myths and sacred symbols."

In their place, he said, society should "spiritualize the material culture to perfect man and society through technology and social planning." He argued for politics supplanting metaphysics "as the language of theology." To Cox, genuine worship did not take place by a parishioner who knelt in church but who took a stand with strikers on a picket line. The book and its arguments were widely discussed and debated during the last half of the 1960s, and it is deemed an important contribution to the intellectual life of that decade (Cox, 2012).

As for myself, I was in college during 1964–1968 and became fascinated with the popularity of Cox's book, although I didn't agree with all his conclusions. Here is my memory of that:

I was on a journey in college to find something worthwhile to latch on to and devote my life to. I tried to do it through churches that pursued secular missions, but it didn't work for me. Late in my sophomore year, I found my niche in student campus movements that were part of what I called the "new evangelism" of the '60s. As I was embracing that end of the theological scale, The Secular City was published and started drawing attention among my peers. We couldn't see how religion could—or should—be secularized. But we understood why this book was so appealing to people at the time. After all, everything was being questioned in the 1960s; especially all forms of traditionalism. I think even for those of us who didn't follow secularism as a worldview or a way to make the world better, Cox showed us the necessity of translating our religious views into terms that secularists could understand; we had to find a way to show how God was relevant to the everyday trials and tribulations that people were experiencing. I remember having several late-night conversations with friends about Cox's book, and I think it helped us understand those who were struggling with seeing how religious faith could solve the everyday problems people were facing. So, in this and other respects, The Secular City helped both faith followers and secularists in America.

After his book became an international best seller, Cox went on to a career as a professor of theology at the Harvard Divinity School where, some say, he moderated some of his *Secular City* arguments but remained committed to exploring the intersection of Christianity and modern religious pluralism.

THE GLOBAL VILLAGE

Four decades have passed since the death of Marshall McLuhan, a once-obscure Canadian English professor who would become one of the most popular intellectuals of the 1960s and 1970s. His signature book, published in 1964, focused on the true nature and power of news and entertainment media in America and was called *Understanding Media: The Extensions of Man*. McLuhan gave America a new understanding of television, movies, and books; how they shrink the world down; and how they affect our processing of thoughts and emotions. Each of these media platforms is not a neutral entity he said; each affects the message being delivered and the effect that message has on us. In fact, it was McLuhan who first coined the term "media" in popular usage. His three most famous ideas, still being studied today in classrooms and boardrooms around the country, are as follows:

1. The media have created a *global village*, grouped around uniform and thus identifiable images and sounds that cut across language.
2. The *media is the message*, meaning—among other things—that the delivery platform of mass-communicated messages is just as important as—if not more so than—the messages delivered.
3. The *medium is the message*, meaning that each media platform shakes us up (massages) in different ways. We process information differently on television than in print or in the movies, and the images and sounds presented on television affect us psychologically and even physiologically in ways different than print media do.

McLuhan also categorized all media as either *hot* or *cool*, depending on the level of audience participation required. *Hot media* do not require much audience participation, while *cool media* do. Hot media are those that are actually extensions of a person's senses, such as ears or eyes, and that extension is in high definition. That extension is packed with information, and he defines images, radio, and text as such hot media. They deliver all the information you need in a straightforward manner. You don't have to fill in the gaps with your imagination. His hot media are the phonetic alphabet, radio, movies, books, other print media, lectures, and books. Since they deliver so much data, we as audience members don't have to participate much in creating meaning.

On the other hand, cool media provide less information (deliver it in low definition, he would say) and require more audience participation. Examples of his cool media are television, telephone, cartoons and comics, seminars, oral speech, ideographic or pictographic writing, and oral speech.

McLuhan's classifications of media moved people away from perceiving media as neutral (as far as audience effect) and from static entities to dynamic ones that constantly evolve. An example would be radio, which was invented for one purpose (point-to-point communication) and wound up being used for another (broadcasting). Computer inventions and eventual usage applications are more current examples. Although McLuhan did his writings before personal computers and the Internet made their appearance, his logic of media classifications and media effects seems to be as relevant today as before. If alive, he would probably have to classify the Internet as an extremely "hot" medium because it provides so much information that we don't have to add any meaning to it. Yes, we spend a lot of time interacting with the web, but interacting with a medium is not the same as participating in creating its messages' meanings.

Here is how I recall the scene as a graduate student pursuing a PhD in journalism at the University of Missouri: I would go to student/faculty parties at night, and we wound up sitting around drinking beer and talking not about what guy was seeing what girl or what prof was over the edge with her grading, but we'd talk about Marshall McLuhan and his hot and cool media! I remember one particular house party where we grouped around a sectional listening to one of the cooler profs talk about McLuhan's beliefs about television. One particular idea fascinated me, although it seemed too far out at the time: "What if," the prof said, "we all think we're sitting there watching TV, but what really is happening is the TV is watching us?" McLuhan actually envisioned what is happening today or something close to it: that television would be able to record our viewing habits and create psychographic profiles of us, probably for marketing purposes. It was heady stuff, or at least it was to our young minds. I loved the intellectualism that was part of the 1960s.

One reason that McLuhan was so important to intellectual discussions of the decade was that television itself had become so important as an entertainment and information medium in America so much so that individuals and families began scheduling their daily routines around television programming. There was a sense—as there is today—that we were being "invaded" by this invention, and we were curious about some of those effects that might accrue as a result of such heavy use.

EXISTENTIALISTS

It was not surprising that in the turbulent 1960s, a decade where the military draft and the specter of the Vietnam War hung over America, an intellectual such as the French philosopher Jean-Paul Sartre would rise to popularity in America. Along with him came more attention paid to fellow existentialists such as Albert Camus, Soren Kierkegaard, and Friedrich Nietzsche. These and other existentialists focused on the absolute necessity of individual freedom, and that was something made even more desirable in a time when the U.S. government was pressing hundreds of thousands of young men into fighting a war that many didn't want to fight. The message of the individual's right to choose what to believe and how to live fit into the larger context of the decade's mantra of young people was "Do your own thing." And it certainly fit into the various pushes for equality that galvanized in the civil rights movement.

But bringing the French writings of Sartre and others to Americans took gifted translators who also understood philosophy. The best of these was Hazel Barnes, a Yale PhD and the first woman named distinguished professor at the University of Colorado. Through her, many Americans discovered existentialism, and one was a young student looking for a major and finding it in philosophy. He was Thomas J. Nenon, who today is professor of philosophy at the University of Memphis. Here is how he recalls the influence she, Sartre, and French existentialism had on his life:

> Hazel Barnes was a Sartre translator, and I found her challenging and fascinating. French existentialism is what lured me into studying philosophy. I read Satre and Camus, and Kierkegaard, and I was influenced especially by the first two.
>
> There was a lot of philosophy coming out of literature classes then, too; maybe more than in philosophy itself. So literature classes were important to me. (Thomas J. Nenon, interview on December 24, 2018)

THE INTELLECTUAL CONSERVATIVE

One of the most articulate intellectuals among political conservatives in the 1960s was William F. Buckley, whose sophistication and urbane wit came across well, especially on television. Many have called him the intellectual heart of political conservatism in both this decade and the 1970s. Even those disagreeing with his conclusions could not dismiss the logic of his thinking or his ability to make his points both orally and in writing. He was a confidant of Ronald Reagan during his years as governor of California, who would ask for his advice during his campaign for the White House and later as president. Reagan believed Buckley to be a most influential journalist and ally in the right-wing populist movement that Reagan himself was part of (Douthat, 2009). His followers and admirers would include future writers of leading conservative magazines and newspapers, from the *National Review* to the *Wall Street Journal*. Many call Buckley the father of modern day conservatism because he was able to bring together leading thinkers among social conservatives, national defense hawks, and those favoring more libertarian policies especially on economic issues. The *Los Angeles Times* wrote in its 2008 memorial to Buckley, who passed away in February that year:

> Buckley was a fierce debater who loved trading savagely lyrical putdowns with his political opponents. But, unlike the conservative pundits who drive talk radio today, he had many personal friends and admirers among his public foes, including such luminaries as the late economist John Kenneth Galbraith and late writer Norman Mailer. Some of his key political opponents, though, had trouble reconciling the two Buckleys—the irresistibly charming raconteur and the talk show host who drew exquisite rhetorical nooses around the necks of his opponents. "You can't stay mad at a guy who's witty spontaneous and likes good liquor," Mailer once said. (Kraft, 2008)

It was Buckley who founded the *National Review* in 1955 and built it into the leading magazine of political conservatism in America. Buckley also authored or coauthored more than 50 books, both nonfiction and fiction, including a series of novels about spies. It was said of Buckley that his twin leading passions in life were language and writing, and he used the former to produce some critically acclaimed books and articles. He would serve in the army during World War II and then go on and graduate from Yale. But while he was still a student there, he demonstrated his intellect and writing ability in a commencement speech that he was never able to deliver because school administrators saw an early draft and demanded he soften it. When he refused, they chose another student speaker. Buckley's planned speech defied tradition and criticized Yale for not living up to its leadership responsibilities as an educational institution. He admonished the college for not demanding that its professors promote Christianity and free enterprise and called on the school to sanction faculty members who promoted socialism or communism. In retaliation, Buckley would later write *God and Man at Yale: The Superstitions of Academic Freedom*, which became a best-selling book that pulled no punches in criticizing his alma mater for what he perceived as its hypocrisy. Predictably, the book was denounced by liberal graduates of Yale and praised by conservative grads.

Starting in the early years of the 1960s, the *National Review* took the lead in developing a new conservative movement that pulled away from the extreme right wing of conservatism as represented by segregationists in the South, members of the John Birch Society, and anti-Semitists. In so doing, he went against traditional political thinking in critiquing groups of his own party. Contrary to others' expectations, however, he was successful in doing it and wound up bringing conservatism back into mainstream politics only a few years after Republican senator Joseph McCarthy of Wisconsin nearly sank it following his censure by the U.S. Senate for his communist witch hunts.

JOHN OLIVER KILLENS

Not exactly a name that is easily remembered by many, John Oliver Killens distinguished himself as a leading African American intellectual of the 1960s. An influential leader in the Black Arts Movement of the decade, Killens had a close friendship with Martin Luther King and was himself an advocate for civil rights in the decade that produced such a positive sea change for equal rights legislation for blacks in America. He founded the Black Writer's Conference that provided inspiration for current and future African American writers and was professor at Medgar Evers College, in Brooklyn. As a writer, he was one of the most lauded authors of his day. He died at age 71 in 1987.

Killens's first novel was called *Youngblood*, and it appeared in May 1954, which was the same month that the Supreme Court decided the landmark *Brown v. Board of Education* case that declared segregated schools to be unconstitutional. *Youngblood* was a novel chronicling the struggle for self-determination by African Americans in the early 20th century and provided enlightenment and a boost for the civil rights movement that would unfold in the following years in America. Killens would go on to write similar books (*And Then We Heard the Thunder, Great Gittin' Up Morning, A Man Ain't Nothin' But a Man*, and *Great Black Russian* to name four). Killens was also the first black writer to achieve solo screenplay credit for a Hollywood movie. That was *Odds against Tomorrow*, which premiered in 1958.

Killens's work depicted the heroic efforts of blacks in American history and put a special focus on community and family settings. His stories carried moral lessons and values that he hoped would offer inspiration and hope to African Americans still living the struggle for equality. Activism, sometimes featuring armed self-defense methods, that resulted in transformation were key parts of a Killens story. He believed all kinds of artists should engage in political activism and use their work to help illustrate and promote their cause. Like fellow activists of the era, Killens was under surveillance at times by the FBI that kept a file on him and his rhetoric and activities.

HERBERT MARCUSE

Although born in 1898, German philosopher Herbert Marcuse emerged as one of the most influential philosophers of the 1960s in America. As one of the leading members of the Frankfurt School, the full name of which was the Institute for Social Research in Frankfurt, Marcuse came to America when the Third Reich arose in Germany and closed down the Frankfurt School. Following the war, Marcuse made America his permanent home, and it was here that he became one of the cornerstones of the "new left" counterculture movement. This native Berliner, who attended Humbolt University, transferred and graduated from the University of Freiburg where he produced a PhD dissertation on *The German Artist-Novel*. It was the start of a lifelong obsession with the role of philosophy and aesthetics in liberating the mind and soul. Marcuse was influenced by philosopher Martin Heidegger, and his interests in German art and literature broadened out to philosophy. He returned to school and produced a second dissertation focused more on philosophy. He and Heidegger, however, broke apart in 1932 when Heidegger became involved with the Nazi Party. In America, Marcuse taught at Brandeis and Columbia University before moving to California to continue his writing.

In brief, Marcuse believed that the artist was a critical person in societal transformation. Artists, he said, lived in a gap between the ideal and the real. Artists could entertain others with the ideal, while having to live in less-than-ideal conditions. Longing for the ideal while living in a society that could be repressive (and he faulted capitalism for some of that) made an artist an alien in his or her own land, and that sense of alienation could be used as an agent of social change and transformation. That kind of thinking found a warm welcome among counterculture followers in the 1960s, which was a decade of social protest and change.

And the idea of an artist as a catalyst for social and political change was not lost on the American government either. For example, in its efforts to help bring down the Berlin Wall that went up in the 1960s, the U.S. State Department used people like former actor Peter Claussen to work with East German actors, artists, writers, and musicians to spread a sense of creative thought and a sense of liberation among those living in East Germany. Here is a description of Claussen and what he did:

> *Claussen, himself a former director and actor and not the most stereotypical state Department employee because of his opposition to the war in Vietnam, would prove helpful in making connections to the very people who were most often leading demonstrations in East Germany. These people were creative artists who, among other things, wanted to be able to express themselves more freely through their arts. It was the job of Claussen and other diplomats like him to make connections with East German artists, develop joint creative projects, and bring the resources of America to help the arts grow in East Germany. The reality was that as the arts flourished there, so did the demonstrations for freedom. And it was these demonstrations that produced the fall of the Berlin Wall.* (Willis, 2013)

Marcuse was a dialectical thinker and realized that art represented the ideal and the desired state, while at the same time being created, analyzed, and distributed in a society and culture that was less than ideal, in some cases a repressed society even in America. It was a society in which liberating forces clashed with dominating power; the two thrusts existed and evolved within a synergistic environment. One force would provide fertile ground for the other to exist. An artist, frustrated, for example, by not getting his message distributed because of economic or market considerations, would push for more change. Meanwhile, as societal powers felt their status quo threatened by unwanted change, they would resist with more insistence that the creative thought had to make money in order to first be widely distributed. And, again, this philosophy found a home among people in the 1960s who were seeking many societal changes.

NOAM CHOMSKY

When I first encountered the thinking of Noam Chomsky, I was in graduate school doing a paper on the role of the state in American society. I wondered what an MIT linguist could know about a political science topic like this, much like I had wondered what an obscure Canadian English professor like Marshall McLuhan could know about the impact of television on our lives. But after spending time with the thoughts of both Chomsky and McLuhan, I realized that it's not one's academic specialty that is important but the clarity of their thought, the breadth of their knowledge, and how they are able to make connections from one field to the next. Chomsky is a guy that I never fully agreed with—especially his leaning toward what I perceived as a preference for anarchy—but I could appreciate the dangers he described that a state could pose for limiting the individual freedoms we enjoy as Americans.

Chomsky, born in 1928, may have started out as a linguist, but his interests and research soon morphed into philosophy, cognitive science, history, and political activism. As of 2018 he had written more than 100 books on subjects ranging from politics to linguistics to the mass media. In the 1960s, Chomsky was one of many intellectuals who stood against the war in Vietnam, calling America's involvement an imperialistic move. He created a nationwide stir with his essay "The Responsibility of Intellectuals" (which became a book), calling on them to voice opposition against the war and articulate their reasons for doing so. As a result of his strident antiwar protests, Chomsky wound up on the infamous "enemies list" kept by President Richard M. Nixon. He used his linguistic background and expertise to show how the media was being used at times for government propaganda purposes and built that into a critical theory. In addition to *The Responsibility of Intellectuals*, Chomsky wrote *American Power and the New Mandarins* in the late 1960s. His focus in this book is that people should be highly skeptical of the idea that those who hold positions of government power because of their technical expertise will govern well for the people. He writes, "Quite generally, what grounds are there for supposing that those whose claim to power is based on knowledge and technique will be more benign in their exercise of power than those whose claim is based on wealth or aristocratic origin? On the contrary, one might expect the new mandarin to be dangerously arrogant, aggressive and incapable of adjusting to failure, as compared with his predecessor, whose claim to power was not diminished by honesty as to the limitations of his knowledge, lack of work to do or demonstrable mistakes" (Chomsky, 1969).

Chomsky had a strong influence on the college protest movements of the 1960s, especially in his writings about the importance of universities to cultural development of the era. The founding document of the Students for a Democratic Society (SDS), the main student protest group on campuses in the 1960s, lays out the central role of the university in a needed revolution. The document is called the *Port Huron Statement*, and it offers some of the same ideas that Chomsky preached about as he urged resistance to the current political system. In part, the *Port Huron Statement* reads:

> From where else can power and vision be summoned? We believe that the universities are an overlooked seat of influence. First, the university is located in a permanent position of social influence. Its educational function makes it indispensable and automatically makes it a crucial institution in the formation of social attitudes. Second, in an unbelievably complicated world, it is the central institution for organizing, evaluating, and transmitting knowledge. (Hayden, 2005)

Chomsky had been speaking and writing about the same key role of the university but, just like the SDS, believed that universities must shake off the corporate and governmental influences that evidenced itself in the kind of "with-strings-attached" funding and grants that universities received from these agenda-driven entities. While universities were already contributing to the social and cultural growth of America, Chomsky and the SDS statement reasoned, they could contribute so much more if they were independent of these outside influences that were really at the base of much of what was wrong with America in the 1960s.

What did all this intellectual introspection mean for the average college student in the 1960s? Generally, it meant one of three things: (1) You ignored the debate altogether; enjoyed life as a college student; and focused on parties, sports, and—hopefully—graduation. (2) You protested the protesters and aligned yourself with the status quo, wondering why these extremists were wanting to overthrow a system that seemed to have so many perks. After all, you and your family and friends seemed to be doing okay, so why protest? (3) You jumped in and joined the protests. And this could be done in at least a couple ways: you could either support the protests intellectually and promote their cause in conversations with your friends, or do that and actually join their marches, demonstrations, and other activist activities. On many college campuses, the SDS made some inroads infiltrating the student newspaper staff and would thus have a venue to focus coverage on the protests and opine about them on the editorial page.

If there was a polar opposite to organized campus protest movements like the SDS, it was probably found in the many Greek fraternities and sororities that flourished alongside protest groups in 1960s college life. These Greek houses tended to be more conservative and focused more on living the good life than on taking the personal risks often associated with student protests.

JOHN KENNETH GALBRAITH

By the 1960s, in the world of economics, few names were as well known as John Kenneth Galbraith. Two years before the decade began, this Harvard economist had published his best-selling book, *The Affluent Society*. In it, Galbraith argued that the United States was becoming rich in the affluent private sector at the expense of staying poor in the public sector and creating roadblocks for those from the lower classes to buy into the American dream. His focus on the inequality this system created in society dovetailed with the civil rights movement that was about to burst open in the 1960s. His ideas, mostly devoid of mathematical models to help prove them, failed to develop many disciples among leading economists. But they did resonate with liberal politicians and with people on the left who were pushing for a government that reached out to help all people. He decried an America that he often said had become a democracy of the wealthy and fortunate.

Largely because of his popularity, Galbraith became a confidant of Presidents Kennedy and Johnson, writing speeches for both of them and helping create Johnson's "Great Society" program aimed at helping the middle and lower classes achieve success. Galbraith, always confident, eloquent, and popular with audiences, perceived and articulated economics as an aspect of culture and society instead of an obscure and complex universe of numbers. He spoke with sadness of an America that had devolved in character from a nation of family-owned farms and local stores to a country of factories and mega-stores. Unbridled capitalism, and along with it more oligopolies, was hurting the very Americans it was designed to enable, he said. He also attacked advertising and marketing tools that were designed to be manipulative, in terms of enticing consumers to buy things they didn't need, rather than being helpful as tools of useful information for consumers wanting to make smart buying choices.

Galbraith continued to influence liberal America's thinking about economics through his life, writing a sequel to *The Affluent Society*, entitled *The Good Society*, in 1996. He would live until age 97, dying in 2006.

MILTON FRIEDMAN

Milton Friedman was to free-enterprise economists what John Kenneth Galbraith was to social democratic followers. Often cited as America's preeminent proponent of free markets, Friedman was honored with the Nobel Peace Prize in economics in 1976 for his work in the fields of monetary history and theory and consumption analysis and for depicting how complex and difficult the policy of stabilizing an economy can be. In the 1960s and early 1970s, Friedman was advisor to President Nixon and led the American Economic Association as its president. He taught economics at both the University of Chicago and Stanford University. Three years before the start of the 1960s, Friedman wrote his benchmark book *A Theory of the Consumption Function*, which argued against the thinking of economist John Maynard Keynes that consumers hold spending levels to their current incomes. Instead, Friedman said people spend on the basis of what they believe their *permanent income*—or average income over a period of a few years—is. Then, in 1960, he wrote probably his most influential work, *Capitalism and Freedom*, in which he made a popular case for a free-market economy with a minimum of federal regulation or mandates. He was passionate especially in promoting the abolition of the military draft to be replaced by an all-volunteer army. Friedman's passion inspired many college students to enter the field of economics. Among the economist's chief contributions was his theory of *monetarism*. Going against established economic theory, Friedman demonstrated that price levels depend on the supply of money and that, over a long period of time, increasing the supply of money will increase prices but will have no effect on economic output. In the shorter run, however, hiking the supply of money can serve as a catalyst to employment and output, with the opposite cause-and-effect scenario to also be true. Therefore, in solving problems of inflation and unemployment, he advocated increasing the money supply at the same rate that the real gross national product increased. Doing that, he argued, would cause inflation to disappear. The book had a strong influence on the economics profession and on the U.S. government's monetary policy.

EVERYDAY INTELLECTS AND EVENTS

These were some of the household names of intellectual giants of the 1960s, but there were many more mentors whose ideas and insights impacted so many Americans in this decade, as they do in all decades. Along with those individuals were the events of the 1960s that were implanted firmly and vividly in the minds of baby boomers. The following memories from Joseph Bogan, who spent a career as a federal prison warden following completion of his PhD in psychology at the University of Oklahoma, are similar to memories most of us from that generation have of those everyday intellectual giants and moments that influenced us. In a 2018 interview for this book, he said:

> *It's interesting and fun for me to look back on the '60s. . . . I was 14 and change at the start of the decade, so that time was crucial to the development of my worldview and thinking. Of course, that thinking continued to evolve after the decade and hopefully is still doing so. While I am sure those intellectuals [mentioned above], as well as others, had an influence on the "zeitgeist" of the '60s, none of them had any influence on me, at least directly. I probably knew of most of them by the late '60s. . . . As far as individuals, my father influenced me most. He was himself an "intellectual" with a BA earned in his 30s at night. He read all sorts of authors widely. Later in the '60s, I would be greatly influenced by my graduate school professors in clinical psychology. Again, I think the influence of the intellectual writers of the time was mediated through my professors. I got my Ph.D. in 1970 at the end of the decade. It was the historical events of the decade, rather than its intellectuals, or "elite" thinkers, that influenced me, along with my personal experiences within that cultural context. Of those events, Vietnam loomed largest. And of course 1968, the year Jane and I married, was the most eventful year between WWII and now. But my unique experiences also did . . . one example would be the year I spent working as a Psychology Trainee at Boley State School for Boys, where 95 percent of the staff and residents were black. That experience forever changed my thinking about race.*

BIBLIOGRAPHY

Chomsky, Noam. *American Power and the New Mandarins*, New York: Pantheon Books, 1969.

Cox, Harvey. *The Secular City*, New York: MacMillan, 1965, as cited by Carl E. Olson, "Modern, Secular Liberalism Is a Religion," *Catholic World Report*, March 2, 2012, as accessed on April 12, 2018, at http://www.catholicworldreport.com/2012/03/02/modern-secular-liberalism-is-a-political-religion/

Degelman, Charles. "Digger Bread," *Retrospect*, December 14, 2015, as accessed on April 16, 2018, at https://www.myretrospect.com/?s=digger+bread

Didion, Joan. *Slouching towards Bethlehem*, New York: Farrar, Straus, and Giroux, 1968.

Douthat, Ross. "When Buckley Met Reagan," *New York Times*, January 16, 2009, as accessed on May 18, 2019, at https://www.nytimes.com/2009/01/18/books/review/Douthat-t.html

Hayden, Tom. *The Port Huron Statement: The Visionary Call for the 1960s Revolution*, New York: Public Affairs Press, 2005.

Kraft, Scott. "William F. Buckley, Jr., 82; Author and Founder of Modern Conservative Movement," *Los Angeles Times*, February 28, 2008, as accessed on May 15, 2019, at https://www.latimes.com/local/obituaries/la-me-buckley28feb28-story.html

Menand, Louis. "Out of Bethlehem: The Radicalization of Joan Didion," *New Yorker*, August 24, 2015, as accessed on April 12, 2018, at https://www.newyorker.com/magazine/2015/08/24/out-of-bethlehem

Willis, Jim. *Daily Life behind the Iron Curtain*, Santa Barbara, CA: Greenwood Press, 2013, p. 175.

4

DOMESTIC LIFE

By the time I graduated from high school in the summer of '66, I was pretty radical, although not an activist. I had seen The Graduate *and* Easy Rider, *and realized things were changing in America. I had already discovered the "beat" culture, had been to San Francisco, and I was into drama. Southern California was not as activist as San Francisco. We had the [extreme right-wing] John Birch Society and flyers on my doorstep supporting right-wing causes. My dad, however, had shifted more to the left.*

So begins the narrative of one Southern California native, Dr. David Esselstrom, who grew up in the 1950s and 1960s and has many memories of life in his corner of America in the counterculture decade. After graduating from high school, Esselstrom went on to graduate from UCLA with a bachelor's degree in theater arts in 1970.

Like everyone else, I thought the world was crumbling and we were in the final stages of collapse of society. Our only hope was in the youth. I remember in 1969 seeing my (military draft) lottery number come up as 42 and joined the California National Guard.

Under the lottery era of the military draft, numbers were allotted to each of 366 possible birthdays, drawn at random. A lower number meant a young man was going to be conscripted into the army, whereas a higher number meant he would probably avoid it. Esselstrom saw his chance of being drafted was very high.

I remember some of my friends being killed, and it made Vietnam very real to me. I didn't want to be part of the war machine, but I didn't feel right about going to Canada. [Many young men in the '60s and early '70s moved to Canada to avoid the draft.] The tragedy of Kent State happened in my basic training. In the military, I felt trapped behind enemy lines. But I finished active duty in the National Guard and graduated UCLA with a theater arts degree. I was disenchanted with the arts in Southern California so I moved to San Francisco in 1971. Right then, I was more concerned with just surviving. I had no real direction. I enrolled at San Francisco State in 1971 in a creative writing Master's degree program.

Esselstrom worked as adjunct professor in Portland, Oregon, for a few years and tried to break into film and television writing. He came close to succeeding on a project, but the producer lost the screen rights to the property and it was never made into a movie. Esselstrom returned to Los Angeles, joined some screenwriting groups, and did some freelancing. Eventually he began teaching English at Azusa Pacific University and got his PhD in English at the University of Southern California.

I was always a seeker in high school. In college I toyed with the idea of religious studies. In the '60s the emergence of the Christian Left was exciting for me. I always had a soft spot in my heart for that. Looking back at the legacy of the '60s, the changes that happened were not the changes that the youth culture expected. The youth movement was pushing for political change. Politically, those changes haven't happened. People latch onto things at different times for different reasons, but the youth movement didn't understand the political process very well.

So what did change, according to Dr. Esselstrom?

The value of diversity was one big change. Another change that lasted was acceptance. That should be a basic Christian value. God loves everyone. There were also many pointed and effective questions about the nature of power and a realization that evil is evil. There is something wrong when you're not letting people move into different areas of your city or neighborhood simply because of the color of their skin.

I was very aware of the changes that were happening in the '60s. It was largely a youth movement, driven by the baby boomer bulge. It was a coming-of-age thing, fueled by outside influences like Vietnam and civil rights. The first march I took part in was the march on Sacramento where we protested [college] tuition when Reagan was in office [as governor]. We were testing different solutions. There was a commitment to testing to see if we couldn't do something a little different. I came to realize that the exercise of care is not something you find; it's something you do. Enthusiasm is not something you discover; it's something you bring. (David Esselstrom, unpublished telephone interview with Jim Willis, September 20, 2017)

Dr. Esselstrom is typical of many young people who did not quite fit either of the stereotypes that society likes to erect for young revolutionaries or conservative traditionalists. Although he held—and still holds—conventional religious beliefs, that doesn't necessarily make him a social conservative. Like many individual thinkers of his generation, Esselstrom takes issues and evaluates them one at a time and does not come out either uniformly conservative or liberal. For those who have talent in the arts, a positive outlook, and an abiding sense of humor like Esselstrom does, young people of the 1960s learned to think outside the box, expressing and applying their thinking in different—and often unique—ways. In many ways, the David Esselstroms of the world remind us of the fallacy in trying to pigeonhole a person into one category or another.

BABY BOOMERS COME OF AGE

The 1960s found America welcoming the vanguard of "baby boomers" into high school and college. This would have a profound effect on life and culture in America and provides part of the answer to the question of why this decade turned counterculture for many young Americans. The baby boomers were those people born between 1946 and 1964, the years that birth trend lines were soaring in America. More babies entered the world in 1946 than ever before in history. World War II was over, and the long-delayed rush to start families began as American troops returned from the battlefields of Europe and the Pacific. The birth numbers totaled 3.4 million, which were a whopping 20 percent more than 1945 alone. Another 3.8 million babies came in 1947, and the trend continued until tapering off in 1964. Altogether by that year, there were more than 74 million baby boomers, comprising 4 out of every 10 Americans (Baby Boomers, n.d.).

The bulge of that early baby boom hit college in the 1960s, and their attitudes and worldviews were reflective of the conditions they grew up in. Of course, those conditions differed based on socioeconomic factors as well as race and ethnicity (racism was alive and well in the 1950s), and also gender (women in the 1950s largely were not involved in the workplace outside the home).

What seemed, on the surface, to have been a placid growing-up decade of the 1950s harbored various kinds of discrimination against minorities and women. The baby boomers had observed this, often silently as children do, and when they reached college age, many wanted to take a stand against those unequal conditions. As for white middle- and upper-class boomers, they had grown up in homes with mostly well-meaning parents who wanted them to have all the material comforts that the years of the Great Depression and war had denied them. Adults in the postwar years looked ahead and saw a future framed in prosperity and ease of living. Business was good in 1950s America, the country's industrial might was strong, and pay was good, with labor unions pushing for even higher wages. The more discerning college-age Americans, however, began rebelling against what they perceived as a growing materialism whose focus pushed aside considerations of inequality in the country. Not everyone had an equal chance at the brass ring, and they knew it. They witnessed many examples of discrimination and racism, and they also witnessed a hugely unpopular war in Vietnam that threatened to deprive them of the very life they had been raised to expect. So many found a welcome venue to vent their frustration and displeasure in the larger protest movements that were a part of the fabric of 1960s America.

THE GROWING SUBURBS

Many teens and young adults in the 1960s had largely grown up in the suburbs, which had also boomed in the postwar years. In fact, suburban life became one of the most noticeable features of the 1950s as large developers would buy up tracts of land outside the cities and begin mass-producing inexpensive homes to house the growing postwar families. Helping to spur this housing boom was the G.I. Bill, which made it easier for veterans to purchase homes, so easy, in fact, that buying a home in suburbia was often less expensive than renting an urban apartment. By 1960, one-third of Americans lived in these suburbs, and that percentage grew more throughout the decade.

In some cases, entire towns and small cities arose from farmland in the postwar years, sometimes because of the land's proximity to a city and sometimes as a result of a new factory or military base being stationed there. Typical of the latter was the new town of Midwest City, Oklahoma, which became a large suburb of Oklahoma City. Midwest City was born in 1943 when developer W. P. "Bill"

Atkinson got word that the U.S. Air Force was going to build a large base on that land, just southeast of Oklahoma City. The town was named for that base, Midwest Air Depot, whose name was later changed to Tinker Air Force Base, in honor of Maj. Gen. Clarence L. Tinker, an Oklahoman who was the first American general killed in World War II. I grew up in Midwest City in the 1950s and 1960s, and my memory of the town and those years goes like this:

In some ways, Midwest City was much like other suburbs of the 1950s and 1960s, but in other ways it was unique. It was essentially a middle-class town, although part of it would be described today more as lower middle-class. Those of us in that group wouldn't have called it that then; it was just our life and we enjoyed it and seldom felt deprived. The typical homes were only about 900 square feet in size, although the more affluent had homes twice that size. None of the housing was older than 15 years by 1960, and we all knew this was a very young town and that made it kind of a pioneering adventure to live there.

We had one movie theater that was a huge draw for all of us, and I recall that, even by 1960, we could get a ticket, popcorn, and a Coke all for about 50 cents. We had two drug stores, two groceries, two sit-down restaurants, and one genuine diner. This town grew faster than others, however, because of the quick expansion of Tinker Field.

What made this town different from the standard suburb in America was it was largely an Air Force town. It seemed like most of the people who lived there were either Air Force personnel or civilians working at Tinker Field. . . . My own mother worked at Tinker in the civil service. We had bombers and jets flying in over our home all the time, because Tinker was a major aircraft maintenance facility. Many streets and businesses in town were named for aircraft or had Air Force-related names. For example, I grew up on Lockheed Drive, our movie theater was the Skytrain, our two drive-in movies were the Tinker and the Bomber drive-ins. We were the Rockets and Thunderbirds at our two junior high schools and we were the Bombers at our high school.

All in all, life was placid and that lasted on into the mid-1960s until the threats of Vietnam and the Cold War with Russia started concerning us. Few of us wanted to go fight in a war we didn't understand, and we all felt that our town would be a prime target in case of nuclear war because of Tinker Field being there. The Cuban missile crisis in 1963 worried us a lot. And, as the decade continued and we started getting word of some of our classmates being killed in Vietnam, that particular threat became more real.

WOMEN IN THE 1960s

The 1960s provided the needed push for women to advance beyond the confines of the traditional roles of 1950s housewives, and several influences made that happen. Keep in mind this was the decade in which the National Organization for Women (NOW) was founded, and the push was on for leveling the playing field for women in America. Among its founders were feminist author Betty Friedan and the first black congresswoman Shirley Chisholm. It has grown to become the largest feminist organization in America and today has 550 chapters nationwide.

The influences of suburban life on women in the 1960s were also telling, especially on female baby boomers. These were young women who had grown up in the 1950s during a time when the mantra "A woman's place is in the home" was often heard, especially by men. Although the mothers and older sisters of many of these boomers had worked during the war years of the 1940s when their husbands went off to fight, the 1950s idea was that women should return to their rightful place as wives and mothers and turn the workplace back over to the men. There were definite roles that men and women were to fulfill, and they were very different roles. Female students in junior high and high school were expected to take classes in "home economics," while men took classes in "shop" and "auto mechanics." College prep courses drew both sexes, but college was seen generally as a starting point for men and a kind of ending point for women. Banter about the "MRS" degree and the phrase "ring by spring" were widespread among college students and sounded humorous but were actual expectations in more cases than not. Statements about women were uttered in the 1950s and 1960s, which would be considered strongly sexist today. One woman who attended the University of Oklahoma in the 1960s described it this way:

> I remember two distinct social gatherings, both held in sorority houses, in which women were explained their roles and limitations with what I considered put-downs even then. One situation was when a campus religious organization was meeting there, and the male leader referred to women as a "speck of intellect on a sea of emotion." In the second setting, the sorority was prepping for the upcoming Parents Day, and the "girls" were instructed by their president to be sure and not talk about sports in the upcoming social gatherings because those were topics for men. But even as I was growing up before college, my own mother would counsel me, "It's a man's world, Anne, so you'd better get used to it."

This family-bound role of women put them in a position of domestic importance in American suburbs, since that's where so many families were migrating in the 1960s. But it also gave them the stereotype of being dependent on their husbands who brought in the money. The idea of a woman as a coequal partner in that venture—as one qualified to earn the same kind of living as one's husband—had not yet occurred to most suburbanites. That had been so especially in the 1950s when female boomers were growing up. Therefore, by the time they started college and began thinking about it all, many women realized how limiting, dissatisfying, and demeaning the 1950s stereotypes of women were. And they began wanting more for themselves. They began talking about it among themselves, listening and reading the thoughts of other women who were championing in a new kind of feminism. One of them was women's rights advocate Betty Friedan, who created a storm in 1963 with the publication of her book *The Feminine Mystique*. In that book, Friedan encouraged women of the 1960s to break the chains that had bound them and their mothers to less-than-fulfilling lives and to blaze new paths beyond the traditional roles society had placed them in. Those paths would take them into careers outside the home where, Friedan argued, they could be just as successful—if not more so than—as men. Friedan became a pioneer of the feminist movement of the 1960s and went on to found the NOW. Friedan was one of two women in the 1960s whose names were on the lips of every woman who wanted more out of life than home-making. The other was Gloria Steinem, who advocated women's rights in articles for *Esquire* and *New York* magazines and went on to found in 1972 the main magazine of the feminist movement: *Ms*.

Margaret Palmer Hellwege is a baby boomer from Oklahoma, who recalls her life in the 1960s and her thinking that later morphed into a more liberal and activist stance on social issues.

I was a pretty straight arrow during the late '60s. After all, I was a wife and mother beginning in '66. While [husband] Steve was in college, we partici-pated in a few anti-war activities but, on the whole, we were just your typical little family. We didn't become part of the "hippie culture" until the early '70s. We met people younger than us who were "anti-establishment" and we found we had a lot in common as far as politics and music especially. That "free love" and "free spirit" ideology is what ultimately led to our divorce. There were lots of drugs involved (mostly pot) and concerts and parties. We had the same friends, so our divorce was friendly and amicable. My girls grew up knowing what bongs, roach clips, and "shotgun kisses" were. We were the only ones [among our friends] who had children so they were very close to all the "stoners" who came in and out of the house. It was a fun time, free and easy. We all worked, but the weekends were pretty wild. Our politics were quite liberal, of course. We all protested capital punishment at a formal rally and regularly campaigned for human rights and equality. That part of my life was relatively over by the '80s. That's when I moved back to Midwest City (Oklahoma) and went to work at Tinker [Air Force Base]. I was tired of being poor as well as stoned most of the time. I never gave up the hippie philosophy, however. I found like-minded friends and we all worked as well as partied together for five years. Then I moved back to Tulsa and, although I'm still friends with all the old crowd, we don't get together very often. Most all had married, had children, and settled down for the most part. Steve and I are still close. (Margaret Palmer Hellwege, e-mail interview with Jim Willis, October 14, 2017)

Another baby boomer who lived through the changes in gender roles was Suzy Underwood, a Harvard graduate who became a successful attorney and insightful writer about her life experiences. Here she recounts memories of the era that helped shape her thinking about gender roles, how it helped make her into the woman she has become and how she has taught her own children:

For my parents, the gender roles were clear. My mother was in charge of the house and the family, my father dealt with the outside world and earned the money to support us. He might have disagreed with some of the decisions she made regarding us kids, but he would have no more told her how to raise the children than she would have told him how to practice medicine. She did all the cooking and shopping—even bought his clothes for him—and he paid the bills, managed the investments, filed the tax returns. Pretty traditional arrangement back in the fifties. Yet surprisingly, their three daughters were NEVER told to follow this pattern. It was made clear to us from an early age that we should have careers that we were passionate about, and whether we married and had children was almost incidental. I think they were truly ahead of their time in this regard.

In college I began to think about gender roles and expectations. With my high school boyfriend, I had expected him to pay for everything on our dates, and also to open the car door for me when I got in or out. I can remember sitting in the car after he got out, waiting for him to come around to my side to open the door, and not budging if he forgot to do it. It seems ridiculous now. Once I got to college, I began to realize that there was no reason for this behavior. Indeed, once sex became part of the equation, it was preferable NOT to have the guy pay for the date, because he then expected sex in return. It was much easier to say no if I had paid my own way—or to say yes if I wanted to, but not out of a sense of obligation.

I joined SDS at Harvard, but never really felt comfortable there. It was only later that I realized it was because all those big deal student radical guys were incredibly sexist. They didn't want ideas from the women, they wanted sandwiches. Gender roles in the revolution! And worse, there is the famous quote from Stokely Carmichael that the only position for women in the movement is prone. He later claimed that it was a joke, but I doubt it. And thus the women's movement was born, out of the sexism of the civil rights and antiwar movements. But that's another story. . . .

In law school I was part of a class that was 48% women. Everyone treated each other as equals and there were no gender roles in the classroom. I remember learning that one of my male classmates, who was married, had his wife type up all his class notes and his briefs. I was horrified! Fortunately, that was the exception rather than the rule, at least in Davis.

When I went to work at the Attorney General's Office, I was certainly not the first woman they hired, but I was the first one to make a big deal about being treated equally. I did not want men to hold the door for me, or to wait for me to get on or off the elevator first. They didn't know what to make of me. Also, I didn't shave my legs or armpits. That was only visible in the summertime, but they couldn't understand that either. And when I got married, I didn't take my husband's name. I came back to work after my honeymoon and everyone asked me "What's your name now?" I said that it was the same as it had always been. By this time, 1983, women keeping their own names was not that unusual, but it still seemed to astonish my co-workers.

In both of my marriages, the division of tasks has been based on ability or interest, not on gender. Except for the fact that I nursed the babies. I suppose I could have pumped my breast milk and had my husband give it to the baby in a bottle, but that seemed like way more work than just giving the baby my nipple. So there was a real biological reason for that gender role, I was the one with the lactation equipment. In contrast, I did not have the cooking skills, so both husbands did most of the cooking. I think I was traumatized by the two years of Home Ec classes the girls at my school were required to take in seventh and eighth grade. (The boys had one semester of Nutrition and three semesters of a free period! Talk about unfair gender roles!)

When my children were small, I always made a point of dressing them in gender-neutral clothes. I would have none of those pink outfits with ballerinas or blue outfits with trucks. I once got chastised by a clerk in Mervyns Department Store when she found out my baby in the little gray velour onesie was a girl. "You can't dress a girl in gray," she said. Oh yeah? Just watch me!

I feel good about modeling relationships of gender equality for my children. I expect that if either of my daughters ever gets married, she will keep her own name. And I think all three of my children take it for granted that gender does not determine who does what in any kind of relationship, whether business or romantic. (Underwood, 2017)

TELEVISION AND FILM PORTRAYALS

A highly celebrated and critically acclaimed television series, *Mad Men* ran from 2007 through 2015 and chronicled the rise of women in the workplace in the 1960s. The series focused both on the fast-paced world of Madison Avenue advertising agencies in that decade and on how women were relegated to positions of secretaries and suffered the daily sexist barbs in this male-dominated career. But it also illuminated the unfulfilling roles of the housewives who were expected to dedicate themselves to their husbands even while those men were having affairs with other women, often while at work.

Another film, which premiered in 2017, that showed the working conditions for women—especially black women—in the 1960s was *Hidden Figures*. This critically acclaimed film followed the stories of three African American women recruited to work on NASA's first suborbital and orbital manned space missions. The substandard ways they were treated—right down to their limited bathroom breaks and locations of those facilities—were typical of the hardships that talented women had to overcome in their attempt to achieve even a semblance of equality especially during the first half of the 1960s.

One woman who became an adult in the 1960s and decided to join the workforce describes her experience, in part, this way:

I became a woman in the 1960s. By the age of 25, I was one of the rarities for the time in that I was divorced and had two young sons to raise. Divorce was very much frowned upon. . . . When I divorced my husband in 1965 there were still some who would practice the tradition of shunning, turn their backs to you as though you did not exist.

. . . I swore that my sons would not suffer for my mistakes and my marital status. I entered the workplace in order to support my sons and myself in 1965. Thus, as an unmarried woman, and more specifically, a divorced woman, I entered an environment in which I had no "protection"—no husband.

. . . I was hired in 1965 by a public municipality which employed some 300 people. Supervision was heavy at this time, with little if any, latitude for the workers. Time clocks were the norm. Permission was needed to utilize the bathrooms and we were timed as to how long it took to go to the bathroom and, how often we went. . .

My work area was a very large room on the first floor with desks filed in various rows by different departments. My department consisted of 4 rows of desks, 3 desks wide. Located in a wide open area in front of glass fronted offices on the side for middle and upper management. Supervisors were seated in the last row of each department, so that they could observe their charges to insure we were all working.

Nonetheless, this environment, as stifling as it appeared, was a fun, often a loving one. We watched out for one another and there were lots of jokes, teasing and stifled laughter. Most employees were honored to be working for the utility and believed that the utility took care of them. For the most part they did.

I spent 7 years at the utility. The longest place of employment in my 30-year career. I still refer to those 7 years as my apprenticeship. (Romney, 2016)

THE PILL

When speaking of women and ways in which the 1960s provided impetus for them expanding beyond traditional roles, one cannot ignore a significant medical breakthrough in 1960: the development of the first birth control pill. The "pill" would become a staple in American life for many women who wanted to enjoy sexual intimacy while greatly minimizing the chance of having a baby. It allowed women and men to plan proactively when to add children to their family. By 1965, one out of every four women was using the pill, and it would prove to be a boon to the "sexual revolution" that began in this decade and would carry into succeeding decades.

The birth control pill was instrumental in the "free love" movement so popular in the 1960s and also the "Playboy Philosophy" championed by the famous magazine's founder, Hugh Hefner. Both philosophies rested on the idea that men and women should feel free to explore sexual intimacy with each other not only for pleasure but also as a way of promoting ideals of love and peace instead of war and hate. The pill caused these movements to grow in widespread popularity, especially among young people. At the same time, the pill introduced a more convenient and surer way for couples—both married and unmarried—to plan for families and decide how many children to have and when. While not foolproof, the pill was often deemed the best form of birth control short of sexual abstinence.

The pill was introduced in the 1960s, after years of research underwritten in the 1950s by Margaret Sanger, a nurse and pioneering advocate for sex education and birth control. The federal ban on birth control had been lifted in 1938 in a landmark case that involved Sanger, and diaphragms—also called "womb veils"—became the method of choice. In 1950 Sanger felt a better birth control method was needed, and she raised $150,000 in funding to research and create the first human birth control pill. The first pill that was approved by the U.S. Food & Drug Administration was Enovid, in 1960. But it would be five more years before the Supreme Court (in *Griswold v. Connecticut*) allowed married couples the right to actually use birth control. The decision stated that birth control was a privacy right protected by the Constitution. That decision notwithstanding, 26 states still had laws banning birth control among *unmarried* women (Thompson, 2013).

INEQUALITY FOR BLACKS

For black Americans, the experiences they encountered and things they witnessed in the 1950s left them not only wanting more for themselves but also angry over the racism that had hurt them, their friends, and loved ones. Those influences would trigger the civil rights movement that resulted in the passage of the National Civil Rights Act in 1964 and that would then take more years to actually enforce. The Voting Rights Act would soon follow and help blacks achieve equal opportunity for voting.

The political power in the South had mandated "separate but equal" as a mantra for schools and public facilities as well as restaurants and public transportation. The problem was these schools and facilities were more separate than equal, and what was needed was integration of blacks and whites and equal access to all facilities. The civil rights movement was focused on achieving that, and this was what consumed much of black America in the 1960s. The movement had its successes, such as the election of the first modern-era African American to the U.S. Senate (Republican Edward Brook from Massachusetts in 1966) and the first African American woman to Congress (Shirley Chisholm from New York in 1968), but it would also have its failures, such as the murder of three young civil rights workers in Mississippi in 1964 and the assassination of Rev. Martin Luther King in 1968.

One African American, Otis Sanford, would grow up in racist Mississippi and arose as an adult to become managing editor of one of the South's largest daily newspapers, the *Memphis Commercial Appeal*. He recalls what life was like for him and other blacks in the 1960s and early 1970s.

> *The civil rights workers killed in the '60s. That kind of stuff was more of an issue for us. It culminated in the death of Martin Luther King. That's when things began to change. The eyes of the world were trained on what was going on in the South. Finally, in 1969 and 1970 where I lived, they said we can no longer sustain this kind of separate-but-equal mentality. Let's not divide our public amenities any more. People started, slowly but surely, to come to their senses.*

There were injustices we all had to overcome to get somewhere; especially the ambitious ones, and I was ambitious. I had good grades in high school and junior college, so Ole Miss [the University of Mississippi] couldn't deny me entrance. In college, "Down with the establishment!" was the black students' theme, too, only the object of our focus was different from white students. We were focused on civil rights, while whites were focused more on the Vietnam War. Black Americans had more reason to protest that war [because of the higher number of blacks drafted] but I did not see many blacks out protesting the war, because we were out there protesting for civil rights here at home. (Otis Sanford, unpublished telephone interview with Jim Willis, September 8, 2017)

A white American, Alan Brooks, recalls his observations of blacks and whites in the 1960s and finds what he calls "incongruity" in the era. He begins by recalling Malcolm X, the African American Muslim minister and human rights activist who was assassinated in 1965.

My parents gave me The Autobiography of Malcolm X *a year after he had been assassinated. He was shot shortly after predicting he would meet such a fate. It was a bit of a joke reading the book; we lived in a white community where one of the choir ladies from the church nearby would drop in to say hello and ask what I was reading. "Oh, he's reading* The Autobiography of Malcolm X," *Mom would reply. The choir lady would laugh because it was fairly incongruous: what did a notorious black radical have to do with a crew cut white boy?*

. . . Which is what I remember about the era: the incongruity of napalm in Vietnam, and at the same time incense in San Francisco. And it continued well into the '70s. . . . A few years before my parents gave me the Malcolm X book, we were walking across a bridge and saw a rare sight in our community: a black person. The incident is vivid because I never saw an African-American before and so my parents asked me what I thought. I replied that I didn't want to talk to him; what makes the memory vivid is their sad expressions, as if to way, "What? Did we give birth to a Klansman?" However I felt no guilt; peer opinion can be even more influential than parental opinion. In school we had been told by older students how African-Americans "lowered property values" and you couldn't argue with students from Rightist families. They were too quick-witted, hard-nosed. Fortunately, the Malcolm X book changed my mind, and such may have been the intent in making a present of the book.

. . . One rather ordinary, although special to me, experience was visiting an African-American family after a riot in 1967. The "why" of the visit is lost in the mists of time, but it was a pleasant visit due to the surreal zeitgeist of that year, soon to change the next year, or the year after. I started having more empathy/sympathy for African Americans then. (Brooks, 2012)

Dr. Marti Watson Garlett, an educator and former television host on a children's show, recalled her coming-of-age experience over the issue of racial equality:

For the first seven years of my childhood, I lived on a dairy farm in Illinois. My wannabe physicist father had found that World War II interrupted his educational plans and by the time I was born in late 1945, he found himself running my grandfather's farm, married with three small children. I was the middle one.

And then in 1952, my father suffered a heart attack in his early 30s. He survived, but he had to change plans once again.

All the acreage of plowing, planting, and harvesting crops and twice daily milkings of a herd of Holsteins had gotten the better of him. Not to mention all the harsh weather he'd had to do his daily chores in. We also had thoroughbreds, pigs, and chickens, and my mother had a huge garden. She faithfully canned vegetables all summer for our winter provisions.

So the summer after my second grade year, our family headed south where weather was milder and the textile industry was growing. My father took an accounting position at Wings Shirt Factory in Greenville, South Carolina, where I entered third grade at the Summit Drive School. Again, the year was 1952; segregation was in full swing. I saw the signs: "COLORED TO THE REAR, WHITE ONLY, COLORED ENTRANCE" (back doors), and so on. I was an aware little girl, and I'd never seen anything like it. This is not to say that before we moved there, I knew there was such a thing as people with dark skin. But I became aware of it very fast.

One day during recess on our school playground, I noticed a group of men spreading fresh tar on the road that ran in front of our school (Summit Drive). It was a hot, smelly job. I crept toward the sidewalk to watch them. What I saw was a really, truly black chain gang wearing black and white striped "coolie" pajamas, each one yoked to another by a big iron ball and chain, and another and another, and so on. White men dressed in khaki uniforms were yelling at them and occasionally raising a whip. These white men also wore guns and holsters on their belts. It was a shocking sight. Many years later I'd see the film Cool Hand Luke *and would shiver at what life must've been like for those powerless black men I saw. It was ruthless, and it was brutal, and I was frightened for them and for me.*

I even wrote a story about it in fourth grade. Well, not a story about it per se. My story (which I wrote on my own initiative, independent of any classroom assignment) was about a black dog who was not allowed to enter a dog show because he was black. Solution? His owner rolled him in flour so he was now white and could enter, and in fact, even win. Then he shook the flour off, and all the judges could see the error of their ways.

The impact of witnessing what I did in Greenville, while Jesse Jackson was growing up in the same city, during the height of Jim Crow has lasted me all of my life. I became a civil rights activist at age 8 but had no idea of that yet.

By the time I entered junior and senior high school, we had returned to the Chicago area, where I had been born. My father took a managerial position in my grandfather's firm. I did not go to school one day in my life between K-12 with a black student. I later learned that the town we lived in had a regulation against homeowners selling to blacks. That was a stunner to me but helped explain a lot.

When I entered college, where there were black students, a girlfriend and I went to sign up to be Mississippi Freedom Riders in the summer of 1964. She later went without me because my parents refused to let me participate. I was by that time 18, but 18 didn't mean then what it means now. They didn't refuse because of safety concerns for me—at least, they never mentioned it—but instead because they needed me at home to babysit my younger brother. I still morally wrestle with that lost opportunity and still blame them, even though they are both long gone.

And then, before that summer came about, JFK was assassinated. His head was all but blown off. It was right before my college's Thanksgiving vacation when I would travel by train back to Chicago, but I couldn't wait. I needed to talk to my father. There was a line-up of girls in my dorm waiting to use the one wall phone on our floor, and finally it was my turn. When I heard my father's calm reassuring voice, I started sobbing and gasping out words that, in essence meant, is the world coming to an end? I was overcome by the hate and rage I heard. (And now here we are in 2017.)

I started following what Martin Luther King was doing, and I'd see the mourning of Bobby Kennedy on the news. I became a staunch advocate for both of them, and sometimes my words cost me what apparently were meaningless friendships. I learned at some point that my politics made me a "liberal," a strange word to me. I always thought and still do think of it as social justice advocacy. When I became a Christian, I thought of it as following Jesus' teachings. And then in the same year, within months of each other, both MLK and RFK were shot dead. I wailed and no doubt startled my then infant son. But I couldn't stop crying for what could have been.

Some idealistic young people say, "I wish I was alive in the '60s, because that's when things mattered." I'm as big a fan as anyone of the freedom songs, "If I Had a Hammer" and "Blowin' in the Wind"—I sang them as fervently as if they were prayers—but I would never want to live through the 1960s again. (Marti Watson Garlett, e-mail interview with Jim Willis, February 2, 2018)

A significant milestone in the march toward equality for blacks occurred in October 1962, when Mississippian James Howard Meredith became the first African American to enroll at the University of Mississippi (Ole Miss). A violent confrontation erupted over this, two people were killed, and President Kennedy called out 31,000 National Guard troops to quell the violence. Meredith would go on to become the first black graduate of Ole Miss and emerge as a key civil rights activist.

THE CANADIAN OPTION TO VIETNAM

An alternative for young men in the 1960s who wished to avoid the military draft, and fight in a war they couldn't endorse, was to move to Canada. Many weighed this decision carefully, with some choosing to go. The government estimates some 100,000 young American men made this move to avoid the draft. Those who did go were not able to return, without fear of prosecution, until the presidency of Jimmy Carter when a pardon was granted in 1977 for those men who had evaded the draft by moving to Canada. Here is the story of one man, A. David Landsperger who wondered if he should take the Canadian option in the mid-1960s.

> *I'd put a lot of thought into military service long before it was time to sign up for the draft when I turned eighteen in 1964. All that thinking led me to the conclusion that it wasn't for me. Not because I had some deep-rooted opposition to all wars, if I'm being honest, but simply that it wasn't in my strategic plan. I couldn't see putting my life on the sidelines for two years while I got the chance to build character marching in formation and sweeping out barracks, or whatever other plans the army might have for me. Then, there was this Vietnam thing slowly heating up, which clinched my decision. The whole thing made no sense to me. The French had been there forever and finally threw in the towel; wasn't this just a civil war in some tiny Asian country a half a world away?*

As Landsperger points out, it wasn't only a young man's opposition to the Vietnam War that made some consider leaving the country to avoid the draft. Many young men had simply worked hard to educate themselves for a career and a life mission that did not include fighting in a jungle war in a country many had never heard of, for a cause that didn't seem to affect America's safety or security. Landsperger continues:

> *I remember our 8th grade history teacher telling us back then that every generation had to have its war and while there was nothing solid on the horizon for us, he was confident that we'd get our chance. This was just before the first U.S. military advisors were killed in Vietnam. My plan was to go directly to college to get my 2-S student deferment in the fall, no year off to bum around Europe or contemplate my navel.*
>
> *Five years later, while Washington was sending more poor kids to the jungles of Asia, I was preparing for on-campus senior job interviews. My*

search criteria were clear: I had to be assured of a 2-A critical industry draft deferment, the job had to be reasonably interesting, and it had to be within striking distance of Philadelphia. I went with a firm seventy miles to the west after their HR guy boasted that they had never been turned down for a deferment request. I broke that streak for them. Shortly, I got a letter from my draft board back in the Pittsburgh area stating that I was to be reclassified 1-A, available for military service, pending a physical exam. Next came the letter to report for a physical as the clock began to tick LOUDLY.

A young man's world could change in a day during this decade, and the most shocking change would often come in the mail with a letter like the one Landsperger received. In a heartbeat, all the plans a young man might have made, the relationship he was building with a special woman, his excitement over living a life he dreamed of would all change with that letter from the draft board. The man's worst fears would be realized in the thought of losing his life in the jungles of Vietnam. It was more than enough to cause men like Landsperger to consider his options. Here is what he did:

I hooked up with an anti-war group in Philadelphia to see what options I had. With no obvious ([well, not obvious to me] physical or mental) flaws, my options were limited. I declined to establish Conscientious Objector status on principle and also took the reserves off the table. My opposition to the war had perhaps grown stronger than my army-less strategic plan or maybe it was my nightmares about dying in a faraway jungle for a cause I didn't believe in but I began to take a hard look at the land up north. I bought a few months by switching draft boards but the notice to take my physical eventually came and a few weeks later the mailman told me I had passed the physical and was deemed ready to serve.

A steel company just across the border in Hamilton, Ontario had openings for engineers and I decided I would head that way if I got a draft notice. Next came tearful letters and phone calls with my parents. My dad, a WW2 vet, said he'd support my decision if it came down to that. Looking back, it was probably naive of me to think I could walk into a steel mill in Canada and be offered a job on the spot. Maybe I'd have driven a cab instead; who knew where a draft dodger would end up?

But, as Landsperger realized, it wasn't that easy to justify that kind of break with all he had known in life. Wanting to go to Canada and actually doing it were two different things. He was facing a moment of truth as the pressure increased. Then, just as it had when he got the letter from the draft board, his life would change again, in another heartbeat.

On December 1, 1969, the government held a nationwide draft lottery in an effort to make the system fairer for all. Each of the 366 birthdates was given a number and I listened in my car radio to KYW as they were pulled out of a cage one by one. The expectation was that anyone below 130–150 would be drafted. I drew 351.

It was at last over for me, but was it really? All these years later I still think about it and even write about it. Do I ever worry that my personal battle caused somebody else to take my place, perhaps coming home damaged or in a box? Absolutely, to this day. Were my motives all righteous and pure with me standing up for exactly what I believed at all times? Probably not. Yes, I had my convictions but I gamed the system and won. Did I ever disrespect anyone who was drafted or enlisted then or now? Absolutely not. I visited Normandy a few years ago and was fortunate enough to shake the hand of a Vet at one of the cemeteries there. It was a deeply moving experience for me.

We all have to make our own decisions based on the information and options we have at hand. Would I have gone to Canada if it had come to that? I'm reasonably certain the answer is yes. Where would I be today as a result? I wish I knew. That's as black and white as I can get on this one.
(Landsperger, 2017)

STAPLES OF 1960s LIFE

In the midst of all the turmoil of the 1960s, many Americans carried on with life as normal as possible and enjoyed many of the leisure-time features of the era. Among them were drive-in restaurants, drive-in movies, and television that had matured from its early 1950s years and was now offering a wide array of programming. Much of it was mirroring the turbulence of the decade, and some of it was pure escapism from that turmoil.

Drive-Ins and Take-Outs

If you've ever seen the classic film of California life in the 1960s, *American Graffiti*, you've seen the role that drive-in eateries played in life then, especially for young people. The film, starring Ron Howard and Richard Dreyfuss, pictured a typical night on "the strip," with a fleet of teen-driven cars parading back and forth as drivers and passengers yelled out to each other in passing. Their destination was often a drive-in like Mel's that the film made famous. Cars and pickups would form a constant entrance and exodus from the diner's parking places as customers would order their burgers and fries over intercoms or hail one of the servers who were gliding around the drive-in on roller skates bringing food and drink to the cars. They would attach metal trays to rolled-down windows, and your car became your dining room. But eating was only part of the drive-in's attraction. Equally important was that it was a gathering place for young people—and often older ones too. A place like Mel's would serve as a hub for nightly social activity year-round, especially in the warmer climates. Relationships would begin or end there, romances would flourish or fall apart. Fights between friends or enemies could break out over disagreements, and, always, news and the latest rumors were exchanged about people you knew or didn't.

Part and parcel of many drive-ins and 1960s diners were the take-out orders, boxed and ready to go. As families started becoming defined by parents who both worked outside the home, there was less and less time for the preparation of home-cooked meals. Enter the take-outs. Here is how one baby boomer, Patricia Zussman, describes her memories of take-out dinners entering her home:

> I was the baby of the family and when I started school my mother went back to work. That meant the veggie garden in the back yard was abandoned, and the canning cellar emptied and was not replenished. I learned to cook and bake at my mom's side, but as she got busier and we kids grew older, she cooked from scratch less and less. We started living on frozen fish sticks and pizza.
>
> Take-out was a real treat and our favorite place was the Totem Pole Drive-In. This Native American-themed, completely un-PC place (slogan: "Heap Good Food") was the casual outpost of a nearby fancy restaurant. My favorite menu items were the "Pocahontas" (French dip sandwich), the "Iroquois" (fried shrimp), and the "Cherokee" (wait for it—frogs legs!). But everything on the menu was great, and it was hard to choose.
>
> My mother came home one Friday evening with five of the iconic white dinner boxes. Those were the days when Catholics didn't eat meat on Friday so we knew they contained fish dinners. Imagine our surprise when we opened the boxes and found not fish but spare ribs!! Surprise and delight from us, consternation bordering on panic from our mother. We could all see she was exhausted from a long week and furious that they had given her the wrong order. Her first impulse was to forbid us to touch them, then slowly, realizing that there was nothing else to eat in the house decided that since we didn't intend to break the law, God would forgive us this once. My mother was nothing if not pragmatic, and she was not going to waste that food or that money. (Patricia Zussman, 2015)

Another story of the Totem Pole Drive-In, and of the drive-in, eat-out culture of the 1960s, is provided by John Unger Zussman, a midwesterner who migrated west to California after college. It goes like this:

My favorite menu item at the Totem Pole Drive-In was the Big Chief Burger, an all-the-trimmings double-decker burger that was similar to but far better than the Big Boy they sold down the street, which itself was infinitely better than the Big Mac that arrived later. . .

The Big Chief sounds standard now: two hamburger patties, two slices of cheese, sweet pickle slices (which I discarded), shredded iceberg lettuce, and a toasted triple sesame bun. The secret was the dressing, which was more refined, more flavorful than its competitors, then or since. I remember it as a perfect blend of mayonnaise, summer vacation, Tom Terrific, rainbows, and ambrosia.

In the late '50s and early '60s, everyone went to the Pole—teenagers on dates, families with kids, frats, greasers. It was the epicenter of the Woodward Avenue cruising scene, which extended from the Pole to Ted's Drive-In in Pontiac, eight miles north. But in the late '60s it attracted a rowdier crowd. After a series of police incidents that culminated in a stabbing (or was it a shooting?), it closed. The next year, it reopened as a Burger King. But you couldn't get a Big Chief at a Burger King. I was in college in Boston by then, but every time I returned to Michigan and passed the place, my mouth would involuntarily start salivating.

What to do? I needed a fix. If I couldn't get a Big Chief, maybe I could get the recipe. I opened the phone book and looked up Mrs. Hund, who owned the place (along with the upscale Northwood Inn and Club Berkley restaurants up the street). There she was! I dialed the number, and she answered! (This was way before call screening.) I explained my dilemma and she laughed. Apparently I was not the first fan who had contacted her. No, she wouldn't give me the recipe. But she had partnered with a food company, and Big Chief Dressing would soon be available at local markets.

Salvation? Each trip back, Patti and I looked in the stores, to no avail. Meanwhile, we tried to reconstruct it ourselves. But what to add to the mayo? We tried everything: dry or prepared mustard, garlic salt, onion salt, Lawry's seasoned salt, pickle relish, a little ketchup. Nothing came close. . .

Then we heard that Mrs. Hund had died, and with her, my dream of ever tasting a Big Chief again. Flash forward a couple of decades. We hear almost simultaneously from Patti's brother and my sister. A new restaurant called Duggan's has opened on Woodward, a few miles north of the old Totem Pole. Apparently they bought the recipe before Mrs. Hund passed, and they are now serving . . . drum roll . . . authentic Big Chief Burgers.

On our next trip, with both eagerness and trepidation, we made our way to Duggan's. It's full of local relics from the '50s and '60s. From the Totem Pole they've got the actual neon thunderbird that topped the building, menus plastered on lighted signs, and vintage pictures of Fords, Buicks, and DeSotos packing every parking stall. . . . But there's more—memorabilia from other restaurants, photos of sports teams, photos of classic cars cruising Woodward, signs from Mohawk and Sinclair gas stations, and an actual Gulf gas pump. It's a boomer throwback, where time apparently stopped 50 years ago.

And the Big Chief? Almost unbelievably, it lived up to expectations. As we bit into our burgers, and the beef and bread and cheese and lettuce filled our mouths and the savory dressing coated our tongues, we looked at each other and we agreed, "This is it. This is how we remember it." It was Remembrance of Things Past if Proust had been addicted to cheeseburgers instead of madeleines. . . .

When we go back to Detroit, it's the Big Chief we want, because a Big Chief is more than food. It's a portal to a time when our parents took us, or we took our dates, out to a drive-in and we had our whole lives ahead of us and all we had to worry about was how to scarf up every morsel of burger and every drop of dressing without dripping on the upholstery. (John Zussman, 2017)

The take-out boxes Patricia Zussman describes ring a bell with me, because we had plenty around our house in the 1960s as well. In fact, my dad became obsessed with the dream of opening his own drive-in with take-out orders. In our town we had one hamburger diner, which was owned and run by a man I only ever knew as "John." It was a favorite spot for my father, and he would take me over on Saturdays for a burger and Coke. The counter was lined with those round-top swivel stools, and my dad liked that. He envisioned those in his own diner and reasoned they were good for business because people wouldn't sit around too long and prevent new customers from sitting down and ordering more food. Get them in and out fast was my father's thinking. Even so, he was probably the kind of customer he wouldn't himself want to have, because he loved sitting on that stool and chatting with John who was always behind the counter, standing over the open grill flipping hamburgers. One day in the early 1960s, John, who sold his burgers for 35 cents apiece, told my dad about a new hamburger place up in Oklahoma City that was selling hamburgers for 15 cents apiece. I remember them both rolling their eyes as if to say, "That will never last!" That restaurant was McDonald's, and it would cause big problems for independent burger places like John's.

The Dawn of Fast Food

The drive-ins and diners would give way to the fast-food franchises, many of which began in this era. McDonald's, as the franchise known today, had begun in Des Plaines, Illinois, in 1955 and began going national in the 1960s. It grew out of a local San Bernardino burger stand named for the two McDonald brothers who actually started it but was transformed and purchased by Illinois entrepreneur Ray Kroc into the largest fast-food franchise in the world.

The McDonald brothers conceived of and implemented a finely tuned logistical sequence of food preparation and in-restaurant delivery to customers that allowed those customers to get their food in a fraction of the time it took the diners and drive-ins to prepare and deliver their meals. The system also helped ensure the food was freshly prepared and that customers actually got what they ordered. Finally, it replaced all the plates, glassware, and utensils needed for sit-down meals with paper plates, cups, and plasticware and replaced dining rooms with in-car eating, although the fast-food dining rooms would later be added to the system. Kroc's vision was to make the McDonald's restaurant and golden arches as much a part of Americana and family values as house rooftops and church steeples. The restaurants would be places for families and not for teenagers cruising the night streets and congregating in the drive-in parking lots. All of this became a reality, and it was firmly in gear by the 1960s.

The fast-food experience grew, and different franchises added their own customized elements. Pizza Hut began operating out of a Wichita home in 1958 and expanded quickly in the 1960s to neighborhood restaurants around the world. Dave Thomas opened his first Wendy's restaurant in 1969 in Columbus, Ohio, naming it after his daughter. Burger King began in 1953 in Jacksonville but was not franchising nationally until the 1960s. Sonic began in 1959 in Stillwater, Oklahoma, and was meant to be only a statewide chain. That began changing in the 1960s, however, and today it is nationwide. Little Caesar's Pizza began in 1959 in Garden City, Michigan. Chick-fil-A opened in Atlanta in 1967.

Suffice it to say, the 1960s was the decade when today's fast-food industry exploded onto the American scene, coast to coast. And America ate it up.

Drive-In Movies

Although drive-in theaters had been in existence since Richard M. Hollingshead Jr. opened one in Camden, New Jersey, in 1933, the outdoor movie-viewing experience waited until the late 1950s and 1960s to hit its stride. Some 4,000 drive-ins operated across America in those years, and they were most popular in rural areas of the country although plenty of them drew in large crowds in the suburbs too (Nelson, 2013).

Drive-ins were great on warm-weather nights for family outings. The family could bring the baby and small children along without fear of having them bother others in an indoor movie theater. Sometimes families would bring pillows and blankets and let the kids fall asleep right in the car. And you could also spread out a little more than in cramped theater seats. Families with pickup trucks would sometimes position the trucks in reverse, with the truck bed pointing toward the screen. Everyone would then hop into the back and spread out. Many drive-ins catered to families by offering the added bonus of a playground where kids could play in the twilight hours before the films began for the night. And then, of course, there was the snack bar where you could go fill up on popcorn and candy and haul it back to the car to eat.

Drive-ins had the same advantage as indoor movies for a couple's date night, but they also had an added advantage of privacy that the indoor theater didn't offer. But the sometimes-amorous activity that took place inside cars made some parents hesitant about turning over the car keys if they knew that was the date destination. The stories about drive-ins as "passion pits" became part of 1960s lore among high school and college-age students. Given this moniker, it is ironic that some drive-in theaters would also rent their space to churches for outdoor Sunday morning services. Other added incentives to customers included charging a flat per-car price for admission on weeknights instead of charging per passenger in the car.

The popularity of drive-ins began to decline in the 1970s, partly because, first, the development of video cassette recorders allowed for the distribution of movies on video that could be seen on home TV screens. Watching movies at home could offer the same advantages of drive-in theaters without having to pay admission charges to a movie or wonder if the weather was going to turn bad in the middle of a film. Second, cable television was starting to develop in the late 1970s, and there was more to see on the home TV screen than before. Third, the rising price of real estate made the large open spaces required by drive-ins less profitable. Added to all this, most of the country adopted Daylight Savings Time in the spring and summer, making days lighter longer and pushing back the start time for outdoor films until 8:30 or 9:00 p.m. Therefore, over the 1970s and 1980s, most drive-in theaters fell into a state of disrepair and few remain today. Some of those properties that haven't been torn down and rebuilt with other businesses today serve as large open sites for flea markets.

Among the latter-day drive-ins to go out of business was the Foothill Drive-In in Azusa, California. This site is a historic landmark today as the Foothill was the last drive-in going west on Route 66. It opened on December 18, 1961, and showed its last movie on December 28, 2001. It was purchased that year by neighboring Azusa Pacific University (APU), which wanted to expand its west campus onto the drive-in site. Trouble ensued, however, when the California Historical Resources Commission placed the drive-in on the State Register of Historic Resources in 2002, greatly limiting what the property could be used for. A compromise was reached, however, as the university agreed to restore the drive-in's neon marquee to its pristine condition if granted permission to tear down the large theater screen and use the drive-in parking lot as a school parking lot for students. So, on the night of October 28, 2005, the movie screen was torn down. The restored marquee is there, however, and is used by both APU and the city of Azusa as a roadside message board that announces upcoming events (Azusa Foothill Drive-in Theater, n.d.).

Writer John Shutkin takes a whimsical look back at what he calls his "one drive-in story," and it illustrates what could happen on a drive-in movie date:

One spring day my junior year in high school, my mother informed me that she had received a call from one of her friends. Her friend's daughter (let's call her Myra, because that was her name) was coming home for the weekend from her girls' boarding school and could I double date with Myra, Myra's date (from a nearby boys' boarding school) and Myra's roommate. I assumed that I was the target of the invitation because I had a car (and a Mustang at that) and was a "good boy." It was really not a question; this was obviously a command performance or, at the least, a clear expectation of my mother's— She Who Must Be Obeyed.

I said OK (good boy, remember?), but was dreading it. Not only did I think I had better plans for the evening with my own friends, but my recollection of Myra from before she went off to boarding school was of a homely and pretty loony kid; in fact, my clearest memory of her was when she "painted" all her fingernails in sixth grade with a pencil and then walked around with the pencil stuck in her ear (or maybe it was her nose).

Things brightened considerably when I showed up at Myra's house at the appointed time. Myra had clearly emerged from her ugly duckling stage and was now very attractive—though she still seemed kind of loony. Even better, however, was Myra's roommate, who was absolutely, drop dead gorgeous. (I forget her name now, but let's call her Angelina.) And even better than even better, both Myra and Angelina were wearing their school uniforms—you know, the white oxford shirt, blue blazer and plaid kilt outfit, with the kilt rolled up at the top into mini length to create the "naughty schoolgirl" look of every adolescent boy's wet dreams. Oh, and of course, Myra's boyfriend was the hunky, jock-y, preppy type who I knew was way cooler than I was regardless of the disparity in our SAT scores.

So off we go to the local restaurant/hang out in New Haven for dinner, it having been announced to Myra's parents that we were first going there and then to a nearby movie theater. However, as we were finishing our respective burgers, the three others (hereafter, the "co-conspirators") informed me that we were not going to that movie theater, but to a neighborhood drive-in movie instead. They even assured me that they had all seen the movie we were supposed to see, so they would have no problem discussing it with Myra's parents if need be. Of course, these brilliant co-conspirators hadn't thought about whether I had seen it or not.

Fortunately, I had seen the movie as well (an early James Bond, probably) and, in any event, was not entirely averse to going to a drive-in with the charming and enchanting Angelina. And it was quite clear to me about 30 seconds into the movie at the drive-in—and I have no recollection of what the movie was—that the whole reason for going to the drive-in was so that Myra and her boyfriend could make out in the back seat the entire time, as they were more than a little constrained by their boarding schools' strict rules on visitation, to say nothing of Myra's parents' that weekend. Meanwhile, back in the front seat, Angelina immediately explained to me that she had just gone through a rough break-up with her boyfriend (Myra's boyfriend's roomie, as I recall) and that she loved being in the company of a really polite, smart conversationalist such as I rather than the kind of rude boys who just wanted to put their grubby paws all over her.

Well, that might sound like a compliment to a parent, but to any boy with half a brain and half a sex drive—both of which I had—that was an unmistakable message to just keep talking and stay the hell away from her. So Angelina and I spent the duration of the movie in undoubtedly scintillating, but chaste, conversation while Myra and her boyfriend went at it behind us. And, of course, I felt totally used.

After the drive-in, we all went back to Myra's house and we were invited in by Myra's parents, where we dutifully had a snack and discussed with them the movie we hadn't just seen. I was at least somewhat rewarded, not by the expected report back to my mother from Myra's mother about what a "nice boy" I still was, but by the sudden and seemingly heartfelt (and tongue included) kiss that Angelina bestowed on me just before we got out of the car. That encouraged me sufficiently to call her a couple of weeks later when she was back at school to see about having a real date. Unfortunately, Angelina explained, and as much as she really, really liked me, she had just gotten back with her boyfriend and he was the really jealous type and, well, you know.

At that point, I realized that I hadn't been just 80% used the night of the drive-in, but 100% used. (Shutkin, 2017)

The Rise of Television

Another reason for the decline of drive-ins was the rise in popularity of television. Pioneering programming in the 1950s gave

rise to greater quality of production in the 1960s and more diverse
story lines for series. The popularity of TV would eventually spell
trouble for both indoor and outdoor movie theaters as more people
chose to stay home. But the influence of television went far beyond
its impact on theaters; television resulted in a major cultural shift
in American lifestyles. The challenge for television was to provide
entertainment that would obtain needed ratings and revenue,
while still being true to its public service mandate in providing
information and educational programming for America. Early in
the decade, in 1961, the chairman of the Federal Communication
Commission, Newton Minow, delivered a stern warning to television executives that TV was at risk of becoming a "vast wasteland"
if the information and public service missions failed.

The black-and-white television programming of the 1950s would
give way to the new world of color TV for baby boomers just as
the last weeks of the 1950s ended and the 1960s began. The show
that came to define color TV for boomers was the popular Western,
Bonanza, which premiered in color on September 12, 1959. Although
limited color TV programming had been around earlier, this show
was the breakthrough and the first nationwide prime-time series
shown in color. The number of color TV sets had mushroomed to
500,000 by 1960 and, by mid-decade, one out of every four homes
in America would have a color set. By the end of the 1960s, most
of America was watching color TV. Networks were soon deliver-
ing their entire programming schedule in color, and this served
as a more powerful magnet to keep Americans home at night and
glued to their television sets (The Color Revolution: Television in
the Sixties, n.d.).

Here's how television affected me in the 1960s:

*Television opened up a whole new world for me, and often served as an escape
from some school years that were stressful. I remember getting hooked on TV
series like* Gunsmoke, The Untouchables, *and* Have Gun, Will Travel,
and would set my weekly clock by when they and others came on.

*But television in the '60s also made me aware of things going on in the coun-
try and the world that I would have not known about otherwise. I remember
watching nonstop the news programming surrounding the Cuban Missile
Crisis in October 1962, and of course of President Kennedy's assassination
and aftermath in November 1963. I remember seeing the civil rights marches
and violence in the South in the 1960s, hearing and seeing Martin Luther
King, and watching the Democratic Party come unraveled at its 1968 Chicago Convention.*

I know it was the influence of television news that helped propel me into the career of journalism. I wanted to be the guy who could break these kinds of important stories to others. I knew I was growing by becoming more aware of the world, and I thought that was a good mission to pursue in my career.

Television in the 1960s served as both an information medium that would rival the importance of newspapers and the escape medium that many Americans were seeking in the turbulent decade. Prime-time programs ran the gamut of shows that connected viewers to contemporary issues and problems—like *East Side, West Side,* and *The Lieutenant*—to those programs—like *The Beverly Hillbillies* and *Mr. Ed*—that offered ridiculous scenarios that simply made people laugh. This latter category was the most popular as far as ratings went. It's important to keep in mind, however, that the decades-old, critically acclaimed news magazine show *60 Minutes* began in 1968. It has dominated Sunday night network ratings ever since.

A sampling of the most popular TV shows of the 1960s would include the following: *The Andy Griffith Show, Star Trek, The Twilight Zone, I dream of Jeannie, The Beverly Hillbillies, The Flintstones, Bewitched, Gilligan's Island, Bonanza, Get Smart, The Dick Van Dyke Show, The Smothers Brothers Comedy Hour, Green Acres, Mission Impossible, The Untouchables, Batman, Laugh-In, The Carol Burnett Show, Hogan's Heroes, The Wild, Wild West, Alfred Hitchcock Presents, The Avengers,* and *My Three Sons.* The bulk of them were comedies and variety shows, possibly reflecting Americans' desires to escape the trouble that the 1960s presented them.

TELEVISION COMES OF AGE

In the 1950s, Americans had begun welcoming television into their living rooms and dens and loved their early black-and-white shows like *The Honeymooners, I Love Lucy, Father Knows Best, Wagon Train, Gunsmoke, The Many Loves of Dobie Gillis,* and *The Ed Sullivan Show.* Viewers put up with what would today be called poor production quality and live-TV bloopers because they were so enamored with this "talking radio." But television was more than just a technological innovation in communication; it ushered in a whole new culture change for America and its family routines, which were now often scheduled around the times that favorite TV programs would be aired in the evenings. Looking back on the role television had played in her young life, journalist Linda Ellerbee wrote an article for *TV Guide* in the 1980s that later became a part of required reading for many language arts students in school. The article was called "When Television Ate My Best Friend," and it recounts in a whimsical way what the delivery of a strange new box to her best friend Lucy's home meant to their relationship. Linda and Lucy spent every day playing with each other and seeing how high they could swing on the playground. Then, all of a sudden, Lucy disappeared after school and seldom came out of her home to play. A portion of Ellerbee's account reads:

> *I knocked on the door every day, but her mother always answered saying Lucy was busy and couldn't come out to play. I tried calling, but her mother always answered saying Lucy was busy and couldn't come to the phone. Lucy was busy? Too busy to play? Too busy to fly? She had to be dead. Nothing else made sense. What, short of death, could separate such best friends? We were going to fly. . . . I cried and cried. I might never have known the truth of the matter, if some weeks later I hadn't overheard my mother say to my father how maybe I would calm down about Lucy if we got a television, too. A what? What on earth was a television? The word was new to me, but I was clever enough to figure out that Lucy's daddy had brought home a television that night. At last I knew what had happened to Lucy. The television ate her.* (Ellerbee, n.d.)

By the 1960s, television production values had come a long way from its initial decade of popularity, and nearly all of America had tuned in to the new media platform. Whereas only 9 percent of American homes had television sets in 1950, some 90 percent had them by 1960. Television was becoming a force to be reckoned with and had already given Hollywood filmmakers a run for their money in snaring audiences away from the big screen. Entertainment was becoming more home centered, and the ramifications were far-reaching for the industry. The introduction of "TV dinners" by the Swanson food company in the 1950s and the accompanying "TV trays" were two big signals that life was changing for American families. America began coming home from work, pulling a precooked frozen dinner from the freezer, cooking it for 20 minutes, and sitting down at a TV tray to eat it in front of their television set to watch evening programs. By the 1960s, that trend had only grown in popularity, especially since wives were joining their husbands in the workplace at a faster pace, making TV dinners a more convenient option at night than coming home and cooking a full meal after a day at the office.

A key development in the decade was the founding of the Public Broadcasting Service (PBS) or the viewer-supported, noncommercial network of stations that began in Boston in 1969. One of PBS's first series would prove to be its most significant, in terms of educating the children of America. The program featured a large yellow bird and was called *Sesame Street*. It would educate a nation for decades to come and is still on the air today.

As it does in any decade, much—but not all—television programming reflected the tenor of the times and the interests and challenges viewers had and faced in their daily lives. There was a continuation of the variety shows and quiz shows of the 1950s (although the latter genre was damaged by the scandals of quiz shows like *Twenty-One* in the late 1950s), and there were the silly comedies like *The Beverly Hillbillies* and *Gilligan's Island*, but there were also provocative dramas that dealt with serious questions and issues of the decade. Shows like *Dragnet*—a holdover from the 1950s—put the spotlight on realistic crime in communities, while *Star Trek* took on social issues dressed up in futuristic space-probe settings, and *Twilight Zone* did the same in a fantasy series that hit too close to home on issues like discrimination and inequality among races, ethnicities, and creeds. The growing violence brought on by crime was reflected in hard-hitting shows like *The Untouchables*, and some of these shows were boycotted by groups believing they were just too violent for the American public. The controversy surrounding the Vietnam War went largely untouched in TV series, although news documentaries did show the brutality and controversy of that war.

Television in the 1960s may be best remembered by many as the decade that began featuring African American actors in television series, and that was certainly a reflection of the civil rights movement that was sweeping the country. Among the TV shows of the 1960s featuring blacks, sometimes as stars and sometimes as featured performers, were the following (MacDonald, n.d.):

- *Rawhide* (1965)
- *I Spy* (1965–1968)
- *Hogan's Heroes* (1965–1970)
- *The Sammy Davis, Jr. Show* (1966)
- *Star Trek* (1966–1969)
- *Mission: Impossible* (1966–1973)
- *Ironside* (1967–1975)
- *Julia* (1968–1971)
- *The Mod Squad* (1968–1973)

I can still recall seeing the first African American in a costarring role on a TV series. I was becoming a television junkie by the 1960s.

Like most white TV viewers, I didn't notice what I didn't notice: the absence of any black actors or actresses with leading roles in TV shows. That changed in 1965 when the clever series *I Spy* premiered. There was the standard good-looking white guy (Robert Culp) in the lead role but, right next to him, there was a black guy who would become an icon in television: Bill Cosby. Culp played tennis star Kelly Robinson, and Cosby played his trainer, Alexander "Scotty" Scott. Both of them, of course, were undercover spies for the government. I immediately found Cosby's Scott to be the real draw of the show, and I think most of my friends did too. It wasn't long before we started forgetting he was black and just saw him for the clever and humorous character he portrayed on the screen. The rest was history for Cosby and television. As for me, you might say *I Spy* began my understanding of the need for diversity and the need to define a person beyond the color of his or her skin.

The first TV drama or sitcom to put a black in the lead role—and to not engage in the stereotyping of that actor—was the revolutionary sitcom *Julia*, which premiered in September 1968 on NBC. It starred the popular singer and actress Diahann Carroll in the title role as a widow, a mother, and a registered nurse who lived in with her young son in a middle-class suburban home. What the show brought to the screen, doing so for the first time, was the depiction of an African American woman with a college degree who was respected as succeeding as a dedicated professional. This was an image and role model that black American television viewers had not seen before, and it helped underscore the hope that the American dream was available to all races and not just white Americans. That said, those same viewers who might be looking for a show that addressed civil rights issues of the day did not find it in *Julia*. For the most part, the creators and producers of the show kept the plot lines in safe territory and did not portray the star or supporting cast members as activists. Nevertheless, simply putting on a show in prime time that starred an African American who was making it in the professional world was a great contribution and a definite turning point for broadcast television.

The most racially integrated prime-time television show of the decade was actually the original *Star Trek*. The show premiered in 1966 and told the continuing story of the crew of the starship Enterprise as they pushed the boundaries of space, finding new cultures and intergalactic tribes of people along the way. The show featured not just one, but two, non-white actors among the leading cast members. The black actress Nichelle Nichols played Nyota Uhura, while the Asian American actor George Takei was Hikaru Sulu. Both characters broke the previous molds for blacks and Asians on the screen, as both were heroic professional scientists in service of humanity.

The Mod Squad was another groundbreaking success, running on ABC from 1968 through 1973. The counterculture crime drama featured not only an African American (Clarence Williams III) among its three leading stars but also a young woman (Peggy Lipton) who was the epitome of an intelligent and forward-thinking woman of the 1960s, fully capable of handling herself well in what was then a man's world. The third star was Michael Cole, a white male actor. Together, these three 20-something took their nonconformist style into a police world that had been more typified by the straight-laced Joe Friday of the popular police procedural, *Dragnet*. The show took a risk in doing so, because in the 1960s there was a cultural gulf between young counterculture Americans and the world of law enforcement. It was a time when the derisive term "pigs" was used by hippies to characterize police officers. The show was about three young, disaffected rebels (a black, a white, and a blonde) who are recruited by the Los Angeles Police Department to go undercover and unarmed and solve crime by their wits, and it was a risk given the cultural tensions of the day. But it was a risk that worked, as the show resonated with young audiences, possibly providing them with greater respect for police.

THE DRAMA OF OUTER SPACE

The 1960s was the decade that humans entered suborbital space, put a man into full orbit, and capped it off by sending astronauts to the moon. Through it all, the American public was fascinated with the achievements of NASA and became engrossed in the stories of these brave men who rode rockets into the new frontiers beyond Earth.

The drama of space began when President John F. Kennedy announced his goal to Congress on May 25, 1961: "First, I believe this nation should commit itself to the goal, before this decade is out, of landing a man on the moon and returning him safely to Earth" (JFK's Moon Shot Speech, 1961). Kennedy's proclamation was spurred on by the Russians who were ramping up their own space program and who seemed a formidable competitor for getting to the moon first. The race for space was on. America's manned space program had already been launched and had notched its first success with the suborbital flight of astronaut Alan Shepard, on May 5, just three weeks before Kennedy's space speech. Shepard was one of a group of high-energy and charismatic astronauts whom NASA had introduced to America in a carefully designed public relations program that the news media loved and transmitted to everyone in America. Here is how writer Tom Wolfe described the introduction of the Mercury 7 to the expectant journalists gathered for an initial group press conference with the young heroes of Project Mercury:

> *With that, applause erupted, applause of the most fervent sort, amazing applause. Reporters rose to their feet, applauding as if they had come for no other reason. Smiles of weepy and grateful sympathy washed across their faces. They gulped, they cheered, as if this were one of the most inspiring moments of their lives. Even some of the photographers straightened up from out of their beggar's crouches and let their cameras dangle from their straps, so that they could use their hands for clapping.* (Wolfe, 1984)

It may seem ironic that a hardened group of reporters and photojournalists from some of the biggest news operations in America were swooning so much at seven men who had yet to distinguish themselves to the public and who were—in fact—all unknowns. Yet that was just an indication of how most of America came to feel about these young space jockeys riding horses that were nearly all automated. The fact remained that these men were risking their lives to push America into space, and that was worth the admiration the country felt. This space program would continue through the full three-orbital flight of astronaut John Glenn on February 20, 1962, and culminating in the lunar landing on July 20, 1969, accomplished by astronauts Neil Armstrong and Buzz Aldrin. As in any ongoing drama, however, the endings are never happy for everyone. Such was the case with the NASA flights in this decade, as three astronauts—Gus Grissom, Ed White, and Roger Chaffee—were killed when a flash fire erupted in their Apollo command module on January 27, 1967, during a launch pad test at Cape Canaveral.

In 2004, NASA's chief historian Steven Dick looked back on Americans' reaction to the 1969 lunar landing and described what it meant for most people. "Putting a man on the moon not only inspired the nation, but also the world," he said. "The 1960s were a tumultuous time in the U.S., and the moon landing showed what could be accomplished at a time when much else was going wrong" (Roach, 2004). In sum, Dick called the mission America's crowning achievement of the 20th century.

And Jeffrey Bennett, an astronomy professor and writer, added that the space program of the 1960s gave Americans hope for the future. "There are many ways to show people the great possibilities of the future, but I'd argue that the visibility of the moon in the sky is more powerful than any other single course of inspiration," Bennett said (Roach, 2004).

I was a 23-year-old seminary student who was on a religious retreat in the mountains the night that Neil Armstrong set foot on the moon. For Wallace, it only added to the spiritual experience of the evening. We had just finished dinner when we gathered around the TV set to watch this. As Armstrong stepped from his landing craft and stepped onto the lunar surface, it was a surreal feeling. We were seated outside in an amphitheater and, instinctively, we all looked up on this clear California night to the brightly lit moon above. It seemed impossible that someone from Earth could be walking its surface, and I wondered if something like this might be taking place on other moons of other planets in the universe. When Armstrong uttered his line, "That's one small step for man; one giant leap for mankind," chills went down my spine. I knew then I was witnessing maybe the most significant event of the entire century. Being a part of that—even as a distant real-time witness—was overwhelming and something I'll never forget. My friends at the retreat seemed to share these feelings. Any doubts we had previously about the value of tax dollars going to probing outer space seemed to go out the window that night. Earth and—just as important to man—America had just put its first man on the moon. When Buzz Aldrin stepped down onto the surface, that was two. If I wasn't a space junkie before that night, I became one from then on.

WHAT WE WORE

One of the most visually distinctive features of the 1960s was what this generation—especially the younger generation—wore. While many moms were still in dresses and pearls like Donna Reed or June Cleaver (from TV shows like *The Donna Reed Show* and *Leave It to Beaver*), and while many dads were dressing like Don Draper of TV's *Mad Men*, the kids were doing something else. In fact, they were doing it into their 20s and sometimes beyond. This was the case especially with young people who had a statement to make—often one of protest aimed at the "establishment." To a great degree, the 1960s experienced a shift in apparel about mid-decade: much

of the classical, conservative styles in the first few years gave way
to more colorful, creative, and provocative (think miniskirts) styles
from 1965 forward. It was as if what we wore reflected the openness and rebelliousness of the decade.

That change didn't come all at once, however, and it didn't come
at the same speed everywhere in the country, as the following comments from these college graduates show about their high school
and college days:

- "In the '60s in high school, we wore dyed-to-match sweaters and
  skirts with short white socks and white shoes. . . . In Kansas, where
  I went to [a public] college, you had to wear skirts and, to church,
  hats and gloves. Campus rule," said Marti Watson Garlett.
- "In the early sixties sorority girls couldn't wear jeans on campus
  at OU [Oklahoma University]," said Jene Cheek. "But it was very
  different in the late sixties."
- "Until 1968 or so, in the [Los Angeles] Valley's LA Unified schools,
  boys were sent to the VP for untucked shirts or untrimmed hair,
  girls for dresses three inches above the knee," recalls Alan Rifkin.
  "Pants Day for girls was once a year. Slacks or cords for boys, not
  jeans. And wing-tipped showed or Hush Puppies. By 1970, my
  first year of high school, it was all a barefoot, jiggle-TV haze of hal-
  ters and miniskirts and Danskins and no bras, and if I was seated
  behind a girl in a backless shirt, I was just as tormented looking
  away as looking at. I've been waiting 45 years to be asked this."
- "At OSU [Oklahoma State University] in 1966 you could only wear
  slacks if it was a blizzard outside," recalls Betty Briggs. "In 1967
  I worked for minimum wage at a stock brokerage company. I was
  required to wear hosiery and keep an extra pair in my drawer in
  case of a run. When I worked as an AT&T operator, you could not
  wear slacks unless you worked the evening shift."
- "In high school in the sixties Kentucky girls could not wear jeans,"
  said Anne Kindred Willis. "I never wore pants to school; you had
  to wear a dress or a skirt and top."
- "In Southern California, we started loosening up our styles earlier
  than other parts of the country," said Todd Jones. "The conservatism of the 1950s was largely gone by 1963, although the beach look
  stayed around for awhile."
- "In high school in New Jersey, on cold days, we wore ski jackets; in
  college we wore pea coats," recalls Kathleen Woodruff Wickham.
  "In high school girls were not allowed to wear pants of any kind,
  no matter the weather. We wore A-line skirts and white blouses
  with knee socks. A Saturday fun outfit in the winter meant wool
  Bermuda shorts and knee socks with Weejuns loafers. Boys were

not allowed to wear jeans. Khaki jeans aka Chinos were problematic for the administration because they were cut like jeans but were khaki. In my freshman year of college girls had to wear skirts to class and could only wear jeans/pants going to the gym and then a raincoat had to be worn over them."

- "After the Free Speech Movement started at Berkeley in the early sixties, the style of dress changed dramatically for college students and even faculty," said Russ Meyer.

An interesting look at how a typical Southern California junior high school handled student apparel issues for its female students is found in its 1967 "Girls Good-Grooming Guidelines," which read in part (Mulholland, 1967):

- Clothing should be wide enough and long enough to be appropriate for the business of school.
- For most girls, the dress or skirt should not be over four inches from the middle (bend) of the knee and for some girls not that much.
- Culottes are allowed only if they are of dress length and look like a dress.
- Dresses with matching bloomers are permitted only if the dress part is at or very near regular dress length.
- Dresses or skirts should always cover undergarments when sitting, standing, walking, and bending over.
- Any garments which distract from the educational program such as low-cut blouses, bare shoulders, midriffs, low backs, spaghetti straps, and extremely slit skirts, or extremes are not acceptable.
- Shoes should have a firm sole; boots should not cover the knees.
- Moderate make-up only is appropriate for school.
- Jewelry should be appropriate for the business of school and should not distract from the educational program.

By the late 1960s, however, things had changed on many college campuses and in some workplaces. People were donned in bright, swirling colors, while tie-dyed tee shirts and psychedelic patterns accompanied beards and long hair on men. Often there would be circular silver peace symbol worn on a long chain, often on an open chest. Some wore capes or tunics. Bell-bottom jeans were ubiquitous, often with large leather belts with silver buckles and designs. Women who weren't wearing jeans were wearing miniskirts. And hats of all kinds and sizes were everywhere. All in all, the latter years of the decade were a fashion rebellion to the decades that had gone before. The British musical invasion, ushered in by the Beatles, brought British fashion to America and added to the wild color combinations and the receding length of women's skirts.

When the hippie culture began around San Francisco, a style of dress was adopted to accompany the counterculture followers. If one wasn't a hippie, then one could at least become a "pseudo-hippie" by looking like one. Said one baby boomer,

> *By the time I went to college in the fall of 1968, my entire clothing style changed. Out of my mother's clutches, I went hippie. Or more accurately, pseudo-hippie. I did not head for San Francisco nor did I live on the streets. But I was dressed appropriately for protest marches, and that's what mattered. We were so sure we were counter-culture individualists. Radicals! Looking back I realize that you cannot be a non-conformist while conforming to a style all your peers have adopted. But it is fair to say, as a group we had left the mainstream. None of this made parents very happy. . . . The new hippie clothes style wasn't great for retailers either. Shopping at the Army Surplus tends to undercut major department stores.*

How to dress like a hippie? These were the guidelines from the Fifties Web (1960s Fashion, n.d.):

1. Do have a flower. I know the song says "in your hair" but the truth is that it's hard to get the things to stay put.
2. No flower? Go for the Pocahontas headband.
3. Hair is long and "unkempt looking." (My mother's words) But it is clean. Yes, we washed our hair. Hey, deep down we were Baby Boomers from suburbia.
4. Women could wear a mini or even micro skirt provided she had decent legs. A chain belt was groovy. Boots or go-go boots were okay too.
5. Men—Jeans, the grungier the better. Leather vests were big too.
6. Fringe—for all. Vest, jackets, pants, shirts. Anything could be fringed.
7. Peace symbol. Every last one of us had at least one peace symbol.

In thinking back on how these different clothing styles affected me and my wardrobe, I'm reminded about the cultural gap existing between traditional young Americans of the day and the young revolutionaries—real or imagined—of the 1960s. I was one of the traditionalists in the 1960s, one of so many young people who grew to a slow awareness of the troubles the country was facing and who didn't understand the urgent need for change that my counterpart hippies felt. Nevertheless, there was something about their boldness—evidenced most readily by what they wore—that started getting to me. Therefore, over time, I began trying out the tie-dye shirts and ties, the bell-bottom jeans, and even a few beads now and then. For the most part, however, I favored the button-downed shirts, the Bass Weejun loafers, and the camel blazers. As the 1960s gave way to the 1970s, however, my styles grew more reflective of the times, complete with the wide-collared, multicolored shirts, the chain necklaces, and the polyester leisure suits in some strange rust and banana yellow colors. Facial hair was a must. If we were to wear all that in later times, we would probably have been arrested immediately for promoting illegal nightlife on the streets.

MILESTONES IN ATHLETICS

As is always the case, America was in love with sports and athletes in the 1960s, and there were plenty of athletic achievements to appreciate and honor. Some new institutions in sports were born in this decade, and others saw records set and broken.

For as long as many Americans can remember, there has been a Super Bowl in professional football, but those old enough will remember that it began on January 15, 1967, when the National Football League's (NFL) Green Bay Packers met and defeated the American Football League's (AFL) Kansas City Chiefs, 35–10, in Los Angeles Memorial Coliseum. At the time, it was called the World Football Championship, and it was also a time when there were both an NFL and an AFL. Professional football would be restructured all under the NFL name (the old NFL would become the National Football Conference, and the AFL would become the American Football Conference), and the name would change to the present-day Super Bowl, but the event was the same: the two best professional football teams were facing off for a winner-take-all game, and it became a bona fide part of the American sports ritual from that day forward. It would sit alongside the World Series of baseball and the NBA Finals in basketball as a time of year when most of America would hunker down in front of their TV sets and watch the best play the best in sports.

Other significant sports achievements in the decade included the following:

- A young Louisville boxer named Cassius Clay defeated heavily favored heavyweight champion Sonny Liston in 1964 to become the world champion and launch a legendary career as Muhammad Ali.
- The New York Yankees dominated professional baseball and the World Series in the first half of the 1960s with home run kings like Mickey Mantle and Roger Maris.

- The Boston Celtics dominated professional basketball and won six straight NBA championships.
- In college basketball, UCLA was the team to beat under legendary coach John Wooden. It would go undefeated in 1964 and stack up NCAA championship after championship.
- In college football, Texas, USC, Notre Dame, and Ohio State were the dominant teams, each picking up at least one or two national championships through the decade.
- At the Olympics, "Bullet" Bob Hayes earned the title of the fastest man on Earth when he won the 100-meter dash in the 1964 Tokyo Olympics and then went on to become the only man to win Olympic gold as well as a Super Bowl, playing receiver for the Dallas Cowboys.
- In professional golf, Arnold Palmer and Jack Nicklaus would emerge as among the greatest names in golf, each notching several major championships, including the Masters, U.S. Open, PGA Tournament, and British Open.

BIBLIOGRAPHY

"Azusa Foothill Drive-In Theater," Roadside Peek: An Adventure in Times, n.d., as accessed on January 13, 2018, at http://www.road sidepeek.com/roadusa/southwest/california/socal/socaldrivein/lacntydi/azusadrivein/index.htm

"Baby Boomers," History.com, n.d., as accessed on January 9, 2018, at http://www.history.com/topics/baby-boomers

Brooks, Alan. "Remembering the 1960s: Racism, Prison, and What Went Wrong?" July 24, 2012, as accessed on January 11, 2018, at https://ieet.org/index.php/IEET2/more/brooks20120724

"The Color Revolution: Television in the Sixties," TV Obscurities, n.d., as accessed on January 17, 2018, at http://www.tvobscurities.com/articles/color60s/

Ellerbee, Linda. "When Television Ate My Best Friend," n.d., as accessed on March 26, 2018, at file:/http://mitford.rockyview.ab.ca/Members/srowe/language-arts-7/7.4-resources/language-arts/sightlines-7/when-television-ate-my-best-friend-text/view

"JFK's Moon Shot Speech to Congress," Space.com, May 25, 1961, as accessed on May 16, 2019, at https://www.space.com/11772-presi dent-kennedy-historic-speech-moon-space.html

Landsperger, A. David, "Should I Stay or Should I Go?" *Retrospect*, October 3, 2017, as accessed on April 16, 2018, at https://www .myretrospect.com/?s=should+i+stay+or+should+i+go

MacDonald, J. Fred. "The Golden Age of Blacks in Television: The Late 1960s," Blacks and White TV: African Americans in Television since 1948, n.d., as accessed on March 26, 2018, at https://jfredmacdon ald.com/bawtv/bawtv10.htm

Mulholland Junior High School Girls' Good-Grooming Guidelines, 1967, Balboa, California.

Nelson, Laura J. "Digital Projection Has Drive-In Theaters Reeling," *Los Angeles Times*, January 19, 2013, as accessed on January 19, 2013, at http://www.latimes.com/entertainment/envelope/cotown/la-et-ct-drive-ins-digital-20130120-story.html

"1960s Fashion," Fifties Web, n.d., as accessed on March 25, 2018, at https://fiftiesweb.com/fashion/hippie-clothes/

Roach, John. "Apollo Anniversary: Moon Landing Inspired World," National Geographic News, July 16, 2004, as accessed on March 24, 2018, at https://byjohnroach.com/writings/space/apollo-anniver sary-moon-landing-inspired-world.html

Romney, Kat. "Women in the Workforce in the Mid-1960s," Letterpile. com, December 20, 2016, as accessed on April 17, 2018, at https:// letterpile.com/memoirs/Women-in-the-Workforce-in-the-mid-1960s

Shutkin, John. "My One Drive-In Movie Story," *Retrospect*, August 11, 2016, as accessed on May 5, 2018, at https://www.myretrospect.com/ stories/my one-drive-in-movie-story/

Thompson, Kirsten M. J. "A Brief History of Birth Control in the U.S.," December 14, 2013, as accessed on June 25, 2018, at https://www.our bodiesourselves.org/health-info/a-brief-history-of-birth-control/

Underwood, Suzy. "Teach Your Children," *Retrospect*, November 7, 2017, as accessed on May 8, 2018, at https://www.myretrospect.com/ stories/teach-your-children/

Wolfe, Tom. *The Right Stuff*, Bantam Books, New York, 1984, pp. 184–86.

Zussman, John Unger. "Secret Sauce," My Retrospect.com, August 10, 2017, as accessed on April 18, 2018, at https://www.myretrospect .com/?s=secret+sauce

Zussman, Patricia. "Forbidden Fruit," My Retrospect.com, December 14, 2015, as accessed on April 16, 2018, at https://www.myretrospect .com/stories/forbidden-fruit/

5

RELIGIOUS LIFE

Recalling how the 1960s began to inform his thinking about the role of religion in society, retired Oklahoma Baptist University librarian Richard Cheek reminisced about how the civil rights movement changed him. The former missionary said he saw how a critical aspect of his faith was anchored in creating equal conditions for all and in helping those in need. He recalls of the 1960s:

> Once the Civil Rights Act was passed and the Voting Rights Act was enacted, I remember thinking, "We got it done. We've done all those things." The 1960s was definitely a watershed period. It didn't solve all the problems, but the civil rights movement raised up the idea that everyone had these rights. And the women's movement and the LGBT movement came out of that. The civil rights movement to me was one that I look back on and say this is what changed America. The anti-war movement unified people, but the civil rights movement changed us.
>
> There was definitely a religious component to my conversion. I'd almost left the church when I first came back from Vietnam. I remember saying I just don't see how I can be part of the church that I don't see living up to the Sermon on the Mount. It took a number of years. It just got to the point that I felt I couldn't take it anymore. I found a group of liberal Mennonites. We do talk politics, and we are likeminded. I got fed up with the Baptist Church and left. The Baptists came out of the counterculture movement in England. Separation of church and state was important to them. Then all of

a sudden they got some power and said we're not so sure about this separa-tion of church and state thing. (Richard Cheek, unpublished telephone interview with Jim Willis, September 17, 2017)

CHANGES AFOOT IN THE CHURCH

Like most other aspects of life in the 1960s, religion was start-ing to undergo changes that would continue to last and evolve on into the 21st century. While traditional religious denominations in the Protestant, Catholic, and Jewish churches and synagogues were carrying on in fairly normal ways, new movements—some of which began in the late 1950s and others that were original in the 1960s—were rising up and about to cause traditional religious insti-tutions to rethink their practices. Some of these movements arose to offer different frames and expressions for long-held beliefs; others of them arose as part of the widespread protest movements of the 1960s and the distrust that people had in the established religious institutions in answering challenges of the day. It was an abrupt shift from the 1950s when traditional churchgoing in America was as much a part of postwar American life as the mushrooming sub-urbs, booming families, and baseball in the park. The 1950s was the age of *Leave It to Beaver*, but that age was about to change.

Reflecting on churches in the 1950s, former Episcopal pastor Robert Ellwood wrote the following about his Episcopal church in Nebraska: "It was a fine time to go church . . . and to build." Americans were enjoying the postwar prosperity and—following the upheaval of the war years—were looking for family normalcy, so much so that many chose to ignore the fissures in America, although some of them such as racial tensions and the walling off from other people that religious sectarianism and denomination-alism can bring. "It was a U.S. denominational society in action. Few of those to whom it seemed so natural realized how strange and unlikely such an arrangement would appear in most of the religious world," Ellwood said. "Religion flourished in the '50s for several reasons partly because of the ever-expanding spiritual mar-ketplace. There were a lot of different options available that would appeal to different kinds of people. Before the war, organized reli-gion was much more restricted."

Ellwood believes the shift in American religion began "amid the double shocks of 1957: the integration of schools in Little Rock and the success of the Soviet satellite Sputnik." These events sig-naled trouble in America and an increasingly dangerous rivalry with Russia, and they burst the normalcy bubble for many Americans. In addition, it was time when the emergence of popular evangelist Billy Graham was bursting onto the scene, and his message transcended denominational lines and churches, calling for a focus on Christ rather than a specific church or denomination (Tucker, 1997).

HIGH-WATER MARK FOR ORGANIZED RELIGION

Organized religious activity in America hit a high-water mark in the early 1960s, according to a multifaceted study done by Religion News Service that tracked such activity over a 60-year period from 1952 to 2012. The news agency compiled some 400 surveys done over the period and pieced together a religious activity index that was based on such criteria as people claiming a religion, church attendance, people saying religion is a major part of their lives, and the amount of time people say they spend in prayer. In the postwar 1950s, trend lines showed what many felt were another "Great Awakening" in American religion that carried into the first few years of the 1960s. The first Great Awakening had occurred when a religious revival swept Protestant Europe and colonial America in the 1730s and 1740s. But as the protests of the 1960s expanded, so did confidence in all institutions—including churches—and the trend line for religious activity began going downward. It did not stabilize until the 1980s, but then it went down again and the decline has been a steep one ever since (Grant, 2014).

In terms of church membership alone, statistics show the Roman Catholic Church and the Southern Baptist Church have increased membership at a rate to match American population growth from 1960 to the 21st century. Interestingly, however, membership in the African American Episcopal Church has more than doubled, and Mormonism has seen a huge increase of 275 percent since 1960. All other mainstream Protestant denominations have either remained stagnant or seen declines in membership since 1960. Methodism has seen a 24 percent drop, while the Presbyterian Church (United States) has dropped 21 percent, and Disciples of Christ is down a startling 56 percent in membership, while the Church of Christ and the United Church of Christ have each seen drops of more than 30 percent. Both branches of the Lutheran Church (ELCA and Missouri Synod) are down about 5–6 percent (Trends in Large U.S. Church Memberships since 1960, n.d.).

SECULARIZATION AND MEGACHURCHES

The decline in most Protestant denominational membership may be attributed to a growing secularization in America and also to the growth of nondenominational "megachurches," usually evangelical in nature, that attract couples who come from different denominational traditions.

The decline in religious identification is also seen among members of the Jewish faith since 1960. Among people who say they are Jewish by religion, the percentage among Americans has dropped from between 3 and 4 percent in the 1960s to 1.8 percent in 2013 (Lipka, 2013).

Whether you were oriented toward either the traditional church culture or the newer iterations of religion often depended on your age or your race. Things weren't changing much for middle-age and older Americans in the churches, and statistics actually show the late 1950s and early 1960s to be high-water mark in denominational church attendance. Younger Americans, however, were attracted toward the new movements that often branched outside the church walls, and blacks were attracted—as were many young whites—to the new clarion call for Christians to fight for the rights of the racially oppressed.

CIVIL RIGHTS MOVEMENT AS AN INFLUENCE

Certainly, the civil rights movement, led by Dr. Martin Luther King in the South, had intersections with how many Americans viewed the role of churches in helping spearhead needed social change and equality among races. In many ways, the civil rights movement was also a spiritual movement that arose out of the black churches in the South and combined the traditions of African American churches with the gospel of social change. The roots of nonviolent protest can be traced to the biblical underpinnings of the black churches in America, and they also drew inspiration from the nonviolent protest movement in India begun by Mahatma Gandhi in 1930 to protest British rule over that country. Says writer Paul Harvey of the American civil rights movement and its association with black churches:

The historically racist grounding of whiteness as dominant and blackness as inferior was radically overturned in part through the re-imagination of the same Christian part that was part of creating it in the first place. In similar ways, the Mexican-American farm movement drew on the mystic Catholic spirituality of Cesar Chavez and brought to national consciousness the lives and aspirations of an oppressed agricultural proletariat that lacked the most elementary rights of American citizens. (Harvey, 2016)

Martin Luther King himself was an ordained minister in the American Baptist Church, and the organization he founded carried its spiritual connection right in its name: the Southern Christian Leadership Conference. Dr. King became pastor of the Dexter Avenue Baptist Church in Montgomery, Alabama, at age 25. From that pulpit he began mounting his crusade for civil rights, believing God intended for all people to be treated equally. In his penultimate call for greater civil rights—his famous "I Have a Dream" speech—King invoked his faith several times. He cited biblical passages such as Isaiah 40:4 ("Every valley shall be exalted, every mountain and hill shall be made low, the rough ground shall be made level, the rugged places a plain") as metaphors to his vision of equality in America.

LIBERALISM AS A RELIGION?

Many who look at the 1960s see the start of modern-day liberalism, and some see liberalism as a new religion for those who so strongly protest existing conditions and instead push for change. Writer and conservative commentator Stanley Kurtz is one who believes this. A senior fellow at the Ethics and Public Policy Center, Kurtz wrote in his essay "Culture and Values in the 1960s":

> *Sometime during the past thirty years, liberalism stopped being a mere political perspective for many people and turned into a religion. I do not speak metaphorically. A certain form of liberalism now functions for substantial numbers of its adherents as a religion: an encompassing world-view that answers the big questions about life, dignifies daily exertions with higher significance, and provides a rationale for meaningful collective action. It wasn't supposed to be that way. Liberalism arose as a solution to the destructive religious wars of Europe's past and succeeded because it allowed people of differing religious perspectives to live peacefully and productively in the same society. Designed to make the world safe for adherents of differing faiths, liberalism itself was never supposed to be a faith. But to a significant extent, that is what liberalism has become.*

Kurtz believes this "de facto religion" undergirds today's emphasis on political correctness, which, he asserts, is something we inherited from the late 1960s. To Kurtz, political correctness is characterized by demonizing opinions as racist or sexist or homophobic that don't align with "left-liberalism." And, he argues, this demonization runs as deep in the thinking of liberals as religion itself does in others (Kurtz, 2003).

Another writer who agrees with Kurtz's thinking is Carl E. Olson, editor of the *Catholic World Report*. Olson believes liberalism is a kind of religion that did arise in the 1960s. In 2012 he wrote, "The religious character of modern liberalism was never far from the surface. Indeed, the 1960s should be seen as another in a series of 'great awakenings' in American history—a widespread yearning for new meaning that gave rise to a tumultuous social and political movement. The only difference was that this awakening largely left God behind."

Olson said he changed his thinking about how the protest movement was more than a "politics of hope" in the first half of the 1960s and became more of a religion to its followers—the counterculture generation—in the latter half of the decade. He concludes that, by 1969, the movement had to do "with a religious crisis of the magnitude of the Reformation. . . . If you clear the public square of what we traditionally call religion—Christianity, Judaism, Islam, Mormonism, Buddhism etc.—we will not have a public square free of religion. We have a public square full of religion fighting under the false flag of 'secular values'—with no opposing sources of moral authority to resist it" (Olson, 2012).

A NEW EVANGELISM

The thinking of Kurtz and Olson notwithstanding, traditional religion was not being abandoned by America in the 1960s. In fact, many of the changes occurring in American religion in the 1960s can be traced to the evangelist Billy Graham, who burst onto the American religious scene in the early 1950s with a breakout tent revival in Los Angeles, promoted heavily by the media baron William Randolph Hearst. Graham was a natural preacher, and it wasn't long before his crusades were being televised across the country. People flocked en masse to his revivals that filled giant football stadiums across the country. As his popularity grew, so did his signature Billy Graham ministries that spread into Hollywood and the making of several contemporary movies with evangelistic undertones. Two of the most popular were *The Restless Ones* and *The Cross and the Switchblade*. The soundtracks of films like these featured original, contemporary Christian songs. That music, in turn, became intertwined with the growing folk music genre of the 1960s, and it quickly found its way into churches and religious gatherings. The composer of many of these songs, the man often called the father of "Christian rock," was Ralph Carmichael, and songs he wrote included *He's Everything to Me*, *Love Is Surrender*, and *Pass It On*. Carmichael was the son of a Pentecostal preacher who loved listening to music on the radio when growing up and became intrigued by the idea of blending contemporary sounds and orchestrations with religious music. Enrolling in what is now California's Vanguard University, Carmichael thought he would follow his father into the pulpit but instead wound up composing a new genre of Christian music, today known as contemporary Christian music. In the 1950s and 1960s, however, his experimentations caused controversy in many churches, who felt musical sounds should retain a sacredness and not be influenced by "worldly" music. Undeterred, Carmichael kept at it and found great popularity with his works, especially after he was hired by the Billy Graham Evangelistic Association to compose music for its films and crusades.

Lest anyone wonder why a chapter on religion would spend time talking about music, the answer is that—since the 1960s—music has fueled many changes in Christian churches in America. What began as the introduction of some contemporary Christian songs into traditional denominational church services has morphed into an entirely new breed of nondenominational churches—often called "megachurches" because of the size of their worship services and because they transcend traditional denominational lines. Worship styles have changed from liturgical and reflective, in which hymns hundreds of years old are highly prized, to "praise and worship" services where the formality of the service is gone. That is replaced by parishioners in T-shirts, jeans, and shorts singing words of contemporary Christian songs projected onto screens. The order of worship has been downsized to several of these songs, often sung over and over again by parishioners with hands in the air, and 20–25 minutes of a pastoral message. In a larger vein, the different preferences in music have caused some to feel closer to God, while others have mourned the loss of the traditions and reflective environment of traditional services. Some churches have split wide open over musical styles, and rebellious churchgoers have created the megachurches.

And much of this began in the 1960s.

As a student at Dallas Theological Seminary, a large conservative Christian seminary, I recall the changes I witnessed firsthand in attending the required chapel services on campus.

I was a seminary classmate with a young musician who would become one of the pioneer songwriters often associated with the contemporary Christian music movement, Don Wyrtzen. Sometimes in chapel we would sing a song that Wyrtzen wrote, and you could tell the difference between it and the traditional hymns we would sing like "A Mighty Fortress Is Our God." Wyrtzen's music was appealing to young people like us because it blended parts of secular music with Christian lyrics that were targeted at the way we felt in the late 1960s and early 1970s.

I remember one day the seminary decided to hold a special chapel session focused on the debate over bringing contemporary music into Christian worship services, and I remember the Dallas students were divided over it. To some, there was a strong sense that the church service and its music should remain separated from secular music and that we should stick with the old hymns. To others, music like Wyrtzen's was a welcome innovation. It offered a way to reach people with the Christian message who might otherwise not wish to hear it. The new musical sounds conveying that message might cause them to actually hear the message for the first time.

Ironically, after a successful 35 years as a composer and concert pianist, Don became professor of church music at Southwest Baptist Theological Seminary, one of the most conservative and traditional Christian seminaries in the country. So, in the end, I guess he won the debate!

In an article in the *Topeka Capital Journal*, Wyrtzen described himself as a musician who loves to draw from different genres for his work, calling himself an "evangelical Leonard Bernstein." His objective, he said, is to make connections with listeners and to impart the gospel message in the process.

"What I would say is the Lord uses all different forms of music to reach different people," Wyrtzen said. "It's the Gospel and the content of Scripture that sanctifies the form of music. I would fight for the right of young people to do their own music. Today, in most cases, I'm happy to say, most of the songs are very biblical and in many cases are Scripture set to music" (Anderson, 2017).

THE CHARISMATIC MOVEMENT

Another religious development of the 1960s was the so-called charismatic movement, and it crossed Protestant and Catholic lines and changed the ways many individuals and churches practiced their worship. While blossoming in this decade, the movement had actually begun in the 1950s when South African Pentecostal pastor David Du Plessis started sharing his message with leaders in mainstream Protestant churches in America. Before long, the more emotional form of worship—including "speaking in tongues"—began appearing in American churches. One particular church grabbed the headlines in 1960 when St. Mark's Episcopal Church in Van Nuys, California, heard their rector Dennis Bennett tell them of the "new work" of the Holy Spirit, and he broke into an unknown language at the pulpit. He explained he was exercising his spiritual gift of speaking in tongues and said others who felt so led should do the same. In response, the church demanded his resignation, and he left and was sent to St. Luke's Episcopal Church in Seattle, Washington. Along with him, he took his charismatic practices of speaking in tongues, prophesying, and faith healing. Also while there, he began writing about the need to exercise these spiritual gifts and traveled to other churches spreading his message. Bennett is credited with planting the seed of what would become a charismatic revival (a similar movement had taken place in the early 1900s) in the Protestant Church, which later moved into local Catholic churches. Bennett was joined in this movement by other pastors such as Larry Christenson of the Lutheran Church, Harald Bredesen of the Reformed Church, and fellow Episcopalian Everett Fullam.

Alongside this stream of the charismatic movement was another one that emerged outside the mainstream Protestant Church. Theologically, it was similar in stressing the benefits of having a fuller, personal spiritual experience with God and exercising spiritual gifts. But in practice, these followers had come to a point of wondering if the traditional church structure was the best way to do that, so they practiced worship outside the local churches, choosing to meet instead in small informal fellowships—that in time grew to larger ones—and which met in the homes of these believers, community centers, or local schools on Sunday mornings. Leaders in this independent fellowship movement were Bob Mumford and Derek Prince. These local fellowships began networking with each other as leaders and speakers would move back and forth between different fellowships and as conferences were held. New musical recordings of praise songs and new books were created and disseminated along the network, adding to the larger community of these local fellowships.

As the charismatic movement gained strength in the Protestant Church, it began moving into the Roman Catholic Church in the late 1960s where the need was felt to connect more with the power of the Holy Spirit and to exercise spiritual gifts that believers had been given. In 1966, some lay faculty at Pittsburgh's Duquesne University began praying for a greater form of dynamic worship and Christian witness in the Catholic Church. A few months later, in 1967, a group of 30 professors and students from Duquesne retreated to a site to focus on the first four chapters of the New Testament book of Acts. As one professor later said, the group felt overcome by the Holy Spirit, began weeping, singing praises, and speaking in tongues. That was the beginning of a larger fellowship at Duquesne that, in turn, spread to other colleges. Then, in September 1967, some 150 students, faculty, and priests convened what would be the first annual National Catholic Pentecostal Conference. Within 10 years, the movement had swept into many Catholic parishes around the country, the annual conference had grown to 30,000 participants, and some 1 million Catholics were followers of this charismatic movement. It would continue to grow globally in the 1980s (Hummel, 1986).

The charismatic renewals in the Protestant and Catholic churches also produced problems for both local churches and the larger denominations they represented. For all the spiritual benefits they offered, the charismatic theology divided some churches and split many apart. Here is how I remember the discussion of it going in one of my seminary classes.

I recall one day our professor talking about the charismatic movement and saying what a good thing it was to stress the closeness with the Holy Spirit. But the specific practice of speaking in tongues, which seemed so important to Pentecostals and other charismatics, was probably the most divisive threat to many Christian churches of the day, he said. His own personal belief was that when Acts talks about speaking in tongues, it was more of a metaphor for early Christians expressing their faith in different native languages. In any event, he didn't feel God would ordain a spiritual gift that would prove to divide Christians instead of bring them together.

A GENERATIONAL DIVIDE

One of the hallmarks of the 1960s was that many of the changes in the decade were triggered by young people, many of them still in college or recently graduated. That certainly was true with the various social protest movements of the day, but it was also true when it came to the changes among religious followers. If campuses had their chapters of the Students for a Democratic Society protesters, the same campuses also had their chapters of Intervarsity Christian Fellowship and Campus Crusade for Christ. Both of these youth-oriented evangelical movements hit their strides in the 1960s, although the former had been founded in 1941 and the latter in 1951. The case of Campus Crusade for Christ (which changed its name to "Cru" in 2011) shows how religion was changing among many college students and how it was also promoted aggressively as an answer to the social challenges facing America.

I was one who was affected by Campus Crusade for Christ, and here is how it changed my mind about religion, at least as a young man in the 1960s:

In high school during the early 1960s I attended church because my friends were there and we were involved in a lot of youth activities. The wounds had not opened in America as widely as they would by 1964 when I went off to college, and we teens were carrying on as usual in the tradition of our parents. Religion was more of an activity and something a family would do on Sunday and maybe one night a week. But for me and my friends it didn't necessarily relate to the issues of the day or make us feel much different inside.

My first year at the University of Oklahoma I found myself trying out different churches and student religious centers on campus, but nothing seemed to work for me. Then in my sophomore year I became involved in Campus Crusade for Christ. That was in the spring of 1966, and they were hosting Thursday night "College Life" meetings in the living rooms of OU fraternity houses.

"Crusade," as we called it then, had been started in the 1950s at UCLA by a businessman turned seminary student, Bill Bright. I always thought he looked a little like Clark Gable, actually. But Campus Crusade had just started hitting its stride in the 1960s on campuses across America. It was an organization based in San Bernardino, California, and it met the spiritual and social needs of a lot of college students. There was a welcoming spirit about this organization, and a lot of popular students on campus participated making it even more "cool" to attend functions. Four other things about it proved even more important, however: First, Campus Crusade made religion a personal thing between you and God; it wasn't just a religious activity out there apart from you. Second, it put religion and faith into contemporary terms through the way God was discussed and through the folk music in which it was sung. This had a way of making it "our" religion as opposed to our parents'. Third, it provided an alternative way to rebel against established religion, at a time when rebellion against the establishment was in vogue. Finally, it offered a way to peacefully protest the growing social concerns in America. The idea was that, instead of changing institutions and groupthink, you work on helping change one individual at a time through the gospel message. Thinking back, it was no coincidence that Campus Crusade for Christ found its traction during the 1960s that would propel it to greater success in later years. The decade was ripe for this kind of religious movement.

Campus Crusade even produced its own singing group, *The New Folk*, who toured college campuses across the country and put the gospel message into the folk music vernacular so popular in the 1960s. The group was professional and very talented. In young Christian circles, its popularity rivaled that of the secular folk music sensation, The New Christy Minstrels. This musical outreach helped spread the appeal of religion among college-age students and 20-somethings.

One particular event, organized by Campus Crusade in the spring of 1967, shows how this kind of college-oriented religious movement intersected with the social protest movements of the day. I participated in this rally that went this way:

> *Crusade organized this huge "blitz" of the most socially liberal and coun-*
> *terculture campus of the day—The University of California at Berkeley—to*
> *show how the gospel message was an answer to America's problems. It was*
> *ironic that Berkeley was chosen as the site for this, because this is the place*
> *the campus free speech movement began earlier in the decade. However, it*
> *was clear that many of the students and faculty didn't appreciate having 600*
> *visiting college students descend on them to spread the message of Jesus as*
> *an answer to the societal problems they were debating.*

Nevertheless, we all came from campuses around the country. A huge phone bank was established with numbers taken from the campus phone book, and we began calling Berkeley students and faculty to make individual appointments to discuss issues with them. Of course, our plan was to show them how Jesus could answer the problems they were facing. So that's what we did, for an entire week, fanning out all over campus and on nearby Telegraph Avenue where many students hung out in cafés and bars. There was even a special edition of the New Testament that some of us carried with the image of a clenched fist on the cover, connoting

Jesus as a rebel to the establishment of the day. All week long there were these one-on-one chats going on, and I recall the campus newspaper coming out with an editorial in midweek saying how hard it was to avoid Campus Crusade students. The finale of the week was a campus rally led by Billy Graham right on the UC Berkeley campus at the Greek Theater. Whether you were religious or not, it was a week you wouldn't forget.

By 2011, "Cru" was active on 1,741 college and university campuses around the world, and it had more than 25,000 missionaries in 191 countries (Goodstein, 2011).

HIPPIES AND RELIGIOUS COMMUNES

The aspect of religion that addressed social concerns was evident in other contexts in the 1960s beyond such organizations as Cru. Two of these were in the hippies-based "Jesus Movement" and in the religious communes that movement inspired. Often used as a generic term for young counterculture people of the 1960s who wore flowers in their hair and dressed in psychedelic colors, "hippies" also connoted a different mind-set from traditional America. As Dr. Timothy Leary once wrote in 1968, "Hippy is an establishment label for a profound, invisible underground, evolutionary process. For every visible hippy, barefoot, flowered, beaded, there are a thousand invisible members of the turned-on underground. Persons whose lives are tuned in to their inner vision, who are dropping out of the TV comedy of American life" (Stone, 1999).

The word "hippie" was coined by Herb Caen, a writer for the *San Francisco Chronicle*. He used it to describe participants in the counterculture youth movement—that attracted mostly teens and 20-somethings—who came in large numbers to the Haight-Ashbury district of San Francisco during the 1960s. Hippies dressed in brightly colored, loose-fitting clothing, usually adorned with flowers and peace symbols. In both appearance and spirit, they evoked resistance to the "establishment" culture of the times. Some of the older hippies were transplanted "beatniks" from the late 1950s, who migrated west to join the new hippie subculture.

Some in the hippie movement latched on to what they envisioned as a rebellious Jesus to augment their message of protest in the 1960s, mixing together Christian evangelicalism, Eastern mysticism, social protest, and a retreat from established society into communes of like-minded discontented people in search of a utopian life lived off the earth. Such communes were not original to the 1960s, although the motivation and objectives of these new communities were different. Utopian Christian communes have a long history in America, dating back to the Shakers or the "shaking Quakers" in the 18th century. Other versions of communes would appear in 19th-century America like the Brook Farm community in New England that focused more on economic equality issues and parallel—to some extent—to what we know as communism. But the 1960s counterculture era provided fertile ground for a new landscape of religious movements and communes. This new breed shared few connections with established Judeo-Christian traditions. Some communes were evangelical Christian in part, but many were based on the Eastern religions such as Hinduism and Buddhism.

Of these various religious communes, California graduate student Amy Hart wrote in her thesis:

> These social concerns came to the forefront for the youthful counterculture in the '60s, which ultimately helped form the new religious movements emerging during the era. In their most extreme form, these religious movements resulted in established religious communities that were at odds with the primarily Judeo-Christian models of the past. Three of these new types of religious communities [were]: Eastern religious communities, New Age spiritualist communities, and communes of the Jesus movement. Each of these types of communities responded to the social and political changes of the '60s differently, but their reactions all represent significant parts of the American countercultural movement, and in many ways, the continued direction of American religion today.
>
> The "hippie movement" of the 1960s often brings to mind drugs, free love, and back-to-nature lifestyles. While all of these elements existed in the hippie-oriented intentional communities of the time, those communities actually comprised a numerical minority of the emerging communal living environments. Most emerging communes of the '60s focused on a strictly defined spiritual aim, particularly the communes based on Eastern religious practice and the communities of the new Jesus movement. Of those who were drawn to the new religious movements of the 1960s, the most dedicated and outspoken members lived in organized religious communities. (Hart, n.d.)

In their book, *America Divided: Civil War of the 1960s*, Maurice Isserman and Michael Kazin wrote, "Nothing changed so profoundly in the United States during the 1960s as American religion" (Isserman and Kazin, 2008).

The communes of the 1960s went beyond the practice of living together, sharing the work responsibilities as well as the communal food and physical assets. There was an intentionality to these communes, a purpose to which the members subscribed and worked to achieve. That purpose was often to create a new "purer" society that was less materialistic and corrupt than what members saw existing in establishment America. And religion played a role in that, according to Hart who wrote, "While the religious shifts of the 1960s are often overlooked in favor of an exploration of the general 'hippie' cultural shifts, they represented a huge element of the shifting social customs of the era" (Hart, n.d.).

Writer Erika Anderson describes what it was like to be raised in one of these communes. Her parents inhabited several communes such as Paonia in Colorado and the Spring Holly Farm in Tennessee, winding up in the largest of the American communes then, known simply as *The Farm* in California. At one time, some 1,500 hippies called it home. Anderson's parents found what they were looking for there, and the commune continued to thrive into the 1970s and 1980s when Erika lived there.

They were out to save the world, or at least themselves. Peace, love, and understanding. Of my sisters, two of us were born on The Farm. My eldest sister has a snowflake tattooed on the back of her neck—she was born in a blizzard in Colorado. My other sister was born in a tent on The Farm (no tattoo). I've said that I should get a trailer inked on the back of my neck, because that's where I was born—in a mobile home my dad brought from Nashville. As with most Farm babies, a midwife trained by Ina May (the sister of the commune's founder Stephen Gaskin) guided me into the world.

Prior to starting The Farm, Gaskin held sessions in San Francisco called the Monday Night Class. This is where he preached his philosophy of the world, Anderson said.

Stephen . . . presided over his disciples from a meditation cushion, a stage, or a tree stump to explore spirituality and the purpose-driven life, much of which was determined by the "vibes." He preached that you could feel when you were telling the truth and when you were not, based on your own energy or the energy of the people around you. He was inspired by Buddhism and Christianity, along with the effects of marijuana, and his classes regularly swelled to 1,000 students, with extended Q&As.

Describing life at The Farm, Anderson said:

Life on the inside had its charms and quirks. A Farm store operated like community-supported agriculture. I remember each house getting a box of cooking oil, Ajax, a bar of soap, margarine, salt, and seasonal vegetables, except most couldn't supplement these with trips to a grocery store. . . . And

*while we were growing up, there was no refrigeration, but there were tele-
phones and a Laundromat. To get in line, you placed a call first thing in the
morning so you could wash clothes for your entire house, which might hold
a single family or 50 people. While men worked in the fields, or off The Farm
to earn money, women had weekly or biweekly "house days." One or two
women would look after the kids in their home, make meals and do the laun-
dry if they could. Then they would spend the other days of the week working
in the community, outside the home. (Anderson, 2014)*

Communes like The Farm grew crops that were then shared in common among the members. Seldom could the harvest feed everyone in the commune, however, and some would feel hunger pangs
from insufficient food intake.

ALTERNATIVE RELIGIOUS TRADITIONS

Along with the questioning of traditional norms and institutions
in America came the questioning not just of how one practiced religion but of whether Western religion was the most credible and
valid religious tradition in the first place. Therefore, many counterculture enthusiasts—especially those in the younger generation—
began investigating Eastern religions such as Buddhism and
Hinduism and the belief systems of Native Americans. It was all
part of the religious changes that permeated the 1960s.

Those in the hippie movement, as well as those who identified
with the nonconformity of the movement, found themselves drawn
to some of the rhetoric and teachings of Eastern religions and
Native American beliefs that seemed to echo the strains of peace,
love, and freedom. It was a common sight in many hippie communes of the 1960s to see these Eastern religions worshipped and
practiced. Helping spur interest in all this were visits to America
by different "gurus" or teachers from Eastern countries who spread
their messages and gained converts. In addition, many hippies felt
that using LSD was another way to get in touch with deeper realism by expanding their minds' horizons.

In Zen Buddhism, followers found its emphasis on internal meditation rather than doctrine to be appealing. After all, it was traditional American doctrine that these young people were rebelling
against in the first place. The idea of taking a spiritual journey to
question tradition and find a new path was something to embrace.
Focus was also on the spontaneous and the visceral experience
rather than the structured, cerebral "logic" of the West. This had

actually been something that had attracted the interest of the previous decade's beatnik followers. Zen was a kind of personal meditation that emphasizes "being" rather than "thinking," and being in the moment was part of hippie culture. It was not just hippies, however, who developed an interest in Buddhism. Actually, many American soldiers who fought in Vietnam came into contact with the religion there, because it was practiced by their South Vietnamese allies. And many of these soldiers, who carried deep worries about surviving the war, found solace in the peacefulness of Zen Buddhism. Those who were attracted to it and who did survive the war brought Buddhism home with them and often spread its principles to others, thereby creating a greater awareness of it in America.

Another Eastern religion catching hippies' attention was Hinduism, the dominant religion of India and neighboring countries that stressed meditation and yoga. Many young Americans first discovered Hinduism in the 1960s when the Beatles visited Maharishi Mahesh Yogi in 1968. The popularity of the British rock band helped the popularity of Hinduism in America. But, like, Buddhism, there was a natural fit between the tenets of Hinduism and the counterculture revolutionaries in America. As with Buddhism, the idea of inward meditation as opposed to creeds felt right to the hippies. Hinduism just added the concept of "transcendental meditation" through yoga, a technique taught by Maharishi Mahesh Yogi, who became famous among hippies in America. His central idea was that, through expanding one's happiness, an individual can find the purpose and fulfillment of life. That philosophy hit the spot for many hippies. Other aspects of the culture of India also caught on among hippies, including wearing the colorful Indian clothing, burning incense, embracing vegetarianism, and meditating through yoga. Many of these practices are still prevalent today and have worked their way into mainstream American culture.

But some hippies didn't have to look beyond America to find alternative spiritual practices they could embrace. They found it simply by learning and finding solace in Native American religious beliefs. Chief among these tenets were a reverence for nature and a communal lifestyle where private ownership gave way to collective use of the land and its fruits. Hippies embraced these ideas of communal sharing, of respecting ancestors and the earth, and of the practice of ritual dances. The idea of hippie communes was often built on the tribal communities of Native Americans. And respect for the earth fit with the environmental ideas of hippies. As they did in embracing the cultural affects of the Indian culture, hippies also liked to take on the appearance of Native Americans by wearing their clothing and jewelry (Peace, Love, and Beyond, n.d.).

CHANGES IN THE ROMAN CATHOLIC CHURCH

In organized religion, big changes were taking place within the Roman Catholic Church in the 1960s. Most of these changes came because of a worldwide council of Catholic leaders in Rome known as Vatican II. This was only the Second Vatican Council in the past 100 years, and it comprised four different sessions at St. Peter's Basilica between 1962 and 1965. The meetings were designed to deal with growing cultural changes and issues that impacted Catholics and, altogether, Vatican II resulted in some 16 documents that defined the basis of the late 20th-century church that carried it into the next millennium. Overall, the focus of the pronouncements dealt with the issue of reconciliation. That was not surprising, given the factious era of the 1960s. Three of the new decisions zeroed in specifically on more ecumenical interactions. Catholics were allowed to pray with members of other Christian denominations, encouraged dialogue and gatherings with non-Christian faith traditions, and allowed languages other than Latin to be spoken during Mass. The driving idea was to make the Catholic Church more relevant to people in the contemporary culture.

"Prior to this time, the church had been almost seen as a fortress, very much concerned about its own internal stability and integrity and engaging the world in terms of missionary activity," said Peter A. Huff, the president of Xavier University. "Pope John wanted to reinforce that missionary mandate, but he also wanted to create an environment of dialogue, where the church would engage in all the forces of the modern world. He wants to see Vatican II as a council of reform but a council that's in continuity with the Catholic past that came before it" (Teicher, 2012).

On the 50th anniversary of Vatican II, the Catholic Spirit website discussed key ways in which Vatican II shaped the Catholic Church today. Among the key points, it summarized the following ways (10 Ways Vatican II Shapes Our Church Today, 2012):

- Vatican II presented a new idea of what "the church" means, and what it means is the people of God. This brought a new focus on lay people.
- The Eucharist is presented as the origin and ultimate peak of the Christian faith.

- Vatican II reformed the liturgy, most notably putting the language of Mass into common-day English, jointly celebrated by the clergy and parishioners.
- It called every Catholic to a life of holiness and missionary service.
- Vatican II stressed the key role of family in the church.
- It rewrote the rules for relating with non-Catholic churches and encouraged these relationships.
- It urged collaboration with other faiths.
- It updated the church by encouraging it to become more open and relevant to the world at large.
- While updating the church, Vatican II called for a renewed commitment to the central traditions of the faith.

Changes occurring in the Catholic Church were often most evident on the campuses of Catholic colleges. Thomas J. Nenon was a student at one such school, Regent College in Denver, and he witnessed many changes firsthand:

"I was an undergraduate at Regent College in Denver, a Jesuit university. Of course writers like Thomas Aquinas were big influences there," Nenon recalled. "I went through all the major changes in the Catholic Church at the time. In the early '60s it fostered institutional segregation and had an authoritarian structure to it. But changes occurred in the 1960s and, by the time I graduated, we had integration, more of a voice as students, and we were marching against the war in Vietnam." (Thomas J. Nenon, interview on December 24, 2018)

EFFECTS ON JUDAISM

Members of the American Jewish community were heavily involved in the civil rights movement of the 1960s. Because of their own history in Germany and Russia, Jews found it easy to connect with, and understand the plight of, blacks who were experiencing discrimination and bloodshed in America. Writer Ben Shapiro notes that about one out of every two civil rights lawyers in the 1960s South was Jewish, while more than half of the white Freedom Riders who rode buses into the South to protest racial abuse were Jewish. In addition, two out of three white volunteers who worked in the 1964 Mississippi Freedom Summer were Jewish, and two of the three young civil rights workers murdered there (Andrew Goodman and Michael Schwerner) were Jews. But that's not all. Civil rights organizations like the National Association for the Advancement of Colored People and the Congress of Racial Equality were beneficiaries of the financial generosity of American Jews (Shapiro, n.d.).

But the biggest change to the American Jewish community came not from within the United States but from outside. The year 1967 was pivotal, because this was when Jews in Israel faced the prospect of being annihilated for the second time in a quarter century. June 1967 was the month of the Six-Day War when Egypt and Syria threatened to wipe Jews off the face of the earth. The threat resonated deeply among Jews in America who felt—as they still do—very strong ties to Israel. Many felt if another holocaust were to occur, that would also wipe out Judaism itself.

Dr. Manfred Gerstenfeld, former chair of the Jerusalem Council of Public Affairs, recounted American Jewish reaction in a 2014 interview:

> *Jonathan Sarna, then 12, remembers watching on TV as Israelis dug mass graves to prepare for potential slaughter. A teenage Yossi Klein Halevi remembers the broadcasts of mass rallies in Cairo calling for Israel's death. But many American Jews, haunted by their failure to act during the Holocaust, didn't just passively watch events unfold—they decided to mobilize. They raised tens of millions of dollars. They held rallies. They lobbied President Johnson. Within days, however, the fear turned to relief. The relief turned to pride when Israel won the war in six days, tripling its territory and taking control of Judaism's holiest sites. The Six-Day War, as it quickly became known, intensified American Jews' love for Israel and imbued them with a new confidence to advocate for their interests at home and abroad.* (Gerstenfeld, 2014)

Some of what motivated American Jews during the 1960s can be found in what writer Steven M. Cohen has called "a matter of obligations." Looking back, he has written that a defining characteristic of Jews—as late as the 1960s—was a deep sense of moral obligation to do the right thing and to help others in need, especially those experiencing discrimination. That sense of duty, coupled with deeply held traditions among members of the Jewish faith, was not conducive to going against the grain. Cohen writes, "One could violate the norms, but then one felt guilty about it" (Gerstenfeld, 2014).

SUMMARY

Overall, the 1960s touched and changed nearly every aspect of religion. Some of the changes caused religious disciples to focus on more fundamental aspects of their faith, while other influences caused followers to stretch their meaning of spirituality beyond the confines of conventional religion. Some used religious precepts as a justification for ending the Vietnam War and creating more equality in the land. For them and others, religion meant getting involved more in social issues and working to create a better temporal world. Still others focused more on the hereafter. And some large religious institutions—like the Roman Catholic Church—experienced all these changes and codified some of them in their new Vatican II pronouncements. And, as just seen, American Jews joined heavily in the push for civil rights and experienced a new wave of boldness and confidence when Israel won the 1967 Six-Day War.

BIBLIOGRAPHY

Anderson, Erika. "What Life Is Like When You're Born on a Commune," *Vanity Fair*, August 28, 2014, as accessed on January 7, 2018, at https://www.vanityfair.com/news/daily-news/2014/08/the-farm-born-on-a-commune

Anderson, Phil. "The Poet of the Piano: At 74, Don Wyrtzen Still Making Christian Music," *The Topeka Capital Journal*, May 19, 2017, as accessed on January 3, 2018, at http://cjonline.com/news/local/life/2017-05-19/poet-piano-74-don-wyrtzen-still-making-christian-music

Gerstenfeld, Manfred. "Changes in American Jewish Identity," Arutz Sheva 7, November 17, 2014, as accessed on June 25, 2018, at http://www.israelnationalnews.com/Articles/Article.aspx/15998

Goodstein, Laurie. "Campus Crusade for Christ Is Renamed," *New York Times*, July 20, 2011, as accessed on January 4, 2018, at http://www.nytimes.com/2011/07/21/us/21brfs-CAMPUSCRUSAD_BRF.html

Grant, Tobin. "The Great Decline: 60 Years of Religion in One Graph," Religion News Service, January 27, 2014, as accessed on January 8, 2018, at http://religionnews.com/2014/01/27/great-decline-religion-united-states-one-graph/

Hart, Amy. "Religious Communities of 1960s America," n.d., as accessed on January 5, 2018, at https://digitalcommons.calpoly.edu/forum/vol7/iss1/9/

Harvey, Paul. "Civil Rights Movements and Religion in America," Oxford Research Encyclopedias, August 2016, as accessed on January 8, 2018, at http://religion.oxfordre.com/view/10.1093/acrefore/9780199340378.001.0001/acrefore-9780199340378-e-492

Hummel, Charles E. "Worldwide Renewal: The Charismatic Movement," *Christianity Today*, 1986, as accessed on March 29, 2018, at http://www.christianitytoday.com/history/issues/issue-9/worldwide-renewal-charismatic-movement.html

Isserman, Maurice, and Michael Kazin, *America Divided: The Civil War of the 1960s*, New York: Oxford University Press, 2008, p. 251.

Kurtz, Stanley. "Culture and Values in the 1960s," *Never a Matter of Indifference*, Peter Berkowitz (ed.), Stanford, CA: Hoover Institution Press, 2003, pp. 31–32.

Lipka, Michael. "How Many Jews Are There in the United States?" Pew Research Center, October 2, 2013, as accessed on January 8, 2018, at http://www.pewresearch.org/fact-tank/2013/10/02/how-many-jews-are-there-in-the-united-states/

Olson, Carl E. "Modern, Secular Liberalism Is a Political Religion," *Catholic World Report*, March 2, 2012, as accessed on April 12, 2018, at http://www.catholicworldreport.com/2012/03/02/modern-secular-liberalism-is-a-political-religion/

"Peace, Love, and Beyond," n.d., as accessed on March 29, 2018, at https://peaceloveandbeyond.weebly.com/spirituality-and-religion.html

Sales, Ben. "How the Six-Day War Changed American Jews," JTA, May 7, 2017, as accessed on June 25, 2018, at https://www.jta.org/2017/05/07/news-opinion/united-states/how-the-six-day-war-changed-american-jews

Shapiro, Edward S. "Blacks and Jews in America: 1960s–1980s," Jewish History, n.d., as accessed on June 25, 2018, at https://www.myjewishlearning.com/article/blacks-and-jews-in-america-1960s-1980s/

Stone, Skip. "Hippies from A to Z: The Way of the Hippy," Hip Planet, Hip Inc., 1999, as accessed on January 4, 2018, at https://www.hipplanet.com/hip/hippies-from-a-to-z-the-way-of-the-hippy/

Teicher, Jordan G. "Why Is Vatican II So Important?" National Public Radio, October 10, 2012, as accessed on January 5, 2018, at https://www.npr.org/2012/10/10/162573716/why-is-vatican-ii-so-important

"10 Ways Vatican II Shapes Our Church Today," The Catholic Spirit, October 11, 2012, as accessed on April 19, 2018, at http://thecatholicspirit.com/special-sections/vatican-ii/10-ways-vatican-ii-shapes-our-church-today/

"Trends in Large U.S. Church Memberships since 1960," Demographia, n.d., as accessed on January 8, 2018, at http://demographia.com/db-religlarge.htm

Tucker, Carol. "The 1950s—Powerful Years for Religion," USC News, June 16, 1997, as accessed on January 8, 2018, at https://news.usc.edu/25835/The-1950s-Powerful-Years-for-Religion/

6

MILITARY LIFE

While debates and protests over the Vietnam War were staples of the 1960s and early 1970s in America, some 3 million men—joined by some 7,500 women in supporting roles, yet still in harm's way—were sent to Vietnam to fight the war that America was engaged in from the early 1960s to 1975. Many of those who weren't in Vietnam were stationed in Europe, and many of those were in the former West Germany, facing off against the threat of the Soviet Union near the border of the infamous Iron Curtain that separated democracy from communism. Armed forces records show that there were some 8.7 million U.S. service members between 1964 and 1975, of which about 2.2 million were there by way of the draft. Some 3.4 million of all service members during that era were sent to Vietnam, according to the Veterans Affairs accounting (America's Wars, n.d.), although other accounts vary from 2.7 million to 3.4 million, depending on who is termed a combatant.

A popular misconception is that most of those who served in Vietnam were drafted, but the earlier statistics show a 4:1 ratio of volunteers to draftees. Of those who volunteered, some did so under pressure from the draft in order to have more say in choosing their military occupational specialty or MOS. Others wanted to finish college and enter as officers through Reserve Officer Training Corps or officer candidate school. Many young men just enlisted out of a sense of patriotic duty, while some wanted to choose their service branch instead of being drafted into the army. And then there were those who chose to try and defy the draft and not serve at all. The government estimates as many as 100,000 draft-eligible men evaded military service altogether by moving to Canada (Chambers, 1999).

BRACING FOR VIETNAM

Among the many stories of men and women who competed tours of duty in one military theater or another in the 1960s, a few of them are the following. The first is from Ray McCormick, a retired university professor of communication studies who entered the army as a young man from his home in Manhattan Beach, California, and was sent to Vietnam. There he was wounded in action and received the Purple Heart. His opening memory shows how dangerous many soldiers felt the pending jungle action would be in their lives:

I had a 2-door '57 Chevy Bel Air which was coveted by car guys and I absolutely loved. Two-tone, white over yellow, and the original black interior. After learning that I was going into a reconnaissance platoon in a mechanized infantry unit, I came home for a quick leave before going to Vietnam. I asked one of my friends if he would like to buy my car because if something happened and I did not make it I did not want my parents having to sell my car. It was not really a premonition, but I was just planning ahead for the real possibility, given my job assignment. My thought was that selling my car would be very difficult especially for my mother. So I sold it to him.

It did not take too long for those of us who went to figure out that we had been sold a political bill of goods about Vietnam. In roaming the countryside, I went through a lot of village that were rural, and isolated. Each village had a small population, a few mud and thatched houses, a water buffalo or two, and farming. For these people, making a living was difficult. They were not going to be any better off if the country was a democracy or a communist state. However for the power players in Saigon the war represented hope to maintain their positions. So my frame of mind became, do whatever you can to get out of this place. (L. Ray McCormick, e-mail interview with Jim Willis, November 29, 2017)

A FATHER'S INFLUENCE

Another Vietnam veteran, Oklahoman Richard Cheek, said his military service was influenced by his father's service, his own sense of duty, but also what he saw while in Vietnam in the late

1960s. An astute and talented young man who was raised by parents who stressed social consciousness, Cheek pursued drama in his Midwest City High School, once starring in the production of the comedy *Harvey* but a few years later finding himself in a various real and serious production called the Vietnam War. His story is not unlike hundreds of thousands of other young men who came of age during the Vietnam era and the mandatory military draft that changed career plans, or at least put them on hold, for men of that generation.

I was in Army ROTC at the University of Oklahoma and went onto active duty a month after graduating in 1967. I did basic training in Georgia and then Ft. Monmouth N.J. and then to Germany and then Vietnam after 18 months. All of the married guys got assigned to Europe somewhere then, but the married guys had to extend for a year if they wanted their wives to go with them. So they got three years out of us rather than the standard two years.

I was first stationed in Manheim, Germany, on one of the routes that Russians would have used [during the time of the Iron Curtain divide in Europe] to get into central Germany. We had top-secret plans on what to do to prevent that. I was with the Communications and Signal Corps. Later, in Vietnam, I was very fortunate. One of the things the Army does is once you work around general headquarters, you are put with another headquarters. Our primary response was supporting Vietnam operations. I saw very little hostile activity; I was about as safe as you can be and still draw combat pay. I was in Lon Bin for twelve months and one day.

It was difficult for [my wife] Jene. She was pregnant when I left for Vietnam. Our first daughter, Jenna, was born when I was there. I didn't see her until she was 3 months old. When I was in ROTC, I had considered the Army as a career. But that's one thing Vietnam changed. Once I went there and came back, there was no desire to be an Army officer. Just the separation was hard enough. And then once Vietnam was over, the Army kicked out all the active-duty reservists.

Cheek said that it wasn't always easy to reconcile his personal beliefs with the military's but that it helped to be the son of an army officer when it came to understanding military life.

I was pretty moderate in my political views. My parents were Democrats. My dad didn't think Eisenhower should have been president; he didn't think a military man should be president. I remember being supportive of Stevenson. I later supported Johnson. When I was still in Midwest City you had to be against Kennedy because he was a Catholic. That was required [in this conservative, mostly Protestant, state]. I did some work for the Johnson campaign against Goldwater. My first election was to vote for Hubert

Humphrey. I always had social concerns; concerns for the poor. That was my mother's influence. Wherever we were she found people to help. But I would say music had as much an influence as anything. Joan Baez especially.

But I grew up in an Army family, and we depended on the government to do the right things. Protests were very minor at OU. Our annual ROTC parade and the end of my senior year was the first time we were told there would be protestors out there. But I was a Bob Dylan fan. We spent a lot of time sitting around singing folk songs, and that was a formative period of my life.

The counterculture in the Army was pretty minimal. Some resisted hair cut rules, etc., but that was about it, except for some protest songs that were played on radio. Drug usage, however, was pretty high. Not so much in Germany as in Vietnam. It was incredible. We did almost weekly inspections to try and keep it out of the barracks. Lots of times the winds would change and you could smell the marijuana, and it was often coming from the barracks. Even among fellow officers. It was used both as a protest and an escape. But because we were relatively safe [at headquarters], I don't think we had as much war opposition as other places in Vietnam.

I had a real negative feeling about anyone participating against the war when I was there. [The National Guard shootings at] Kent State happened when I was there, but we heard everything over Armed Forces Radio Network. So we didn't get the kind of coverage of the war nor see the same things as people in America did. What really changed me to start thinking, "I've got to get out of this place," was when I saw the politics in the military and the career concerns of some officers who thought "we have to get ourselves positioned to survive until the next war. What am I doing to do when I leave here; how am I going to maintain my position in the military?" The Army is a very good war machine. They're not so good in peacetime.

The final straw was the whole Vietnamization push [turning the war over to South Vietnam allies to fight]. We saw through that and knew it wasn't going to happen soon. Vietnam wanted our help and our material. (Richard Cheek, unpublished telephone interview with Jim Willis, September 17, 2017)

A GENERAL REFLECTS

Many Vietnam veterans like Cheek retain vivid memories of Vietnam and what it meant to them then and now in looking back on their tour of duty there. One Vietnam vet, who wound up spending four decades in the air force as a career and retired as a four-star general, is Roger A. Brady, who noted the following about going to college in the 1960s and joining the air force during the Vietnam era.

We used to laugh a little bit about things in the '60s. This was the era when people grew long hair. But very few people did in my state. Oklahoma was a conservative place then, and it is now. Until my junior year in college I had a hard time finding Vietnam on the map. When there was a protest, I doubt it ever reached more than 50 people.

ROTC was a very big thing of necessity. It was the draft era and serving in some way seemed inevitable. If you were going to go, many of us thought, you wanted to go as an officer. That would have been part of my family makeup anyway to serve. My father served in WWII. I didn't sense a debate that was widespread. We were so wrapped up in our college lives, if something happened in the world, it would be a few days before we knew about. Our general level of awareness was very low. By the time I was a junior or senior we started watching films and writing reports in AFROTC and seeing footage of the war.

For many of us, military service was more of a tradition than anything. A lot of our parents served, so we thought we'd follow in their footsteps. I was attracted to the fact that it was a team, and I liked that. I was also attracted to the ethic and the discipline of it, as well as the predictability—or seeming predictability—of it. As a student [at the University of Oklahoma] a great benefit was when they [ROTC] started paying us as a junior—fifty dollars a month—I was rich!. But I was a fairly patriotic guy, so what was there to not like?

Brady, who did not set out to make the military a lifelong career but who came to feel it was a good enough fit to stay for 41 years, said the air force tried to pay attention to the needs of its men, hoping the devoted and talented ones would stay in beyond their initial enlistment.

The Air Force is a retention force. We try to keep as many as we can. The Army and Marines are attrition forces. They recruit a huge number of people, but the majority leave after their first term of enlistment. During my first five or six years (from 1969) we had guys hanging round that we knew weren't staying. You knew who was just picking up a paycheck every week. There was not a lot of debate about the war, within the military itself. After the war there was a lot of debate about whether you ought to stay in. The debate was about whether to stay or go, not about the war itself. Among the enlisted men, however, there was more dissension. They bore the brunt of the war. At the base movie theater of DaNang Air Base, some of the troops would refuse to stand during the playing of the national anthem that took place before every movie started. Many would boo them, but there was no action taken. It was a strange time.

In Vietnam, we were very much into the music. There were bands that came and played at the clubs. The NATO nations did not support us in the VN war. But Australian and NZ units were embedded. But the music was good. I used to have a complete Beatles collection. Reel-to-reel tapes. We had growing issues of race and drugs. The military reflects society. All

*the challenges that society had, came into the military. It was done ran-
domly among troops. A lot of people had jobs in VN that were pretty boring. Some drank heavily and some turned to drugs that were easy to obtain.
Consequently, the services instituted mandatory drug testing—we called it
"Operation Golden Flow," and random drug testing continues to this day
in the services. And there were significant levels of venereal disease. In the
early '70s, continuing post-Vietnam, we had race riots at two or three of our
AF bases. The '70s were an interesting time for the AF. In my view, we were
not a very professional force in VN. We were competent but we weren't very
professional. In the '70s, adultery was not something that people were very
concerned about. That's a death knell today.*

Brady feels today's military has come a long way, in terms of
professionalism and accountability, from the 1960s. As the nation
was evolving, so was the military. It had to respond to changing
demands and conditions, and many of the changes it made were
good ones, the general recalls.

*The U.S. military now has been the most respected institution over the past
25 years. That was not true in the post VN days. There were a lot of changes
that took place. We cleaned up our act in drugs; we cleaned up our act in
race, although that challenge remains with us. In my career the single largest
change to the military was the influence of women in the force. Until 1975,
only 2 percent could be women. Now it hovers around 20 percent of the force.
We could not today sustain an all-volunteer force without women.*

*Out of that turbulent came some good—not the least of which was an
increased sense of accountability. We would see that play out in a big way
with Watergate. There was an accountability . . . and a professionalism that
came out of it.*

Like other military officers who served in Vietnam, Brady realized this war was very different from previous wars in a number
of ways. One big difference was it has been called America's first
"living room war" where reporters could roam virtually anywhere
to report, and their stories would appear—along with images of
dead troops—on television across the country. It became obvious
that these images increased the distaste many Americans had for
fighting this war, and it became hard to sustain a war without public support.

*Vietnam was the first war that we could watch every night on our TV
screens with near-live coverage. Guys like Dan Rather were embedded with
combat units and saw bad things happen first hand. It took well into the '70s*

before the AF saw that it was the right thing to do to be as transparent as possible with the media. As a lieutenant I sat in a briefing in which a senior officer discussed having the press fly with us. He was very clear, saying, "Those guys are the enemy—never let them see a napalm strike." Over time we learned the painful lesson that covering up garbage never makes it smell better, and it's simply the wrong thing to do.

The '60s set the stage for a lot of the transparency that we have today. (Roger A. Brady, telephone interview with Jim Willis, September 15, 2017)

LIFE AT SEA

My own brief military experience, cut short by a hearing loss, was mostly spent at sea with the navy in the late 1960s, and these are some memories of that:

I was assigned as a first-class midshipman to a Gearing Class destroyer, the USS Benner *(DD807), whose homeport was Long Beach, California. The ship was launched in 1944 and named for Marine 2nd Lt. Stanley G. Benner who had been killed in the Battle of Guadalcanal in World War II. But the ship didn't spend much time there in the late '60s and saw action in the waters off Vietnam. The crew spent long periods of time at sea in support of the war.*

One of my most vivid memories involved the loud and jarring sounds of its six 5-inch guns, especially when I was inside the gun housing firing them. The barrel of the gun was no more than a foot from my ear. When the guns exploded, it felt as if the Benner *itself had just taken a hit. Another memory was of the luxurious taste of ice cream after dinner, the few times we had it, because it was way down the list of food supply items that would come aboard. Refrigeration of large amounts was a problem.*

Life at sea was different than anything I had ever experienced. Since it was an all-male environment at the time that amounted to a crew of only 330 men who were cut off from everyone else on the earth while on station in the Pacific, the Benner *had its own civilization. Overseeing it was the captain, but, on a day-to-day interactive basis, it could be a little raunchy and depressing. We were in very tight quarters. Even though I lived amidships in "officer country," I still had only one bunk (the top one) and one desk to my name. I shared roughly a nine-foot square space with one other officer.*

The navy's antidote to boredom was work, so you would usually be working a couple shifts a day, not leaving much time for idle thought. Good thing, because sometimes those thoughts would turn dark, as loneliness set in. For some poor souls, that drove them to attempt suicide, and the easiest way was to just take a walk over the side of the ship and into the ocean when no one was looking. That happened once when I was aboard the Benner. *It was in the middle of the night, and the sailor was not noticed missing until the next morning. Our ship, along with help from another destroyer, circled back for hours trying to find a sign of life in the vast waters, but we found no one. After that experience, I decided to stay as busy as I could to fight my own boredom and loneliness. I was actually glad when it came time for anti-submarine warfare or gunnery drills, because they broke up the shipboard monotony.*

Adding to the problems was the fact that your world was shrunk for weeks on end to the length and width of one of the navy's smaller ships. And walking around on deck was not always the safest thing to do, especially in a disquieted sea. Then there was the grayness. The ship was gray, the sky was often gray, and the sea was gray. It's no wonder we all lived either for some action at sea or for pulling into port somewhere and taking shore leave. In between those stops, at least you find some escape, off-watch, listening to The Fifth Dimension *or* The Supremes *back in your cabin.*

All that said, it's a pretty heady thing to be the junior officer on deck in the middle of the night issuing orders to the helmsman to keep this multimillion-dollar ship on course and on station. At times you realize, "Here I am, 22 years old, and I'm responsible for where this United States Destroyer is headed and in charge of getting it to its next station on time."

SIGHTS, SOUNDS, SMELLS, AND FEEL

Whatever one's memories about Vietnam, it is hard to find a veteran from that war who still doesn't remember the sights, sounds, and feel of his year in the jungle and the highlands of this Southeast Asian country. One marine veteran, Arnold Punaro, recalls it this way:

What surprised me about Vietnam was how wet and cold you were all the time due to the monsoon rains. My unit operated in the Que Son Mountains and it got very cold at night and we did not have warm enough sleeping gear. We were also exposed to Agent Orange but did not at the time know what it was or how harmful it would be.

I recall on Christmas Eve 1969 stopping and digging in for the night on the side of the mountain. Due to the rain and mudslides we ended up sliding down to the bottom of a B-52 bomb crater and the troops asked, "LT [Lieutenant], what is that orange color in the water?" It was of course Agent Orange, [a dangerous chemical defoliant used to clear away ground cover to make it hard for enemy troops to hide] *and we ended up sleeping in it that night. Only later did we realize the harmful effects of Agent Orange. I've gone to far too many funerals of fellow troops with Agent Orange-related diseases in recent years.* (Exter, 2016)

In fact, some 20 million gallons of Agent Orange were sprayed from low-flying helicopters over the jungles, highlands, and rivers of Vietnam from 1961 through 1971. The chemical would cause health problems and contribute to the deaths (often from cancer) of many Vietnamese and also U.S. military veterans who were exposed to it. Punaro's account of this and other hazards is typical of what more than two million American men—most of them below the age of 30—experienced while fighting the Vietnam War. Punaro was one of the lucky ones, in that he survived. One out of every 10 who served there was a casualty. At least 2.7 million American combatants went to Vietnam, and more than 58,000 of those died while another 304,000 were wounded. The average age of those killed was 23. Altogether, 9.7 percent of their generation served in Vietnam (Hack, n.d.).

Many of the American troops, scattered in the jungles, highlands, and mountains of this Southeast Asian country, did not have enough of the basic things needed to keep them from being cold, hot, wet, or hungry. As Punaro recounts, the supply lines were not reliable and troops were never sure when a good supply of heat tabs or dry socks would arrive. The new socks were needed to prevent "jungle rot" from occurring on a soldier's feet, while the heat tabs were needed to warm up the canned C-rations that he described as "horrible to inedible." One of his more memorable anecdotes was that some men were so tired of cold C-rations that they would actually pinch off a piece of their C-4 to heat that food. And that, of course, was dangerous because C-4 was a plastic explosive.

Punaro concluded: "We really did not have any contact with what we called 'the real world' back home. No Internet; no radios for news or music in the jungle; no papers; we lost track of time and the days of the weeks and even months. It's a very surreal experience to lose track of time like that and just have your platoon, patrolling the jungle, day in and day out" (Exter, 2016).

Another Vietnam vet, who identified himself in a Public Broadcasting Service online post only as "TomH47," said the following about his 13 months there.

I wrote to my family as often as I could, and I always apologized for not writing more. My mom and older sister saved my letters. I wrote home a lot—I guess it just seemed like I didn't. I "sanitized" my letters, didn't go into the details of combat, the horrific sights, the constant fear, etc. But rereading them did bring back some memories of my tour that I had lost. . . . My brain could be protecting me from those details. So instead of every night night-mares of Vietnam, I have some conglomeration of fearful events that make no sense. . . . I am a Vietnam veteran, served in the USMC for four years, 13 months [of that] in Vietnam. And for the last 40+ years have been living and trying to stay alive. (TomH47, 2010)

One infantryman described what it was like spending so much time traveling over the war zones at low altitudes in helicopters and the dangers that posed.

We were the river people, but we also spent a lot of time on helicopters. I was a radio operator in the 9th Infantry Division, based in the Mekong Delta south of Saigon, wrote Bill Lord in a 2018 op-ed piece for The New York Times. *By the time I left, someone told me I had made more than 50 combat assaults via chopper. Most but not all of them were routine insertions that could happen as often as three times in a day. Occasionally there was light resistance. A few times there was a good deal of shooting. And since you never really knew if and when the shooting would start, we all developed our own little formula for when, under fire, we would decide to jump out of the helicopter.*

You could jump from very high up and maybe break your legs. The for-ward speed of the chopper was something to take into account. The landing area might be water, mud or dry land. All were factors. You wanted out of that chopper in the worst way because the chopper was the target. Still, you didn't want to get panicky and jump too soon. So each individual had his own leap point. Mine was probably about the height of jumping from the roof of a one-story house. Survivable and a good middle ground balancing all the risks. (Lord, 2018)

THE DRAFT ENDS

The Vietnam War was the last war that American combatants fought before the age of the all-volunteer army. In 1969, President Nixon created the Commission on an All-Volunteer Force, often called the Gates Commission, and that body recommended that the United States bring the military draft to a close and begin an all-volunteer military in 1973. That news brought a great sigh of relief to millions of young men who had previously worried about being required to serve two years in the military and probably have to go to Vietnam. The war was increasingly unpopular to many Americans, and it was obviously dangerous for those serving there.

Nevertheless, the government knew it would be a hard task to sell young Americans on volunteering for service after so many years of bad press for the military. To help with that effort, the military hired advertising agencies to soften the image of the army, navy, air force, and marines and to make that image fit with the individualist spirit that young Americans were showing. These ad campaigns took place in the early 1970s and met with mixed success.

The slogan for the army that was approved by a hesitant chief of staff Gen. William C. Westmoreland was "Today's Army Wants to Join You." Involved in that was a clear catering to individuals who would be the vanguard of what would be called the "Me Generation." The air force developed a similar slogan: "Find Yourself in the U.S. Air Force." And for the navy it was "If You're Going to Be Something, Why Not Be Something Special?"

THE NEW LAID BACK ARMY

But the "rebranding" program didn't stop with the external ad campaigns. There were also internal reforms like Project VOLAR (Volunteer Army). In this program, the army experimented with changes at some of its bases that included fewer barracks inspections and efforts at giving troops more individual privacy, fewer bed checks, an easing of military discipline, and even permitting the sale of low-alcohol beer in the barracks and mess halls.

Mother Jones magazine described one other part of the campaign, instituted just after the 1960s came to a close. "In 1971, a couple of recent enlistees hit the road on their motorcycles on a new kind of recruiting mission. 'Rapping with kids on street corners, at dances, at bowling alleys and high schools from New York to Baton Rouge,' according to the *Soldiers* magazine, the duo talked up the perks of the new, laid-back Army. At one high school, Specialist Mike Speegle boasted about his two-person room: 'I had black light posters, peace signs, a little styrofoam beer cooler in the corner'" (Gilson, 2017).

COMING HOME

The hardships of military life in the 1960s and early 1970s were not exclusively confined to time spent in the Vietnam War theater. As it turned, out, coming home was no picnic for these returning veterans either. The America they returned to was one ripped apart by divisions in attitude about the Vietnam War, and the protest voices were loud and sustained, and they were often directed at anyone wearing a uniform. Many returning vets found no hero's welcome at the airports and hometowns when they came home. On the contrary, some found themselves the objects of scorn by those who felt the war was unjust and those who fought in it were too. This was not a uniform reaction to all returning Vietnam vets, but it was the kind of reaction that occurred many times.

One veteran who experienced this jaded homecoming was Karl Marlantes, who wrote of his experiences in his book *What It Is Like to Go to War*.

> *I returned to America in October of 1969 after 13 months as a Marine in Vietnam. While I was there, I would comfort myself by imagining all the girls I ever knew hugging me in a huge warm group embrace. Somehow, I thought something similar would be waiting for me when I came home. I was totally unprepared for what actually happened. My big brother picked me up at Travis Air Force Base in California. As we started to leave the terminal he put his hand on my shoulder and warned me that there might be trouble outside.*
>
> *"Trouble?" I asked. I'd just gotten back from Vietnam. But the war held no hurt or humiliation like what happened as we drove through a crowd of protesters shouting obscenities at us, flipping us the bird, and pounding on my brother's 1960 Valiant with their fists and protest signs. I can still see the hate-filled face of a protester snarling at me through the passenger-side window. I can still feel my utter bewilderment and pain.*
>
> *There were no hugs. My long imagined safe harbor was sown with mines of hate.* (Marlantes, 2011)

What did Gen. Roger A. Brady, then a lieutenant, remember about returning home after Vietnam to a divided nation? "That part was disappointing. But if you were [staying] in the military, you were insulated from it a little bit. There's a camaraderie about that, and you don't encounter a lot of people who get in your face about it" (Roger A. Brady, telephone interview with Jim Willis, September 15, 2017).

One marine vet describes his homecoming experiences this way.

> *I came home from Vietnam at the end of October, 1968—thirteen months from arriving [there]. It was like I was never gone for all those I left behind: the family house—same; the family—pretty much the same; my friends—the same; but I wasn't. I had different interest in what my friends . . . had and once they found out I had been to Vietnam the questions were difficult and the "looks" I got (or felt) were uncomfortable. One particular difficult time with them was a party where someone thought it was funny to shoot off*

firecrackers and even more funny that I "hit the desk." I found a new group of friends, mostly about ten years younger, and Vietnam didn't come up and I didn't bring it up.

It was not a comfortable homecoming, not what we had imagined in the bush of Vietnam. We used to say, "Just make it through the Nam and the rest would be gravy." How little did we know that home, what we called "THE WORLD," was not what we left and not many cared about what we saw and experienced. (TomH47, 2010)

Another veteran, still evidencing the area of a throat scar from shrapnel, recalled, "When I came home, they called me a baby killer" (Stow, 2016).

And one other veteran, Thomas Conrad, summed up the experienced by just saying, "The worst part of Vietnam was coming home" (Conrad, 2010).

Over the years, the Vietnam vets finally got the respect they deserved from most of the country. Today, according to the veterans group, U.S. Wings, 87 percent of Americans hold Vietnam veterans in high regard.

WOMEN IN VIETNAM

Not all Americans who served in Vietnam were men, although certainly the overwhelming majority were. Sometimes unforgotten were the unsung women—approximately 7,500 of them—who volunteered to serve in support roles in Vietnam and who made just as easy of a target as many of the male soldiers there. Women were not subject to the military draft, and the ones who served did so of their own free will. Although not listed as military combatants, many of these women were put in harm's way. Some 6,000 of them served as nurses and medical specialists, and some of those were assigned to field hospitals near the ever-changing front lines of jungle fighting.

Women veterans who returned from Vietnam often encountered similar homecoming experiences. As the BBC reported, "Women especially learned to keep silent about being in 'Nam. Many just tried to get on with life, career and families, burying their inward and outward scars, shame or pride, horror or honour, all mixed up with memories of friendships forged and loves found. Many have died without daring to reveal they served in Vietnam. All believe it changed their lives, for better or worse, but certainly forever" (Stow, 2016).

"I HAD TO GO AND LOOK FOR MYSELF"

Claire Brisebois Starnes was one of the women who served in Vietnam. She had enlisted in the Army's Signal Corps at age 17 in 1963 and, in 1969, she volunteered for a duty tour of 13 months in Vietnam. "I went there to see what was going on," says Starnes. "I had to go and look for myself. I saw it was not the military running the war, it was politicians running the war." Serving first as a translator and then as a photojournalist who wound up supervising a section of the military's public information operation in Vietnam, Starnes said she will never forget what she witnessed there. "I had no idea how bad it would be. When I took the pictures, I never let myself feel anything. You had to tune out emotionally. It was only when I got home that I started to realize what I'd seen."

Starnes said she spent a lot of time traveling over the battlefields in helicopters that were easy targets for enemy anti-aircraft guns below. She found some protection by sitting on her military-issued flak jacket, hoping it would provide some degree of safety from any shrapnel that might hit the underside of her chopper. Even with all of this, however, Starnes wound up doing five tours in Vietnam, nearly to the end of American involvement there in 1975. For her work, she was honored with the Vietnam Service Medal with Silver Star, Republic of Vietnam Campaign Medal, and Republic of Vietnam Gallantry Cross. And, as many Vietnam vets did, she tried to forget what she saw and attempted to bury the images. Finding that didn't work too well, she found help in veteran support groups but eventually left her group because she was experiencing verbal abuse by the male vets who discounted the danger women troops faced. She tried to explain that no one had been safe in Vietnam and—because of that—everyone was a combatant. No one seemed to want to listen, however, so she left the therapy group and never returned. For some time, she has sought out other women who served in Vietnam and encouraged them to tell their stories. She and fellow women vets eventually founded Vietnam Women Veterans, Inc., a nonprofit organization created to honor the role women played in that war (Stow, 2016).

The story of Stearns and other women who did tours in Vietnam is told in the book *Women Vietnam Veterans: Our Untold Stories* by Donna Lowery, a 26-year veteran of the military who served for nearly 20 months in Vietnam.

A popular television drama series *China Beach* aired from 1988 through 1991 and depicted the life of army nurses and Red Cross colleagues at a field evacuation hospital in Vietnam during that war. The series starred Dana Delaney as nurse Colleen McMurphy. When the series began, the Vietnam War had been over for America since 1975, but it was the first time the prime-time television spotlight had been cast on the role of women in that war.

Women who served recall the recruiting brochures and posters trying to attract them into volunteering for the military. Some of these materials held out the promise of "challenging jobs with unlimited opportunities," although most of those kinds of positions or "billets" were reserved for men. Even if a woman had the needed technical skills, she would often be retrained for a billet that the military deemed more appropriate for a woman. Therefore, a woman joining the army would find that Women Army Corps were no longer trained to bivouac nor given firearms training. Those joining the Women Air Force were instructed in things like how to apply lipstick properly, while those joining the marines "were told their lipstick and nail polish had to match the scarlet braid on their uniform hats," according to historical documents on women in the military kept by George Mason University. In addition, "Even in Vietnam under combat conditions, women were told to dress in skirts and pumps rather than boots and field clothing in order to project a neat and feminine image. Their careers were further limited because women were allowed few promotion opportunities and none could serve as admirals or generals." Those supporting women and their contributions to the service were focused on seeking acceptance—not necessarily equality—for women in the armed forces. Changes would come, however, and they began in 1967 when President Lyndon Baines Johnson signed Public Law 90-130 that allowed women officers to pursue and achieve higher ranks—including the ranks of general and admiral—and raised the ceiling on how many women the military could recruit for service. Today, there are some 70 women generals and admirals in the armed forces and some 200,000 women serving in uniform (The Women's Memorial, n.d.)

In 2008, the army had its first-ever woman four-star general, Ann Dunwoody, who was the first in any of the service branches to break through to the pinnacle of military ranks. Four years later, she would be joined by the woman second four-star general, Air Force General Janet Wolfenbarger (Thompson, 2012).

MILITARY LIFE IN OTHER REGIONS

While Vietnam was the duty destination of some 3 million troops during that war, uniformed Americans also served in other regions of the world and faced different kinds of lifestyle issues. Two of these regions that drew significant American military presence were South Korea and the former West Germany. The first location was important because America had just fought a war between 1950 and 1953, which ended only in the signing of a truce. Some hostile action remained until 1955, when the final truce became effective. Starting with the construction of the demilitarized zone (DMZ), America has helped guard the northern border of the U.S. ally South Korea along the DMZ that separates the two Koreas. West Germany was strategic because of its adjacent proximity to communist East Germany and the other central and eastern European countries that were states of the former Soviet Union. The 1960s was a key decade of the Cold War era, and the Soviet Union and North Korea were both countries under communist rule. Therefore, what was it like being an American soldier stationed in one of these Cold War regions? The following anecdotes are examples.

Along the DMZ

Here's how a writer for the *New York Times* described a soldier's life in South Korea, along the DMZ, where some 1,200 American troops have been stationed at a time, bolstering some 10,000 South Korean troops (Haberman, 1983):

Somehow, winter's first dusting of snow this week softened the landscape and made it less bleak. Not much less, though. At its best, the Korean demilitarized zone has little to offer, unless one has an insatiable appetite for craggy terrain and minefields and concertina barbed wire stretching across more miles that the eye can take in.

It can be boring.

Most of the time, the American and South Korean soldiers on one side of the two-and-a-half-mile-wide [and 151 miles long] DMZ do little more than peer through long-range lenses at the North Koreans on the other side. They get to do this in summers that are airless and in winters that have no pity.

It can be scary, too.

The combination of boredom and danger is not uncommon in war theaters, but a false sense of security can creep over soldiers who are involved in action where fighting is only sporadic, at best. And this has been the case along the DMZ. One former army lieutenant who served on the DMZ at the end of the 1960s would sometimes speak of what his year there was like.

We lived near the DMZ and spent most of our working days standing guard along the Z. In the winter it was cold, and in the summer it was hot. In all seasons it was boring, but that boredom was punctured occasionally by reports of a skirmish or confrontation with North Koreans. I remember losing one or two men from our unit to incidents along the DMZ, and that kept us all on guard for a while. Then we would sink back into a complacency.

Actually, my most vivid memory is of ping pong. There was no real entertainment in our off-duty hours, so we played ping pong. In fact, we organized tournaments. I played so much and became so good that I wound up winning the whole divisional ping pong championship. But I would gladly have traded the title for leaving the DMZ and going home. (Robert L. Willis, interview on March 19, 1999, with Jim Willis, Memphis, Tennessee)

In West Berlin

America kept a military presence in Germany during the post–World War II years, helping its former enemy rebuild and find a sense of normalcy. But the situation was more complicated than that. Germany had been divided, east and west, after the war. Two countries were officially created in 1949 (East Germany and West Germany) where one had existed before. The new East Germany came under the Russian sphere of influence and became one of the countries aligned with the Soviet Union. West Germany, now allied with America, would be a good thing not only for the United States but also for western Europe as well inasmuch as Germany had always been a world economic power. But America was also there to oversee operations in the designated American sector of West Berlin. Although the city of Berlin was in East Germany, the city was deemed important to be handed over to one World War II ally or another, so it was divided up into sectors controlled by Russian, American, French, and British forces. Military garrisons from each of these countries controlled their sections of Berlin in the immediate postwar years. Eventually the three western-controlled sectors merged into one, and then control was ceded back to the West Germans. However, the American military continued to maintain a strong presence in Germany for many years to come and still has a sizeable force in Germany today.

The friction between East and West Berlin became more pronounced when the East German government, under the strong influence of Russia, began constructing a barrier that split the city and became known as the Berlin Wall. That construction began during the night of August 13, 1961, on a day that became known as "Barbed Wire Sunday"; the city was divided in half, with the wall encircling what was essentially the free democratic portion of

Berlin. Passage out of East Berlin was denied for its residents and, for 28 years, many East Germans would be cut off from their loved ones and friends on the western side of the wall. Conflicts grew between the Russian and American troops, each guarding its city border stations or "checkpoints," and that friction kept American troops on their toes in a constant state of alert. Several confrontations and incidents along the path of the wall arose, with the most significant being a 1961 confrontation at Checkpoint Charlie.

American troops were readied for more confrontations, as training for riot-control drills and military encounters was stepped up for the U.S. garrison in West Berlin. Companies of soldiers would trade their uniforms for civilian garb and pose as rioters to test the mettle of uniformed troops, and all this was purposely done under the watchful eyes of the East German and Soviet border guards so the leaders of those countries would have a clear understanding of U.S. readiness to defend the borders of West Berlin. In fact, the East German border guards built a special observation tower to get better view of the U.S. troop exercises.

One American lieutenant colonel even acknowledged that he was glad the East Germans and Soviets were watching. "We want them to know that we're here to stay," he said (Jordan, 2015).

In a real sense, the ground-zero point for East–West tensions that—in global sense was called the Cold War—was situated along the Berlin Wall in this divided city of Berlin. American military leaders, in concert with U.S. intelligence agencies, wanted to know what the Russians and East Germans were planning to do next. No one knew the extent of the designs of the Soviet Union, but certainly Russian leaders had been making serious threats about expanding communism into the West. At the front lines of these covert listening-post operations along the wall were American soldiers. Here is how one writer who was a part of one such operation describes what happened:

> *Graduates of the crash course in German at Monterey's Defense Language Institute were usually assigned to one of four shifts or "tricks" rotating through days, eves, and mids. Each tour lasted eight days—six on with two off. After finishing one cycle of days, eves, and mids, a trick crew had a week to recuperate before starting over again. . . . During days, it was busy. Lights were flashing and there was traffic to be recorded. There were tapes to be pulled and sent to the scan room, and replacement tapes to be put on the tape recorders. The OPs (cryptologist linguist operatives) were kept busy and time passed quickly.*

The downside is that rotating tours cause any number of sleep disorders. Although shift workers had one week a month to recuperate, the disruption of their circadian cycle and the nature of work in Room 2, made recovery difficult. Far from staying sharp, the resulting problems with sleep made them less able to concentrate. And the related physiological effects included confusion, depression and irritability. In extreme cases, they could mimic psychosis. Trying to cope, many trick workers started self-medicating, and when the Supreme Court effectively de-criminalized marijuana in Leary v. United States *(1969) it became very popular [among soldiers in Berlin]. The reversal of the Supreme Court decision by Nixon's Congress [in 1970] did little to diminish week's popularity. But the renewed fear of discovery and punishment made some sleep-deprived users, especially those who had moved on to more dangerous drugs, almost paranoid.* (Jordan, 2015)

BIBLIOGRAPHY

"America's Wars," U.S. Department of Veterans Affairs, n.d., as accessed on May 3, 2018, at https://www.va.gov/opa/publications/fact sheets/fs_americas_wars.pdf

Chambers, John Whiteclay. *The Oxford Companion to American Military History*, London: Oxford University Press, 1999.

Conrad, Thomas. "Coming Home: Comments," PBS, April 22, 2010, as accessed on April 20, 2018, at http://www.pbs.org/pov/regard ingwar/stories/untitled.php

Exter, Julie Ann. "Session with Arnold Punaro," Quora, October 20, 2016, as accessed on April 20, 2018, at https://writingsessions.quora .com/Session-with-Arnold-Punaro

Gilson, Dave. "These Early '70s Ads Tried to Convince Kids the US Army Wasn't Totally Uptight," *Mother Jones*, May 27, 2017, as accessed on June 16, 2018, at https://www.motherjones.com/media/2017/05/ army-ads-recruitment-advertisements-draft-seventies/

Haberman, Clyde. "Life in Korean DMZ: Boredom Has an Edge," *New York Times*, November 21, 1983, as accessed on June 16, 2018, at https://www.nytimes.com/1983/11/21/world/life-in-korean-dmz-the-boredom-has-an-edge.html

Hack, David. "Vietnam War Stats, Facts, and Myths," n.d., as accessed on March 16, 2018, at https://www.uswings.com/about-us-wings/ vietnam-war-facts/

Jordan, C. B. *Advisors, Ambassadors, Agents, Ops and Spooks*, Create Space Publishing, 2015, pp. 317–18.

Lord, Bill. "The Chopper Pilots," *New York Times*, March 20, 2018, as accessed on March 26, 2018, at https://www.nytimes.com/ 2018/03/20/opinion/the-chopper-pilots.html

Marlantes, Karl. "Coming Home to Less Than a Hero's Welcome," November 11, 2011, NPR All Things Considered, as accessed on March 22, 2018, at https://www.npr.org/2011/11/11/142096696/coming-home-to-less-than-a-heros-welcome

Stow, Lee Karen. "The Women Who Served in Vietnam," BBC News, May 6, 2016, as accessed on March 22, 2018, at http://www.bbc.com/news/in-pictures-36574698

Thompson, Mark. "Female Generals: The Pentagon's First Four-Star Women," *Time* magazine, August 13, 2012, as accessed on March 23, 2018, at http://nation.time.com/2012/08/13/female-generals-the-pentagons-first-pair-of-four-star-women/

TomH47. "Coming Home from Vietnam," PBS, April 20, 2010, as accessed on April 22, 2018, at http://www.pbs.org/pov/regardingwar/stories/untitled.php

"The Women's Memorial," as accessed on June 7, 2019, at https://www.womensmemorial.org/

7

THE ROLE OF DRUGS

In 1993, the famed 1960s folk singer Judy Collins was doing a concert at Bridgewater State University near Boston. She began talking with the audience about the ways she would try—through her music—to take them back to that decade. Then she paused and said, "As I think about it, however, if you can actually remember the 1960s, you probably weren't there."

Collins's tongue-in-cheek reference is to the widespread use of mood-altering drugs in the 1960s—most notably marijuana and LSD (lysergic acid diethylamide)—and the tricks they played on the minds of users. The use of drugs, especially by young people, was a part of the rebelliousness of the age and a way some found to cope with the threats of Vietnam and other pressing issues of the day.

A DEFINING CHARACTERISTIC?

It is popular lore in America that drug use was a defining characteristic of the 1960s and that drug use was more prevalent in that decade than in any other before or since. That may not have been the case, however, according to historical data kept by the Gallup organization that began surveying people about drug use in 1969. Those earliest of Gallup surveys showed 48 percent of American respondents worrying that drug use was a "serious problem" in their community. But, when Gallup asked respondents about their own use of drugs, the results indicated that drug abuse was an abnormal practice in America and relatively rare. In fact, respondents to the 1969 poll showed that only 4 percent of adults in America claimed to have smoked marijuana. However, most marijuana use seemed to be taking place on college campuses, and only about half of all high school graduates even attended college. About a third of Gallup respondents said they were not aware of the ways marijuana affected users, and 43 percent believed it was smoked mostly by high school students. It is interesting, however, that just three years later—in 1972—6 out of 10 respondents believed marijuana to be addictive in a physical sense, even though research shows it can only be psychologically addictive and even then not for all users (Robinson, 2002).

One 1969 college graduate who became a child custody officer said the popular thinking that marijuana was consumed mostly by high school students led to what she called "scare tactics" by school administrators to keep students from using it. "My generation was told that marijuana caused acne, blindness, and sterility," said Alana Anderson. "It was a scare tactic rather than an education tactic" (Myth No. 2, n.d.).

Did those tactics work? No, said Gary DeBlasio, a teen counselor in New Jersey. "Scare tactics are a big disaster," he said. "They don't work, especially if you use them on kids who have used drugs" (Robinson, 2002).

Reading a two-part series from one of the country's leading magazines in the 1960s, however, gives you a different picture than the one from the Gallup data about how widespread drug use was, at least on college campuses. Citing example after example of how marijuana is easily obtained at college, the *Saturday Evening Post* called marijuana "this generation's illicit pleasure," replacing the campus "booze parties" of F. Scott Fitzgerald's 20s generation. Experiments with drugs by college students were rampant, the *Post* said, adding, "Administrators deny it, and alumni doubt it. But the police know about it. Health officials and school psychiatrists are aware of it. The students themselves are not only sure it exists but they can usually tell you where to find the action." The *Post* writer provides many examples, including the following:

> At Harvard, a student stands beneath a bulletin board that offers cars and typewriters for sale, and points out a cryptic message: "Ride wanted to Antioch—this weekend. Will pay expenses." This,

the student claims, is a general plea for marijuana. The offer to pay expenses is a declaration of solvency. A local pusher will phone the number given and make an appointment. (Goldstein, 2017)

Other examples are shown at the University of Wisconsin and the University of Texas. In the first case, a student walks into a women's dorm and yells he is from the "U of C" (University of Chicago) and is looking for a date. But the U of C is known to be a place where Wisconsin students went to get marijuana. Therefore, it is understood the visiting student is selling. In the Texas example, a student is selling campus maps to freshmen and tells them they can buy a special one with an "X" drawn on locations of marijuana patches. And yet a third example shows how a particularly enterprising student at the University of California at Berkeley sells marijuana. He takes regular road trips to Mexico, and in his trunk are several scuba diving tanks. Once in Mexico, he buys the weed on the black market and begins the process of bleeding out the compressed air and blowing in marijuana smoke. Back at Berkeley he sells the smoke-filled tanks that are passed around and inhaled through the mouthpieces at campus parties. The practice gave new meaning to the concept of second-hand smoke.

MARIJUANA USAGE

The *Post* called marijuana "the most popular intoxicant in the world." It added, "The long-haired element on campus is often a major source of marijuana, but it is a grave mistake to assume that these students are the only ones who use drugs. Drugs have begun to invade 'respectable' areas of campus life, like Fraternity Row.... When so many are certain that the law is wrong, illegal activities become a huge game like the activities many Americans indulged in during prohibition. . . . Pot smokers, to a man, find their vice 'enjoyable' and 'harmless.' They deny that student users graduate to heroin" (Goldstein, 2017).

Although police believed nearly a third of all heroin addicts got hooked through marijuana, drug enforcement officials rejected that belief. One former commissioner of narcotics at the New York City Health Department issued findings that 9 out of 10 of the city's heroin addicts never got to college and, in fact, never finished high school. He went on to assert that it was rare for college students to experiment with addictive drugs. Many medical experts have stated their belief that marijuana is nonaddictive and that alcohol produces far more negative hangovers than does pot.

And why did so many students try marijuana? Although the reasons seemed to vary from group to group, most of the students surveyed said it just gave them pleasure; each time they smoked it was a pleasurable experience. Others smoked it more to identify with the counterculture group they hung out with or protest movement they followed. Among hippies, marijuana use ran very high.

Here is how one of the decade's college students, Suzy Underwood, describes her experience with marijuana and how it fit with the young person's culture—and the music—of the day (Underwood, 2017):

1967. The Summer of Love was the summer between my junior and senior years of high school. I was going to turn sixteen at the end of August—which meant that I had been claiming to be sixteen for months. I thought I was very sophisticated and wise. Retrospect readers may have already seen the poem about my summer program at Syracuse University entitled With a Little Help From My Friends, written in response to the prompt Altered States.

I would have loved to go to San Francisco that summer, it was talked about in all the media and so many popular songs. If only I could have thought of an academic reason to go, my parents probably would have let me. It was pretty far away from New Jersey though. I had never been farther west than Michigan.

Instead I went to Syracuse to learn physics, because I didn't have room for it in my high school schedule since I was taking both Latin and Spanish. I ended up learning a lot more about drugs than I did about physics—maybe I should have taken chemistry instead, it might have been more useful!

The first time I ever smoked marijuana was at a party in one of the Syracuse dorms. I knew how to inhale, since I already smoked cigarettes (all of the cool kids at my high school did, and I was desperately trying to be cool). So I took a toke when the joint came around without any embarrassing coughing, and learned from watching the others that I needed to hold the smoke in instead of just exhaling immediately like you would with a cigarette.

Sitting around in a circle on the floor at that party, I didn't feel stoned, although I wasn't sure what that would feel like anyway. I had been drunk once, in 10th grade, when I drank an entire six-pack of beer at a party. I didn't like the way that had felt—room spinning, nausea—so I was glad I wasn't feeling that way. I just felt incredibly happy and in love with the world. I was singing along with all the songs that were being played on the stereo. Then the song "You Keep Me Hangin' On" started. It was so low, and s-o-o-o-o s-l-o-w that I couldn't believe it. Wow, I thought, I must be really wasted after all! Then I found out it was NOT the Supremes singing, but rather a group called Vanilla Fudge, four white guys from Long Island.

*So maybe I wasn't that wasted, but the song was amazing! I will never forget
the feeling I had listening to that song.*

*There were lots more parties and lots of amazing music that summer.
I heard "Sergeant Pepper" for the first time at Syracuse. "Carrie Anne,"
by the Hollies, is another song I strongly associate with that period. One of
the college guys was making a short film, and he asked my roommate Amy
and me to be in it. I think he had the hots for Amy. As I recall, we were both
wearing little minidresses, and he filmed us walking away from the camera. Several times. The soundtrack was "Hang On Sloopy" by the McCoys.
I don't know if there was a plot to it or not.*

LSD USAGE

As it happened, the effects of marijuana paled in comparison to
the use of hallucinogens like LSD. The call to "turn on, tune in, and
drop out" was issued by Harvard psychologist Dr. Timothy Leary
in 1966. He used it to promote the psychedelic experience of hallucinogenic drugs like LSD. Leary preached that a person could "turn
on" by taking LSD and, in the process, engage the body's neural
system. That would then allow the person to sensitize himself or
herself to the different levels of consciousness in the mind and
body and enter into a more all-encompassing experience with life.
According to Leary and his devotees, turning on would allow you
to become harmonized with your environment and allow you to
articulate your own unique internal worldview in different ways.
The final step in the process—dropping out—connoted a voluntary
way of detaching oneself from commitments the world was trying
to thrust on one. It allowed one to become more of an authentic
individual and to rely more on self rather than other stimuli from
the world. Leary summed it up by saying, "Like every great religion of the past we seek to find the divinity within and to express
this revelation in a life of glorification and the worship of God.
These ancient goals we define the metaphor of the present—turn
on, tune in, drop out" (Leary, 1966).

Leary became the guru of the young generation seeking to find
mind-expanding fulfillment in taking hallucinogenic drugs and to
escape the mess they believed the "establishment" was making of
the country. If the stories of LSD users are accurate, this drug was
one way to escape that world at least as long as "the trip" lasted. One
"acid guide" described the process of tripping as often gathering a
group of friends together and giving them LSD. The "guide" would
help them make sense of their new experience as they might roam

the room and view it through their unfiltered (unconscious) mind. This altered reality, LSD advocates say, is created by the mind and has few—if any—limits. It is something like what happens when you're sleeping and dreaming. The only difference is that you are actually awake. Therefore, it's possible to see those dreams by projecting the dream onto the reality of the room you are in.

This kind of "trip" can also be obtained through the use of cocaine and methamphetamines, but LSD can get you there quicker. There are dangers, however, because when one opens up the unconscious mind, there is a possibility of activating the darker or psychotic side. Therefore, a "fun" trip can morph into a psychotic one. It is the job of the acid guide to lead you to safe places, to steer your projections to safer ground and avoid the dark places. If the guide is that important, it can obviously be a dangerous thing for one to trip alone. In any event, once the drug wears off, the mind-bending trip comes to an end and reality returns. For some, however, those trips may recur at unexpected times, and that especially seems so for people who try LSD too many times. The problem is no one knows for sure how much is too much, because people react differently to it. And, as for "guided trips" with cocaine or methamphetamines, they don't exist because you can't guide those drugs (Kidd, 2017).

It is ironic that the drug adopted by many counterculture enthusiasts in the 1960s was the drug that had been experimented with by the federal government in the 1950s. The CIA, under its project called "MK Ultra," tested hallucinogens such as LSD on some of its own personnel beginning in 1953, as well as on selected military personnel, college students and faculty, patients in mental hospitals, and even those persons frequenting brothels. The goal was to see the possible effects LSD might have in securing confessions during the process of interrogating prisoners and also to see if it could be used in brainwashing and/or reprogramming those who might be used as assets. Here is how one such alleged operation was described:

> In one related operation known rather appropriately (or inappropriately) as "Operation Midnight Climax," the CIA reportedly set up several brothels in San Francisco and filmed the experience of LSD-dosed johns who frequented the brothels. Former Nazi "mind scientists" once responsible for Hitler's propaganda effort were suspected to be behind the research. To what extent this and other allegations regarding MK Ultra are grounded in fact or are more the stuff of conspiracy theory will remain unclear, thanks to the destruction of MK Ultra files in 1973 by the then head of the CIA, Richard Helms. (LSD Statistics and Facts, n.d.)

MK Ultra, directed by chemist Dr. Sidney Gottlieb, did not always produce desired results, as is alleged in this situation: "One CIA operative who received LSD in his morning coffee reportedly ran across Washington in a psychotic fit, convinced that monsters were chasing him. Another test subject, Dr. Frank Olson, a CIA scientist, leapt to his death from a thirteenth-story window nine days after being dosed with LSD. MK Ultra scientists eventually dismissed LSD as too unpredictable to be used in intelligence operations, and by 1962 would move on to 'superhallucinogens' like BZ, which were seen as more promising mind control tools" (LSD Statistics and Facts, n.d.).

Other uses of LSD in the 1950s had included testing for treatment of alcohol addiction and also of mental disorders (actor Cary Grant was reported to have used it as part of his psychotherapy treatments). LSD was also tested for its possible use in enhancing creativity of artists. Author Aldous Huxley reportedly took it. Ironically, Huxley's best-selling work, *Brave New World*, was a novel predicting a happy and conformist society kept in line by imposed medications.

Another well-known writer who experimented with LSD was Ken Kesey, who participated in the CIA's MK Ultra research project and then took a job working in a mental ward of a hospital. The result of his experiences with LSD and working among psychiatric patients was his novel *One Flew over the Cuckoo's Nest*. Following the book's success, Kesey became a promoter of LSD's positive value.

As the 1960s wound to a close, LSD had become the most popular hallucinogenic drug of the counterculture and hippie movements, and ground zero was San Francisco's Haight-Ashbury's district.

Despite these studies that tested potential beneficial uses of LSD, the drug was declared illegal in 1966, and the government classified it as a Schedule 1 drug with the passage of the Controlled Substances Act. Schedule 1 substances are categorized as drugs that can be easily abused and that have no accepted medical use. Despite this classification, the recreational use of LSD continued to grow in the 1960s.

The use of LSD began fading in the 1970s, as worries about its unpredictable effects grew and as law enforcement stiffened against its distribution. According to the website LSD Addiction, the drug is "not very widely used today," although some 200,000 people do try it for the first time every year, according to the National Survey on Drug Use and Health. Nevertheless, only 1 in 10 Americans over the age of 12 has ever used LSD in his or her lifetime (LSD Statistics and Facts, n.d.).

DRUGS IN THE MILITARY

Some 2.7 million American military personnel served in the Vietnam War during the 1960s and early 1970s. These men—along with some 7,000 women noncombatants—gave up 13 months of their lives to stand in harm's way in a country many had never even heard of before the mid-1960s. They were in a dangerous jungle environment, operating under oppressive heat and monsoon-like rains, often confronting an enemy who knew the terrain much better and were expert at hiding and striking at a moment's notice. Most of these troops had been drafted into the military and were not there by choice. Many of them didn't understand the reasons for the war, although they understood the bond of brotherhood and often fought more for the man next to them rather than for a cause. Given these circumstances, it is understandable that many of the troops turned to drugs to cope with the war. Most of that drug use was relatively harmless, with marijuana as the drug of choice. But others turned to harder and more addictive drugs. In 1971, two congressmen released a study stating that 15 percent of American troops fighting in Vietnam had become addicted to heroin. In responding to growing drug use in the late 1960s, the military adopted a policy of court-martialing personnel who either possessed or used illegal drugs, and a dishonorable discharge awaited those convicted. But the military also provided an "out" for soldiers who asked for help in dealing with drug abuse. Any of these volunteers could be granted amnesty from prosecution and was given some rehab treatment. The results of the policy were mixed, since some troops were too addicted for quick treatment, or the threat of dishonorable discharge, to do any good. Six weeks after it was adopted, this policy was changed to one where troops would take urine tests to detect heroin addiction. For those testing positive, treatment would follow immediately. The court-martial part of the policy was dropped. There were no reliable statistics to show whether this revised plan worked (Drug Use in Vietnam, 2001).

In a 1976 study for the U.S. government's National Institutes of Health, Dr. M. Duncan Stanton reported that two stages of Vietnam drug use were discovered: a period in the 1960s where marijuana use increased among the troops and a second period starting in 1970 of increased use of heroin whereby 20 percent of the troops became addicted at some time during their Vietnam experience. The report stated:

The major contributing factors appear to be: (1) the need of troops in stressful combat situations for self-medication, escape, and hedonistic indulgence; (2) the relaxation of taboos against drug use in the United States, and (3) the availability of illicit drugs at low cost which was apparently was the result of profiteering by a number of South Vietnamese officials. Related to the above was the growing disenchantment with the war and the progressive deterioration in unit morale. These drugs are seen as serving many of the functions performed by alcohol in earlier military conflicts. There is no hard evidence that duty performance in Vietnam was seriously affected by drug use. Since 95% of those who were addicted to narcotics in Vietnam have not become readdicted, the situation does not appear to be as severe as originally supposed. Myths as to the persistence and intractability of physiological narcotic addition were dispelled. A major negative effect has been the difficulty that soldiers with less-than-honorable discharges due to drug abuse have had in obtaining jobs. Other long-term effects from drug use are less clear and are difficult to separate from the overall effects of the war. (Stanton, 1976)

Another study of heroin use among U.S. Vietnam veterans, conducted by Washington University researcher Lee Robins, confirmed the problem of heroin use among soldiers in Vietnam. Robins found "high rates of heroin use (34%) and symptoms of heroin dependence (20%) among US soldiers while serving in Vietnam. In the first year after returning to the United States, only 1% became re-addicted to heroin, although 10% tried the drug after their return" (Hall and Weier, 2016).

A "PHARMACOLOGICAL WAR"

Added to the use of illicit drugs by soldiers in Vietnam was the distribution of drugs by the military itself to its troops headed out to long-range deployment. The reason was the belief that amphetamines would add a positive aspect to the soldier's performance in the field. Keep in mind the many ambiguities confronting an American combatant in a war where it was hard to even see the enemy or know when he might spring up in your face or set booby traps for you. To minimize the stress of all that, and to try and keep soldiers alert, the military often supplied the men with "pep pills" or "speed." Therefore, some historians have called Vietnam the first "pharmacological war." One British philosopher, Nick Land, called it "a decisive point of intersection between pharmacology and the technology of violence" (Hall and Weier, 2016). The army issued standard dosage instructions of 20 mg of dextroamphetamine per 48-hour mission, and many soldiers repeatedly ignored those instructions and overdosed on pills that some said were handed out like candy.

A report by a House of Representatives committee on crime showed that the different military branches in Vietnam had used 225 million stimulant tablets, mostly dextroamphetamines. This is a drug that is listed as having two times the potency of Benzedrine, which had been used by troops in World War II. Here is how one Vietnam veteran described the situation:

"We had the best amphetamines available and they were supplied by the U.S. government," said Elton Manzione who served in a long-range reconnaissance platoon. He said a Navy special forces fighter told him the drugs "gave you a sense of bravado as well as keeping you awake. Every sight and sound was heightened. You were wired into it all and at times you felt really invulnerable." (Kamienski, 2016)

A medical kit issued each combatant in platoons stationed in Laos, on missions lasting four days, contained a variety of drugs, including 6 tablets of Dexedrine, 24 codeine pills, and a dozen tablets of the painkiller Darvon. In addition, those troops going out on longer missions received steroid injections. While amphetamines did help keep soldiers awake and alert, many veterans also said that they increased their aggressive tendencies and that these symptoms lasted beyond the missions and after the drug's efficacy had faded (Kamienski, 2016).

These and other psychoactive drugs were meant not just to increase the fighting capacity of soldiers but also to protect them from feeling the psychic pain of combat and reduce the threat of a mental breakdown resulting from combat stress. Different sedatives and neuroleptics were issued for these purposes.

THE LEGACY

Given the extreme hardships visited on American troops who were transported to the jungles of Southeast Asia and left there for a year to fight a deadly war most didn't understand, it's no wonder that drug use was so prevalent in the military in the 1960s and early 1970s. When you're in that kind of a harsh, threatening environment where the heat alone is enough to dehydrate and kill you, let alone the enemy soldiers who know the terrain much better than you, any kind of mental escape is attractive. After the tours of duty had ended, however, the drug addiction that many troops fell into was hard to escape from itself. Many were able to leave drug use behind, but, for others, it stayed with them and caused problems for a long time to come.

It would be good if we could say that once the Vietnam War ended, so did drug addiction in the military, but such is not the case. Heavy drug use remains a problem today in all branches of the military. Separation anxiety from loved ones back home is a contributing factor, and it is, therefore, not surprising that the U.S. Navy has discharged more service members (some 3,400 since 1999) than any other of the armed forces branches. Loneliness and frequent boredom for long periods on sea duty are difficult to deal with for many navy personnel. But all of the services branches experience drug addiction among troops. Since 1999, according to the Michael's House drug treatment facility in Palm Springs, California, more than 17,000 service members have been discharged from the military because of drug use. Failed drug tests have risen 82 percent in the air force and 37 percent in the army (Michael's House, n.d.). But drug addiction doesn't always start while one is in the military; some young men and women enter the military hoping to get "clean" from the addiction they formed in civilian life. The thought is that a more structured and disciplined lifestyle will help them get past the drugs. It doesn't always work that way, however.

The good news is that the vast majority of military troops are able to avoid drug usage and certainly drug addiction. As a huge institution, the military is probably no more susceptible to members falling victim to drug addiction than any other large organization.

BIBLIOGRAPHY

"Drug Use in the Military: Is It Affecting Our Troops?" Michael's House, n.d., as accessed on June 27, 2018, at https://www.michaelshouse .com/featured-articles/drug-use-military/

"Drug Use in Vietnam," Encyclopedia of Drug, Alcohol, and Addictive Behavior, The Gale Group, 2001, as accessed on March 27, 2018, at https://www.encyclopedia.com/education/encyclopedias-almanacs-transcripts-and-maps/vietnam-drug-use

Goldstein, Richard. "Drugs on Campus: Why Marijuana Use Soared in the 1960s," *Saturday Evening Post*, July/August 2017, as accessed on March 27, 2018, at http://www.saturdayeveningpost.com/ 2017/06/22/in-the-magazine/marijuana-use-surged-1960s.html

Hall, Wayne, and Megan Weier. "Lee Robins' Studies of Heroin Use among U.S. Vietnam Veterans," Society for the Study of Addiction, June 30, 2016, as accessed on April 22, 2018, at https://www .researchgate.net/profile/Wayne_Hall/publication/308386214_ Lee_Robins%27_studies_of_heroin_use_among_US_Vietnam_

veterans_Robins%27_heroin_studies_of_Vietnam_veterans/
links/57eaf67208ae5d93a4815d01/Lee-Robins-studies-of-heroin-
use-among-US-Vietnam-veterans-Robins-heroin-studies-of-Viet-
nam-veterans.pdf

Kamienski, Lukasz. "The Drugs That Built a Super Soldier," *Atlantic*,
April 8, 2016, as accessed on April 2, 2018, at https://www.the
atlantic.com/health/archive/2016/04/the-drugs-that-built-
a-super-soldier/477183/

Kidd, Billy. "Interview with a 1960s Acid Guide," Owlcation, February 14,
2017, as accessed on March 26, 2018, at https://owlcation.com/
social-sciences/Acid-GuidePart-One

Leary, Timothy. Press Conference in San Francisco, 1966, as accessed
on March 26, 2018, at https://www.history.com/topics/history-
of-lsd/speeches/timothy-leary-on-mind-expansion

"LSD," Addiction.com, n.d., as accessed on March 27, 2018, at https://
www.addiction.com/a-z/lsd-history/

"LSD Statistics and Facts," LSD Addiction, n.d., as accessed on March 27,
2018, at http://www.lsdaddiction.us/content/lsd-statistics.html

"Myth No. 2: Cannabis Causes Schizophrenia," PROHBDT.com, n.d., as
accessed on May 17, 2019, at https://prohbtd.com/myth-2-cannabis-
causes-schizophrenia

Robinson, Jennifer. "Decades of Drug Use: Data from the 60s and 70s,"
Gallup, July 2, 2002, as accessed on March 27, 2018, at http://news
.gallup.com/poll/6331/decades-drug-use-data-from-60s-70s.aspx

Stanton, M. Duncan. "Drugs, Vietnam, and the Vietnam Veteran: An
Overview," *American Journal of Drug and Alcohol Abuse*, 1976: 3(4):
557–70, published in PubMed.gov by the U.S. National Library of
Medicine National Institutes of Health, as accessed on March 27,
2018, at https://www.ncbi.nlm.nih.gov/pubmed/1032764

Underwood, Suzy. "A Whiter Shade of Pale," *Retrospect*, July 26, 2017,
as accessed on December 18, 2018, at https://www.myretro
spect.com/stories/a-whiter-shade-of-pale/

8

ECONOMICS

I remember the 1960s as a time when a gallon of gas cost 30 cents and the whole car—brand new—cost $3,000. You could get a new home for $14,000 and a fast-food burger for 20 cents, and you could get into the movie for a buck. Of course, on the downside, minimum wage was only $1.25, and the average income was only about $6,000. Still, it seemed like a dollar went further then than now.

That was my memory as I went through high school and college in the 1960s, a decade that experienced a booming economy that had begun in the postwar years of the 1950s. The Dow Jones Industrial Average trended upward during the 1960s and climbed above the 1,000 mark for the first time in history in 1966. Also in that year, the economy grew at a robust rate of 6.6 percent, spurred by a rebuilt Europe that wanted more and more American products and by tax cuts under the administration of President John F. Kennedy. It would be awhile before a resurgent Japan caused trade deficits to spike and before China started causing problems for American manufacturing. In sum, the 1960s proved to be an era of growth in both jobs and the standards of living in America. Nevertheless, economists point out that Americans today have more real spending power than in the 1960s.

A *Wall Street Journal* poll of business, done in 2016, showed that 8 out of 10 economists "say [living] standards are higher today than during the 1990s or earlier." Added to that, "Between technology and health care advances, today is much better than in 1960s," according to Amy Crews Cutts, chief economist at Equifax. And *Forbes* magazine noted in 2016 that "life expectancy has soared since that time, while inflation-adjusted income is 55 percent higher today than in 1960" (Matthews, 2016).

CHANGES IN THE RETAIL SECTOR

Nevertheless, changes were occurring in business and industry both at the executive level and among the workforce as a whole. The decade saw a rise in individual corporations becoming larger by merging with other corporations to create giant conglomerates. This was so especially in the retail sector as giant chains of discount stores, restaurants, and clothing and home goods stores were created and began shoving the independent stores to the background or out of existence entirely. For example, here is a sampling of today's large retail chains that either were launched or grew enormously in the 1960s:

- Sam Walton opened the first Walmart in Rogers, Ark., in 1962.
- Best Buy began as the Sound of Music in 1966 in St. Paul, Minn., before its popularity morphed it into its present-day dominance among electronics stories.
- Toys "R" Us began its enormous growth starting in the late 1960s and continuing on through the next two decades.
- The first Kohl's department store opened in 1962 in Brookfield, Wisc.
- The first Target department store opened in 1962 in Roseville, Minn.
- Lowe's hardware and building supplies stores went public in 1961 and began growing exponentially during the 1960s. (Allen, 2011)

The shift from shopping at sole-proprietor stores to retail chains and big-box stores brought about major changes by the end of the decade to towns and cities and the people who populated them. In smaller towns and cities, once-thriving main streets with local businesses gave way to bypasses that encircled the town and drew shoppers to the emerging Walmart and Target stores. In larger cities, the retail trends were to start clustering stores into large indoor suburban malls, continuing the trend of pulling shoppers away from independent stores and restaurants strewn around various locations within the city. Going to the mall offered the possibility of doing your shopping, dining, and moviegoing all in one location. According to the National Real Estate Investor, "The 1960s was the decade when the shopping center format caught on with Americans and spread across the country. The suburban shopping center was not an entirely new concept but, by the early 1960s, sales in the new suburban form edged out their downtown rivals by a decided margin" (Freeman, 1999).

Melvin Simon, founder and cochairman of the huge Simon Property Group, has noted: "While almost every decade of the shopping center industry has been marked by tremendous change, I believe the 1960s marked a seminal change in the way retailers related to their customers. The decades to follow really represented an evolution of the [shopping center] concept that was formed in the 1960s" (Freeman, 1999).

Helping along this transition were a number of factors:

- The number of American consumers was mushrooming thanks to the baby boom that had begun in the mid-1940s and that was continuing.
- Cash and store credits at independently owned stores were being replaced by the rise of credit cards like MasterCard and Visa that were good at any store.
- Network and local television had expanded into an advertising giant, luring more Americans out to shop at national and regional chains.
- States and cities were backing away from so-called blue laws that banned shopping on Sundays. Eventually Sunday would become one of the biggest shopping days of the week at many chain stores.
- Stores found the value of keeping stores open until 9:00 or 10:00 p.m., and shoppers began flooding to the malls at night.
- The interstate highway system, complete with loops around cities, was nearly complete, making access to suburban malls—often located just off these interstates—accessible.
- The stores were located in an indoor mall, usually built around an attractive atrium, so the weather would not be a factor in walking from store to store to shop.

Two pioneering malls, built in the latter years of the 1950s, would serve as prototypes for the malls built in the 1960s. These were the Southdale Center in Edina, Minnesota, and the Northgate Shopping Center in Seattle. The 1960s saw an explosion of malls patterned after these. The concept was simple: build the mall near an interstate, usually in a suburb; group all the stores around one or two "anchor" stores like a Sears or Montgomery Ward (now defunct); and lure in customers from the entire region to this shopping and eating hub. The result was that these malls boomed during the 1960s and into the 1970s.

Simon notes about this expansion era, "It was during this chaotic period that a number of really first-class developers began to emerge." As an indication of what he meant, by 1969 suburban Houston was seeing a giant 2.1 million square foot mall rise from the ground, known as the Galleria Mall. Even today the Galleria ranks as one of the largest shopping malls in America (Freeman, 1999).

My experience was typical of many others who grew up in the 1960s and saw the impact of the changes Simon described. My memories of that time are as follows:

> *I grew up in a suburb that had a locally owned drug store, a couple independent clothing stores, and a local bank where everyone knew your name and your parents' names. Even as a kid of 11 or 12 I can remember walking a couple blocks to the drug store to pick up something for my mother and just telling the cashier, "put this on my mom's account," and that's just what she did. No questions asked. My dad and I would go to the local lumber yard on Saturday morning to drool over new power saws. I dated the daughter of the man who owned the men's store in town and got an immediate discount there. All that started to change in the '60s when the first indoor shopping mall opened in Oklahoma City with big Sears and Montgomery Wards anchor stores. Our hometown shopping turned to mall shopping and, along with it came a more impersonal shopping experience. More things to choose from, but fewer smiles and good wishes greeting you from behind the sales counter. Those memories are bittersweet for me, as a result.*

Another result was that with the high volume of business that the big chain stores did came the dramatic increase in inventory of consumer goods in these stores. I recall a time when I waited a month just for our local sporting goods store (the only one in town) to get the face mask I ordered for my school football helmet. A few years later, I had my choice of stores to buy sporting goods in, and I could count on those items being in stock when I needed them. The waiting period had shrunk to zero but, along with that, so had the wonderful anticipation that came from finally getting something you'd been waiting for and wanting for so long.

Staff members of the retro MeTV channel, which features programming from the 1960s, described their experiences with malls this way:

> *In the heyday of the indoor mall, one could go buy a ham and go ice skating. Storefronts were elaborately decorated to look like barns and castles. The*

malls were our Amazon.com. While malls certainly still dot our landscape, some of the magic is missing with these stores no longer existing.

They were speaking of stores like the following:

- **Camelot Music.** In our local mall, Camelot had a stone façade that looked like the entrance to King Arthur's Castle.
- **Chess King.** This young men's shop dates back to the 1960s, and its founder figured boys liked chess and racing, and came up with Chess King.
- **Contempo Casuals.** What Chess King was for boys, Contempo was for girls. Also started in the 1960s, CC boomed in the 1980s, when it became the place of choice for big, colorful clothing to match big, colorful hair.
- **Hickory Farms.** Now this brings back memories. Mostly smells. The big red barns sold encased meats and fat chunks of cheese. It was particularly of note for the broke kid wandering the mall, as they often had free samples of summer sausage and whatnot. The brand still exists, but you certainly no longer stroll past farm structures in the mall.
- **Service Merchandise.** This store was a catalog you could walk inside. For those of us who grew up dreamily flipping through Wish Books, it was a heaven filled with video games, calculator watches, cordless phones and diamonds. (MeTV Staff, 2016)

MOVING TO HIGH TECH

Overall, America in the 1960s began moving away from industrial and manufacturing foundations of the economy to fast-moving developments in higher-tech electronics. Here are some technological developments that came out of the decade, which would have profound influence on the digital age to come:

- **Telstar.** This 1962 venture was the first commercial communication satellite put into space by a consortium of companies, including Bell Labs, AT&T, France Telecom, and the U.K. General Post Office, working with NASA. The significance of Telstar was huge. This was the first time a satellite was used to relay phone calls, fax images, and television pictures through space. The first transatlantic TV feed came from Telstar. Even though the signals were only good for 20 minutes at a time, Telstar set the stage for continuous satellite relay signals that would follow just three years later. Telstar's effective life was only seven months, but some 400 signals were relayed during that time.
- **The DRAM chip.** The 1960s brought us to the early stages of the computer age, at least for business and industry, and one of the

critical puzzle pieces was invented in 1968 by Robert H. Dennard and was called the Dynamic Access Memory (DRAM) chip. In and of itself, it didn't look like much, but what it did was to increase enormously the memory capacity of computers while doing so inexpensively. The DRAM chip, in turn, opened the door for a variety of more sophisticated high-tech products to become market ready. In essence, it opened the door to personal computers for home use. Even today, some variation of DRAM is a part of the inner workings of various electronic devices, including computers, cell phones, gaming consoles, and digital cameras. On the business and industry side, this memory chip produced big benefits for companies as it lowered the entry hurdles for companies to blend their operations into the capabilities and power of computers.

- **BASIC programming language.** This development gave keyboarders the language to interact with their computers. Although the first output from keyboard users would be teletype printers and punch tape, "video display screens" were not far behind. Today's computer monitors, keyboards, and the mice or touchpads used with them began with BASIC language. Like the development of the DRAM chip, BASIC language would open up the use of computers to everyone, giving access to computer technology to anyone, whether you owned a computer or just sat down at one at a public library to do your work. This "democratizing" effect was huge not just for the computer industry but for the world as a whole, allowing more people to connect to worlds of information.

In sum, the 1960s helped usher in today's information age. In the process America began turning away more from its traditional reliance on manufacturing and industry and instead turned toward high-tech industries and, soon, the services (e.g., Internet providers) that attended the rise of communication technologies. More jobs went indoors and were desk oriented, and fewer jobs were outdoors or involved assembly-line work in factories. The computer age would also usher in the possibility of working from home and offering young mothers a chance to pursue their career aspirations while staying close to their children. As the 1960s turned into the 1970s and 1980s, those possibilities would increase more and more.

A BUG, A BUS, AND A MUSTANG

One thing that seemed to remain the same in the 1960s, as it had in the 1950s, was America's love affair with cars. Auto sales continued to boom, although there were more imports on the road and they were usually smaller, more fuel-efficient cars. The 1960s, for example, was the decade that America fell in love with the compact, rear-engine Volkswagen Beetle or "Bug," and this car also fit with the free-wheeling persona of young America. If you were into rebellion, driving a Bug was a way to show how different you were from your parents, who were probably driving what America today would call a huge boat. Like other icons of the 1960s, the VW Bug came to symbolize young, independent Americans, and these cars were often seen plastered with floral decals. Despite its small size, the VW Beetle emerged as the number one selling imported car in America and, in 1972, raced past Ford's venerable Model T as the best-selling automobile worldwide. More than 15 million of the Bugs were made (VW Bus, 1950).

It wasn't long before Detroit began realizing the future of small fuel-efficient cars—especially as gas supplies began tightening and prices went up—and started mass production of its own economy cars and compacts, some of them rivaling sports cars in appearance if not power.

But the VW Bug wasn't the only popular Volkswagen of the 1960s. It's big sister, officially called the Volkswagen Type 2, was more commonly known among young Americans as the VW Bus. It was the bus, or more accurately the van, that helped define the counterculture generation of the decade. Developed by Dutch businessman Ben Pon, Volkswagen called it various things—the Microbus, Transporter, Combi (for "combination vehicle"), and Splitti (for its split windshield)—and actually put it into production in Germany in 1950. But when it migrated to the states, it became the favored form of getting around for hippies and those identifying with the hippie movement. In fact, this boxy vehicle with minimalist styling became known in the states as the hippie bus or van, since it was often used to haul teens and 20-somethings, complete with camping gear, to rock concerts, protest marches, or rallies. The vans were often decorated with flower decals and peace symbols.

One particular story seems especially revealing and is found in the book *Bug* by Phil Patton: "When musician Jerry Garcia of Grateful Dead fame died in 1995, Volkswagen distributed an advertisement featuring a drawing of the front of a VW bus with a tear streaming down it" (VW Bus, 1950).

Probably the most successful of these smaller, sportier cars of the 1960s was the Ford Mustang. Making its entry midway through 1964, the Mustang sported great styling with a long hood and short deck. It was instantly popular and has stood the test of time, enjoying great popularity today as well. Like the VW Beetle, the

Mustang proved to be an iconic car for the 1960s, and its popularity was helped immensely by the box office success of the 1968 crime thriller *Bullitt*, in which title character Steve McQueen was behind the wheel of a high-powered green Mustang GT Fastback in the mother of all car chase scenes, dueling a hapless Dodge Charger to the latter's demise. It seems everyone who owned a Mustang has a story to tell, and here is writer John Shutkin's:

> *I inherited my brother's purely functional Chevy II when he went off to college. (A family friend tested cars for Consumers Reports and he was able to buy his test cars very cheaply and so passed on to us at cost a Chevy II he had just tested.) But in the spring of 1966 (my junior year in high school), my father rewarded me for being a pretty good kid by saying that I could trade in the Chevy II for a Mustang. As I recall, Mustangs listed for about $2,100 then and convertibles for $2,400, though I knew that the guy who owned the dealership was a patient of my father's and that there was probably some sort of a deal involved (that's why they call it a "dealership," right?). Having thoroughly researched the topic—i.e., read the brochure inside and out—I chose a metallic blue convertible with the optional 289 engine; after all, why not have a teenage boy drive a truly overpowered car? I do not have a picture of my car, but the attached picture is exactly what it looked like.*
>
> *I used to drive some of my pals from my neighborhood to and/or from school most days. My favorite passenger was Katy, whom I had known for years. In fact, she was my first "girlfriend," but then had the audacity at age 6 to abandon me for first grade, since she was a year older than I was. Nonetheless, we remained good pals forever. It also helped that she was beautiful and incredibly cool, even if too old for me. I even remember that her senior year she was doing research for a paper about this hallucinogenic drug that the US Army had experimented with in the 50's. It was called LSD. And she looked so sexy and sophisticated smoking, I even let her light up in the car, much as I hated the smoke.*
>
> *When I mentioned that spring morning that I was going off to the Ford dealership right after school to pick up my new Mustang, Katy asked if she could join me. Thank you, God. So we went to the dealership and I did the paperwork to trade in the Chevy II, get the Mustang and have them transfer the plates. As soon as Katy and I got into it, we put the top down—though it was still pretty chilly—and, of course, found the local Top 40 radio station. We joked that the first song we would hear had to be "Mustang Sally," which Wilson Pickett had just released. No such luck, but it was the Beach Boys' "Sloop John B," which was almost better. So off I drove, with the top down, pedal to the metal, radio blaring, and beautiful Katy next to me, smoking (in several senses of the word). That was, of course, decades before cell phone cameras, but, if there had ever been a perfect moment for me to take a selfie, that was it. (Shutkin, 2017)*

It is hard to describe what an impact the Mustang has had on car enthusiasts over the decades and still has today. The iconic styling and marketing of this sporty roadster started a chain reaction among other automakers to try and emulate it—Chevy's Camaro and the Dodge Challenger were two examples—but no other car quite caught the free-spirited imagination of the auto buyers looking for a reasonably priced sports car for everyday use. It is telling that, in 2018, the Ford Motor Company announced it would stop making all but two passenger cars and shift its attention to trucks and SUVs. The Mustang and the Focus Active were the two surviving cars.

GASOLINE PRICES LOW, BUT . . .

Although there was interest in smaller, fuel-efficient cars by the end of the 1960s, it certainly wasn't spurred on by steep increases in gasoline prices. From 1960 to 1969, the price of a gallon of gas had risen only 4 cents, from 29 cents a gallon to 33 cents. Adjusted for inflation, that would equate to about $2.40 per gallon in 2018 or roughly where gas prices were nationally in this latter year. It wasn't until later in the 1970s and early 1980s that OPEC (Organization of Petroleum Exporting Countries) began slowing production and driving prices up that the price of gas doubled and continued to climb. And that's when Detroit began its shift to downsizing car engine sizes as Americans looked for ways to living with the high gas prices.

As the 1960s came to a close and gas prices spiked in the early 1970s, here's how one California writer, David Middlecamp, described the situation:

> Stories about fuel economy and gas shortages became common in late 1973 and early 1974. At that time, it was a shock when gas prices climbed to 55 cents per gallon. The new national speed limit would be 55 miles per hour.
>
> The crisis lifted when OPEC increased production, but it was a suspicious era. Under a cartoon depicting Nixon and his cronies beating up House of Representatives investigators, the Telegram-Tribune editorialized on March 26, 1974, under a headline "Was the gasoline crisis for real?"
>
> Excerpts from a Feb. 9, 1974, story by Jim Hayes show consumer expectations have evolved slightly in four decades: "In those halcyon days [the 1960s] before the energy crisis dawned on all of us, the number of miles one could squeeze out of a tankful of 29-cent regular was of interest only to a few automotive engineers, the fabricators of TV commercials for a couple of major oil companies and salesmen who were pushing the virtues of gnome-size cars. Now consumption is everybody's business."

> *Statistics compiled by the U.S. Environmental Protection Agency last year in air pollution studies by certified engineers show that the "average" American-built car got less than 13 miles to the gallon. Examples: A Ford wagon, 8 mpg; an Old Cutlass, 11; a Chevrolet Impala, 12; a Ford Pinto, 21.* (Middlecamp, 2013)

PROTESTS AFFECT BUSINESS

The counterculture movements of the 1960s did have an effect on American business and, therefore, to some extent on America's economic production. Industries and individual companies that were receiving government contracts to manufacture and supply war material—like Dow Chemical that made napalm and Agent Orange—were often made the target of student protests when they would arrive on college campuses to recruit future graduates. Napalm was a highly flammable sticky jelly used in incendiary bombs and flamethrowers, consisting of gasoline thickened with special soaps. Agent Orange is a defoliant chemical used by the American military in Vietnam.

Also often targeted were students' own universities, which, activists believed, were economic partners with companies like Dow in offering research help to develop deadly chemicals for warfare.

Such noted protests took place on the University of Michigan and University of Wisconsin campuses in the mid-1960s and then spread to hundreds of other colleges across the country. Dow is headquartered in the state of Michigan, and the napalm it produced for the military was one of the most controversial war weapons used in Vietnam. Indeed, one of the most remembered photos of the Vietnam War was a young, naked Vietnamese girl running down a dirt road screaming as she tried to flee a napalm attack. One University of Wisconsin student said in a 1967 documentary: "It [napalm] has a complete reference to the zyklon gas, the gas used in concentration camps. It felt like chemical warfare at its worst" (Resistance and Revolution: The Anti-Vietnam War Movement at the University of Michigan, 1965–1972: Dow Chemical, n.d.). And Dow was the exclusive supplier of napalm to the military, so student activists set their sights on this company. In its defense, Dow maintained that the military was responsible for how it used napalm and that Dow was told it was being used only on enemy targets in battle. Critics and protestors, however, charged that the highly flammable chemical was also being used on civilian targets, whether on purpose or by accident. Therefore, in many campus demonstrations like those at the University of Michigan and the University of Wisconsin, napalm was made the symbol of perceived U.S. action in Vietnam, raising concerns about the ethics of how the United States was waging that war.

Learning of a planned University of Michigan protest on August 8, 1966, Dow corporate management mailed a letter to the employees of its targeted Midland, Michigan, factory that produced napalm. The letter alerted employees to the expected demonstration and explained the company's reasoning in producing napalm. Dow management also asked employees to refrain from engaging in any kind of conflict with the protestors. The letter also reiterated its belief that Dow was not "profiteering" from the Vietnam War and framed its production of napalm as its patriotic duty since it had been summoned by the government to help win its war against communist aggression. The letter noted, "We feel that simple good citizen requires that we supply our government and our military with goods they need when we have the technology and the capability and have been chosen by the government as a supplier" (Resistance and Revolution: The Anti-Vietnam War Movement at the University of Michigan, 1965–1972: Dow Chemical, n.d.).

The targeted protests of Dow, however noteworthy they were, did not appear to negatively affect the company's bottom line or standing among other Fortune 500 countries during the 1960s. *Fortune* magazine's own database shows that Dow rose eight places in Fortune 500 rankings (from 58th to 50th) from 1960 through 1969. In addition, Dow's revenues and profits more than doubled during that otherwise-turbulent decade, from $705.4 million in revenues and $62.9 million in profits in 1960 to more than $1.3 billion in revenues and $130.9 million in profits in 1969 (Fortune 500 Database, n.d.).

"CSR" IN SPOTLIGHT

Although the protests and demonstrations of the 1960s may not have damaged the bottom line of companies like Dow, the media attention these demonstrations received did help spur on more interest for what came to be known as "corporate social responsibility" or "CSR" as it is commonly called. Although the concept began being discussed in the late 1950s, it didn't start becoming widespread until the 1960s, and the protest movements seemed to help that. A watershed moment in CSR came as a result of all the attention paid to it in this decade: in 1971, the Committee for

Economic Development (CED) formalized a model called Social Responsibilities of Business Corporations, which became a kind of ethical code for business and industry to follow. The CED is a nonprofit, nonpartisan, public policy group that acts as a committee of business and industry's Conference Board. It is led by business executives and produces well-researched analysis and reasoned solutions to what it deems America's most pressing issues. In 1971, one of those critical issues it tackled was the need for greater CSR. The committee produced a three-tiered model (Thinking Shift: The Evolution of CSR, 2007):

- The Inner Circle: the basic responsibilities an organization has for creating profit and growth.
- The Intermediate Circle: an organization must be sensitive to the changing social contract that exists between society and business when it pursues its economic interests.
- The Outer Circle: the responsibilities and activities an organization needs to pursue toward actively improving the social environment, such as poverty or urban crowding issues.

The interest in CSR was advanced in the 1960s by two seminal books. The first was written by Joseph W. McGuire in 1963 and was entitled *Business and Society*. Its thesis was that any corporation has more than just economic or legal obligations to fulfill; it also has social responsibilities as well because of the footprint it leaves on that society. The second book was written in 1967 by Clarence C. Walton and was called simply *Corporate Social Responsibilities*. In his book, Walton connected CSR with a company's need to acknowledge the debt it has to consumers and to the society it is privileged to operate within. Therefore, a firm has responsibilities and relationships beyond the "corporate fortress" (Thinking Shift: The Evolution of CSR, 2007).

VIETNAM AND THE ECONOMY

A popular idea in the Vietnam era was that corporations made money off the Vietnam War, and many Americans found jobs working for defense contractors that might otherwise not have existed. That appears to be true, although some businesses paid the price for contributing materiel to the Vietnam War. One man who lived through the times, Ken Kahre, puts it this way:

There were of course, a great many defense contractors who supplied such things as arms and ammunition that had to be used during the course of the war. They made money. Some made the aircraft that had to replace the ones that were lost due to attrition. At first glance of course, they made money. But the big picture shows a different story. As the war progressed, as technology changed, those aircraft were replaced by fewer, more expensive models. Aircraft manufacturers found themselves unable to compete in an ever shrinking market. Some went under, some merged. . . . In my hometown, Monsanto sold to the military a product known as Agent Orange. At first a lucrative contract, this came back to haunt them in terms of lawsuits and never ending PR problems. In the long run, I'm sure they wished they never heard of it. . . . Some companies made a profit. For others, it was a bite in the ass. (Kahre, 2017)

In a report for the Institute for Economics and Peace, researchers concluded about the effects of the Vietnam War on the U.S. economy that this war began differently than previous wars in that America got into it gradually, over a period of years. Therefore, there was no initial rush to churn out war supplies as had been the case with World War II or even the Korean War. Therefore, the American economy was able to adjust gradually. Further, it was a war that was largely paid for by a hike in federal income tax rates and with an expansive federal fiscal policy that would eventually lead to inflation. Another unique aspect of the Vietnam era is that consumer use of nonmilitary goods and services stayed the same as before the war; there were no cutbacks or rationing programs as there had been in World War II. The gross domestic product (GDP) grew, and the stock market stayed steady. The war proved less expensive than previous wars, peaking at 9.5 percent of the GDP in 1968. The Korean War had cost over 14 percent of GDP, while World War II had peaked at close to 80 percent of GDP (Economic Consequences of War on the U.S. Economy, 2011).

ENOUGH TO GO AROUND

Overall, most middle-class families in the 1960s lived lives relatively free of economic hardships. While there usually wasn't much money left over after paying the bills, there still seemed to be enough to have a good Christmas and take a family vacation in the summer. I can think of at least four reasons for that.

First, the lack of extra family money could partially be attributed to the fact that women were just beginning to join the workforce in larger numbers. As a result, in more families than not, only one spouse worked, and it was usually the man. Changes that would transform most households into two-wage-earner families and provide greater spending power for families were afoot, but that day had not arrived by the end of the 1960s. Certainly the protest spirit of the decade propelled many women out of traditional housewife roles and into the workplace, but there was great inequality in salaries between women and men, so even if a woman did work outside the home, she was not able to contribute as much to the finances as she would when that pay gap started narrowing and when the glass ceiling for women was raised to higher levels.

Second, a typical American family was probably more thrifty than they would be in later years. Expectations in what a family might afford were lower than they would be, because the norm in retailing was to pay cash for what you bought, unless you put it on a layaway plan and didn't pick it up until it was paid off. This wasn't because families didn't want to buy more, but they were restrained from doing so because credit was tighter and was limited to in-store accounts that were not usable in other stores.

Third, the modern-day credit card was in its infancy through most of the 1960s. Early efforts at developing credit cards that could be used by different merchants were the Diners Club card and the American Express card, but it wasn't until Bank of America issued the first multiuse Visa card in 1958 that American shoppers had access to a card that could eventually be used everywhere to buy things and pay later. But only a small percentage of America was using any of these three early cards until the 1960s were almost over. Indeed, the modern-day MasterCard would not make an appearance until Citibank issued its Master Charge in 1968–1969. Therefore, the credit card phenomenon waited until the 1970s to find traction among many Americans. Until it did, the shopping culture was to either find a merchant willing to "put it on your tab" or just pay cash for it.

Fourth, Americans did not have the plethora of entertainment products that exist today, largely because many of those products were still in the research-and-design stages in the 1960s or simply a dream in the minds of the eventual innovators. As noted earlier, the electronics industry was starting to turn out the processing devices that would be needed to run the computers of the late 1970s and 1980s. But even the rudimentary video game of Pong would not make an appearance by the Atari company until 1972. For in-home entertainment, there was broadcast television, with most markets receiving only a half-dozen channels, if that.

All this notwithstanding, the 1960s was a good time for most kids to grow up. The absence of distractions like video games, cell phones, and virtual reality games meant families had to do the things they had always done like enjoy evening meals together, play football or baseball in the backyard, go on family vacations and outings, and sit together behind what was usually the only television in the home watching the same channel. All of this was happening while much of the country was embroiled in protests over the specter of unequal treatment of races and the Vietnam War, which few Americans really understood.

BIBLIOGRAPHY

Allen, Scott. "The Origin of 11 Big Box Stores," November 25, 2011, as accessed on January 19, 2018, at http://mentalfloss.com/article/29336/origins-11-big-box-stores

"Economic Consequences of War on the U.S. Economy," Institute for Economics and Peace, 2011, as accessed on April 24, 2018, at http://economicsandpeace.org/wp-content/uploads/2015/06/The-Economic-Consequences-of-War-on-US-Economy_0.pdf

"Fortune 500 Database," n.d., as accessed on February 22, 2018, at http://archive.fortune.com/magazines/fortune/fortune500_archive/full/1969/

Freeman, Tyson. "The 1960s: Prosperity Spurs Malls, Hotels, in Technicolor Dream," National Real Estate Investor, September 30, 1999, as accessed on January 19, 2018, at http://www.nreionline.com/mag/1960s-prosperity-spurs-malls-hotels-technicolor-dream

Kahre, Ken. "Did the Vietnam War Make Profits for the US Economy in Any Way?" November 11, 2017, Quora, as accessed on April 24, 2018, at https://www.quora.com/Did-the-Vietnam-War-make-profits-for-the-US-economy-in-any-way

Matthews, Chris. "Americans Think the Economy Was Better in the 1960s," *Forbes*, May 15, 2016, as accessed on February 20, 2018, at http://fortune.com/2016/05/13/americans-economists-1960s/

MeTV Staff. "13 Bygone Mall Stores We Want to Shop at Again," MeTV, January 11, 2016, as accessed on January 19, 2018, at https://www.metv.com/lists/13-bygone-mall-stores-we-want-to-shop-at-again

Middlecamp, David. "1973 Oil Crisis: When Gas Prices Shot up to 55 Cents," *Tribune*, October 25, 2013, as accessed on February 22, 2018, at http://www.sanluisobispo.com/news/local/news-columns-blogs/photos-from-the-vault/article39459306.html

"Resistance and Revolution: The Anti-Vietnam War Movement at the University of Michigan, 1965–1972: Dow Chemical," n.d., as accessed on February 22, 2018, at http://michiganintheworld.history.lsa.umich.edu/antivietnamwar/exhibits/show/exhibit/military_and_the_university/dow_chemical

Shutkin, John. "Mustang Katy," *Retrospect*, November 14, 2017, as accessed on April 24, 2018, at https://www.myretrospect.com/stories/mustang-katy/

"Thinking Shift: The Evolution of CSR," March 27, 2007, as accessed on February 22, 2018, at https://thinkingshift.wordpress.com/2007/03/27/the-evolution-of-csr/

"VW Bus, Icon of Counterculture Movement, Goes into Production," History.com, March 8, 1950, as accessed on April 23, 2018, at https://www.history.com/this-day-in-history/vw-bus-icon-of-counterculture-movement-goes-into-production

9

THE ROLE OF MUSIC

Every generation of young people embraces a genre of music that helps define who they are and, just as important, who they are not. And often "who they are not" means they are not their parents or their parents' parents. All teens and 20-somethings want to feel like theirs is the unique generation that will see the world differently than their elders and make more of a positive difference as well. It has been one of the givens of American culture and has especially been the case in the 20th and 21st centuries. The lighthearted and whimsical romantic songs of the 1890s gave way to the jazz and swing of the 1920s, 1930s, and 1940s. The innocent—some would say naive—long songs of the early 1950s gave way to rock and roll, Elvis Presley, and then to a resurgence of folk music and a folk/rock mix of the 1960s, which gave way to the British invasion of the Beatles and the protest songs that cut across the boundaries of musical genres.

Other musical explorations into hard rock, new age, rap, hip-hop, and curious blends would follow. In each case, the new musical styles were embraced by the young, while parents and grandparents were left scratching their heads over why anyone would want to listen to this stuff. And, in a more extreme reaction that is often common among parents, warnings have been issued to the young that the music—at least the lyrics—is often dangerous to established cultural values and norms. And, of course, the younger generations have always reveled in being seen as rebels by their elders.

As music historian Robin Hilton wrote in 2008, "Every generation has its own soundtrack" (Hilton, 2008).

A Cambridge University study supports Hilton's thesis. "Teenage years are often dominated by the need to establish identity, and music is a cheap, effective way to do this," said Dr. Jason Rentfrow, senior researcher on the study. "Adolescents' quest for independence often takes the shape of a juxtaposed stance to the perceived 'status quo,' that of parents and the establishment. 'Intense' music, seen as aggressive, tense and characterised by loud, distorted sounds has the rebellious connotations that allow adolescents to stake a claim for the autonomy that is one of this period's key 'life challenges'" (Lewsey, 2013).

THE UNIQUENESS OF 1960s MUSIC

Arguably, no other decade was so affected by new musical styles than was the 1960s. Teens and 20-somethings weren't just another generation making a statement that they were different as previous generations had. They were facing situations that could genuinely be life threatening, and their peers were facing the same threats. If you were African American, you were confronting racism, bigotry, and—still—the possibility of being killed just because you were black. Even after the passage of the Civil Rights Act in 1963, it would take a long time for blacks to feel safe in certain parts of the country. And, if you were black or white, you faced the possibility—probability for many young men—of going to fight in a war you didn't understand in a place called Vietnam where American casualties reached staggering numbers in the mid- to late 1960s and into the early 1970s.

CHANGING TIMES

These two threats alone were enough to cause the 1960s to be known as the protest era, and music was a favored way of articulating outrage over a government and culture that willingly allowed bigotry and discrimination while putting all eligible young men in harm's way just as these people were trying to start their adult lives. In 1964 when eventual-Nobel Laureate Bob Dylan sang "The Times They Are-A Changin'," he wasn't just talking about a new crop of high school graduates bursting into a world they hoped to change; he was describing the onset of an era that would prove extremely dangerous for those young people. The lyrics of what would become a defining song of the 1960s say it plainly: "Then you better start swimmin' or you'll sink like a stone" (Dylan, 1964).

Dylan seemed to be predicting changes that were afoot in America as the younger generation was questioning the authority and validity of traditional values. In their place, he foresaw a society where the new generation would create more tolerance and equality. Power would go to the people. His message about the need for societal change has been relevant to every generation since it became popular in the early 1960s. Change is a constant in America, and some generations feel it is needed more than others. The song is still sung at rallies today where people are protesting policies and values in society that they want to see changed.

"EVE OF DESTRUCTION"

The year after Dylan released this song, another singer stepped forward with what was widely seen a protest song that sang of danger in even plainer language. His name is Barry McGuire, and it was his first major solo effort after spending several years with the original folk singing group, The New Christy Minstrels. McGuire's song was actually written by a 19-year-old staffer on his record label whose name was P. F. Sloan. Although Sloan would later write that it was meant more as a love song to humanity, the song was received by the public as a no-holds-barred fire alarm called "Eve of Destruction." It was so anti-government that many radio stations around the country refused to play it, which fueled its rise to become a number one hit in 1965. An index of how powerfully it resonated in America is seen by the fact it knocked the Beatles song "Help!" off of that lofty perch. The song, originally recorded on an album by the Turtles, was released within two years following the Cuban Missile Crisis when fears of nuclear war were high. The doomsday movie *Dr. Strangelove or: How I Learned to Stop Worrying and Love the Bomb* had just appeared in 1964. "Eve" seemed squarely aimed at young men of draft age when he sang, "You're old enough to kill, but not for votin'" (Sloan, 1965).

Recalling what the song was intended for and what the immediate reaction was, songwriter Sloan said:

The song contained a number of issues that were unbearable for me at the time. I wrote it as a prayer to God for an answer. . . . I have felt it was a

love song and written as a prayer because, to cure an ill you need to know
what is sick. . . . The media claimed that the song would frighten little chil-
dren. I had hoped through this song to open a dialogue with Congress and
the people. The media banned me from all national television shows. Oddly
enough they didn't ban Barry. The United States felt under threat. So any
positive press on me or Barry was considered unpatriotic. A great deal of
madness, as I remember it. I told the press it was a love song. A love song
to and for humanity, that's all. It ruined Barry's career as an artist and in a
year I would be driven out of the music business, too. (Sloan, 1965)

Among listener reactions to "Eve of Destruction" were the
following:

- "For me, Barry McGuire's gravelly voice was perfect for rousing
  people off their couches and paying attention to the dreadful foreign and domestic policies the U.S. was pursuing during the mid-
  1960s. Oversimplified and too commercial, perhaps, but it had to
  be, didn't it? If it were going to make a dent on the hit parade. That
  line about 'old enough to kill, but not for votin' still resonates, and
  it augured a major change in legislation."
- A former master sergeant who fought in Vietnam wrote: "Walking
  a perimeter in Southeast Asia in 1971, we Air Force SP's would
  watch troops coming back from their patrols at dawn and crossing
  the wire . . . one of my troops put this on a cassette and played it
  as they came past us. They loved it. I'll always think of this as my
  generation's ballad" (Eve of Destruction, n.d.).

"Eve of Destruction" was the only hit single for McGuire,
although he would resume his career later as a contemporary
Christian singer and even rejoin a revived edition of the old New
Christy Minstrels.

"FIXIN'-TO-DIE RAG"

Another song cited by many returning Vietnam War vets as the
best-known anti-war song was one called "I-Feel-Like-I'm-Fixin-
to-Die Rag" by Country Joe and the Fish. The signature line from
the 1967 song went as "One, two, three, what are we fighting for?"
(McDonald, 1967).

Like other war protest songs, McDonald attempts to place blame
for the Vietnam War on Congress, military heads, and corporate
CEOs whose companies benefited from it. The song deflects blame
from the actual troops fighting the battles and portrays them for
what many of them were: reluctant draftees who would have

rather been anywhere else. It uses a form of dark sarcasm or "GI humor" of the kind seen in the 1970s film and TV series *M*A*S*H* as a means soldiers used in dealing with the horrors of war.

"GET OUT OF THIS PLACE"

General Roger A. Brady recalls the role that one song in particular—"We Gotta Get out of This Place" popularized by Eric Burdon and the Animals—played for him and his fellow officers in Vietnam. He recalled:

> *I was just thinking about a song that was very popular when played by the bands that came to the O-Club. I can only remember the lyric that resonated so much with us—"We gotta get outta this place, if it's the last thing we ever do." In this case, in an officers' club, it was a sort of gallows humor. Some of the officers considered themselves professionals, while others were just serving out their obligation, which is not to say they were necessarily opposed to the war. That said, all of us would rather have been home, and the song seemed to capture that sentiment.* (Roger A. Brady, telephone interview with Jim Willis, September 15, 2017)

General Brady was not alone in that sentiment. This 1965 song, written by Barry Mann and Cynthia Wall, was generic enough in its protest to be used by anyone in a bad situation. But it had special meaning for the fighting forces in Vietnam. It was one of the most requested songs of disc jockeys working for the American Forces Vietnam Network. Decades after the war, in 2008, two researchers from the University of Wisconsin polled hundreds of Vietnam vets and discovered that "We Gotta Get out of This Place" resonated with troops at the time more than any other popular song did. Said one of the researchers, "We had absolute unanimity in this song being the touchstone. This was the Vietnam anthem. Every bad band that ever played in an armed forces club had to play this song" (Mattmiller, 2007).

Similar memories came in an interview with Steve England, a University of Oklahoma graduate and enlisted soldier who did a tour of duty with the army in Vietnam. Looking back nearly 50 years later, England recalled the role that music played for him and the other troops stationed in the Southeast Asian country. In his own words, here are those memories:

> *From July 1969 until July 1970 I was in Nam, 364 days to be exact. My Military Occupational Specialty (MOS) was 35K2I, Senior Avionics Mechanic.*

*As such I was one of the "Techno-Geeks" in the Army, with Radio repair,
Radar repair, Electricians and such. My training was primarily at the Army
Signal School, Ft. Gordon, Georgia. Our training battalion was not your
typical GIs. Very top heavy with college graduates. In fact one of my classmates was from Boston with a master's degree in Electrical Engineering. He
literally slept his way through class, as the aircraft and helo mock ups in our
class rooms had lots of places to hide. The best being in the tail fuselage of the
OV-1 "Bird dog." But that's another story.*

*"I'm Fixing to Die" by Country Joe and the Fish was very popular in our
school battalion. Some of us had a sense of impending doom, but most just
liked the music. One of the techno-geeks actually built a radio station inside
his footlocker. It only broadcast through the electrical wires in the barracks.
He would play lots of The Doors, Smith, Country Joe, Jefferson Airplane
et al. The local Augusta Georgia radio stations broadcast mainly C&W and
Rock and Roll, so all of the "Big City" GIs listened to the "bootleg" music as
our command referred to it.*

*When I went to Nam, I was assigned to the 242nd Assault Support Helo
Company, in Cu Chi. Our territory extended roughly from Saigon, North
West to the "Parrot's Beak" aka Cambodian border. I lived in the Allied Shop
hooch, along with other Avionics, Radio, Hydraulics, Electrical, Engine and
Machine Shop specialists. Again I was with the most educated enlisted men.
High "Amp" stereo systems, mainly reel to reel tape drives were always blaring
in our hooch, at all hours of the day and night. I remember a lot of Led Zeppelin,
the Beatles, Iron Butterfly, Rolling Stones and Jim Morrison.* [Cu Chi was
considered a dangerous area and the territory over which a large network of underground tunnels had been built by North Vietnamese
forces to travel and strike South Vietnamese and American forces at
will.]

*We had an Enlisted Men's Club on the corner of our unit. There were fre-
quent shows of traveling musicians. Without fail, the most sung and popular
song was always "We Gotta Get Out of This Place" by Erik Burdon and
the Animals. Our unit especially liked Burdon's "Sky Pilot" as it related to
helos. Radio Saigon was listened to on the flight line, and over FM radios on
our Chinooks while in flight. That music was controlled by "the man" and
I don't recall any specific war protest tunes.* [The tension between army
radio disc jockeys who wanted to play songs popular with the troops
and military brass who wanted to prevent protest music from becoming popular was depicted in the award-winning film *Good Morning
Vietnam*.]

*The most popular song during 1969 was "Honky Tonk Women" by the
Rolling Stones. It remains to this day one of my most favorite songs. I carry
with me a "Viet Nam Trilogy" of songs: "If You're Going to San Francisco"
by Scott McKenzie recalls that I (and almost every other Nam Vet) left, and
returned thru San Francisco. The second song is the previously mentioned
"We Gotta Get Out of This Place" for obvious reasons. I have often said,*

"On July 17th, 1970 I left Viet Nam, and I haven't had a bad day since."
My final song of the trilogy is "Bridge Over Troubled Water" by Simon and
Garfunkel. The line "Sail on Silver Girl" is an indirect reference to the "Sil-
ver Bird" that we all talked about as we neared the end of our tour of duty.
(Steve England, e-mail interview, October 23, 2017)

PROTEST MUSIC BACK HOME

Although popular music—protest songs included—found its
way into Vietnam where more than a half-million American soldiers were stationed all at one time, the main effect of protest music
was played out back in the states where so many were showing
their utter disdain for this war. In his essay on protest music for
the Gilder Lehrman Institute of American History, documentarian
Kerry Candaele notes that music has always had an important place
in times of American wars. Going back even to the Revolutionary
War, Candaele points out the role that songs like "Yankee Doodle"
played in bolstering the spirits of the American revolutionaries
during the dark days. In the 19th century, songs like "Battle Hymn
of the Republic" and "Dixie" supported the fighting spirits among
soldiers fighting for the blue or the gray during the civil war. And
songs like "Over There" and "God Bless America" undergirded the
spirits of Americans during World War I, just as songs like "Don't
Sit under the Apple Tree" did during World War II.

But the war in Vietnam fostered a different kind of music: songs
that were not meant to unify the war efforts but that were meant
to unify those protesting the war as being wrong and unjust.
Although a few patriotic songs like "Ballad of the Green Berets"
and "Okie from Muskogee" became popular during the Vietnam
War, there were many more protest songs that hit the charts and
helped solidify thinking against the war. Some of the more notable
ones have already been discussed. But there were many others.
Candaele explains:

Youth "counterculture" carved out new spaces for experimentation and
alternative views about what constituted a good society, while a New Left
made up of civil rights and anti-war activists developed as the war in Viet-
nam dragged out and became increasingly bloody, confounding, and ulti-
mately unpopular. This was the context in which popular music in general,
and certainly anti-war music specifically, became a space for cultural and
political conflict and dialog, and at times a product and resource for broad
movement against the war. The Vietnam War was accompanied every step of
the way by an anti-war soundtrack that touched on every tone—melancholy

*and touching, enraged and sarcastic, fearful and resigned—and that cap-
tured the long demoralizing impact of this war. And like the anti-war movement itself, it began without a significant audience in the early sixties, but
grew to a critical mass by the war's termination.* (Candaele, n.d.)

According to the book *We Gotta Get out of This Place: The Sound
Track of the Vietnam War* by Doug Bradley and Craig Werner, the
top 10 songs of the war were the following:

10. "Green, Green Grass of Home" by Porter Wagoner
 9. "Chain of Fools" by Aretha Franklin
 8. "The Letter" by The Box Tops
 7. "Dock of the Bay" by Otis Redding
 6. "Fortunate Son" by Credence Clearwater Revival
 5. "Purple Haze" by Jimi Hendrix
 4. "Detroit City" by Bobby Bare
 3. "Leaving on a Jet Plane" by Peter, Paul, and Mary
 2. "I Feel Like I'm Fixin' to Die Rag" by Country Joe and the Fish
 1. "We Gotta Get out of This Place" by The Animals

Dr. Ray McCormick, a retired college communication professor
who served in the army in Vietnam and came home with a Purple
Heart, said the following of these songs and the roles they played
for him and other soldiers:

*This list sort crystalized my thinking on the issue. Looking at the list, most of
these songs represent the unrelenting desire to get out of war and get home.
Green Grass, The letter, Dock of the Bay, Leaving on a Jet Plane, and We
Gotta get Out of this Place speak to some element of returning to a normal
life and are not really political or protest in nature.*

*I must admit that protest songs had little impact on me while in country.
Two reasons: I was in the field so much that there was little opportunity to
hear them. One stretch I was in the field for three months which meant total
media shutdown except for mail but no radio. When in base camp, maintenance, drinking, and resting had much more priority than paying attention
to the word of songs. So the songs reflecting a simple yearning to get home
had primary impact. The second reason that protest song did not have a huge
impact is that I felt they were rather simplistic in their outlook.*

*When I got home, protest music was part and parcel of the culture that
I was walking back into. So for me, it was not the motivational prompt that
it was for the war protest movement. I was much too jaded to trust either
leadership of the establishment or the protest folks. I knew things were not
right, but I did not trust anyone to fix it. So musically, I did not put much
emphasis on protest music. Fortunately for me, Crosby, Stills, and Nash, the
Moody Blues, Chicago, and the Eagles appeared on the scene.*

One comment on the "I'm Feeling Like I am Fixing to Die Rag." I first heard this song when I was home from Viet Nam waiting to go to Ft. Benning, Georgia, to serve my last 6 months. At first I thought it was fun little commentary until they got to the last stanza. I was very offended when they blamed the parents. Pack your son off before it is too late. Be the First on your block to have your son come home in a box. While the college protesters may have gotten a hoot of this part, it was far too close to home for me. Many parents were mourning the loss of a son as a result of the Selective Service [draft] obligation and to accuse them of complicity in the act is extremely offensive. I saw too many sent home and knew the pain of the families' loss. So that song was off my list. (Ray McCormick, e-mail interview with Jim Willis, November 29, 2018)

CIVIL RIGHTS MUSIC

It wasn't just the war that was being protested in America, however. Among African Americans, much protest effort was directed at civil rights abuses and massive evidence of discrimination, violence, and even murder, especially in southern states but also in northern cities. Music played an important role in the progression of the civil rights movement of the 1960s. Genres included African American spirituals, gospel songs, folk music, and a blending of all three at one time or another. They all helped inspire leaders and followers of the movement, helped them organize for maximum effect, and helped keep civil rights marchers resolute when things turned dangerous for them, their friends, and loved ones.

And it wasn't just the musical artists responsible for this. Musicians and singers would sometimes collaborate with song collectors and ethnomusicologists in finding and getting these songs out to the frontline activists and protest organizers. Conferences and workshops would be held for this type of musical exchange, and songs would also be disseminated in various publications read by civil rights activists.

Speaking in an interview with the Civil Rights History Project, conducted by the Library of Congress, folksingers of the 1960s shared their experiences with civil rights music. Guy and Candie Carawan wrote and sang the songs "Eyes on the Prize," "Tree of Life," and "We Shall Overcome." They recalled working at the Tennessee-based Highlander Folk School, a place that drew civil rights activists from across America, gave them training in nonviolent methods of protest, and taught them protest songs. Candie Carawan noted, "There were songs for every mood. You know, there were the very jubilant songs. There were the very sad songs when someone was killed. You know, there were the songs you used at parties. There was all the humor where you poked fun at people; the satire" (Music in the Civil Rights Movement, n.d.).

Folk singing legend Pete Seeger, who cowrote the modern version of "We Shall Overcome" with Guy Carawan, said music was vital to the civil rights movement. Seeger participated regularly in fundraising efforts for the movement, often by performing at benefits, singing at places like the Highlander Folk School. He was also in Jackson, Mississippi, in 1964 to lend his backing to the student Nonviolent Coordinating Committee's Mississippi Freedom Summer Project. While he was there, three young civil rights workers disappeared while they were helping motivate and organize blacks in the state. The bodies of the workers, Michael Schwerner, James Chaney, and Andrew Goodman, were later found dead. They had paid the ultimate price for protesting racial discrimination in the South.

Recalling that time, Seeger said: "I was singing to about two hundred people in a church when they gave me a piece of paper that said, 'They've found the bodies of Goodman, Schwerner, and Chaney.' And I made this announcement. There was no shouting. There was no anger. I saw lips move in prayer. And I think I sang this song that Fred Hellerman made up, 'O healing river, send down your waters. Send down your waters upon the land.' . . . It's a beautiful song" (Music in the Civil Rights Movement, n.d.).

Also interviewed for the Civil Rights Project, gospel and folk singer Jamila Jones said she left Alabama to attend the Highlander Folk School for training in nonviolent activism. The school was not a popular place with the establishment in Tennessee, she said, and local police raided it one night and shut off all electricity coming into the building, plunging everyone into darkness. She and others were frightened, but it was music that helped them get through the ordeal as they began singing "We Shall Overcome." They added a new, substitute phrase for the title that went "We Are Not Afraid," and it seemed to work. "And we got louder and louder with singing that verse, until one of the policemen came and he said to me, 'If you have to sing,' and he was actually shaking, 'do you have to sing so loud?' And I could not believe it. Here these people had all the guns, the billy clubs, the power, we thought. And he was asking me with a shake if I would not sing so loud. And it was that time that I really understood the power of our music" (Music in the Civil Rights Movement, n.d.).

"We Shall Overcome," originally a gospel song written in 1900 that was later transformed into a protest song in the early 1960s by

Seeger, Carawan, and Joan Baez, was aimed squarely at civil rights abuses and the need for greater equality among races. In effect, it became the anthem of the civil rights movement in America. Many historians credit this song with inspiring needed changes in equal treatment of African Americans that continue to this day.

Richard Cheek is an Oklahoman who graduated from high school in 1962 and has always considered himself a blue state voter in the midst of a state of red. But he believes music affected everyone in the 1960s and inspired those seeking to change the world. The son of a career army officer who would become an officer himself during Vietnam, Cheek often references the social consciousness stirred in people by music. "I was a Bob Dylan fan, too. We spent a lot of time sitting around singing folk songs. And that was a formative period of my life. It helped influence my thinking about helping others," he said. (Richard Cheek, telephone interview with Jim Willis, September 17, 2017)

WOMEN'S RIGHTS MUSIC

The other civil rights movement—women's rights—began getting a foothold in the 1960s as well, and music helped launch it, just as it had the movements protesting the war and racial discrimination. One of the most memorable female singers of the day—Aretha Franklin—charted a number one song that gave women's rights a huge push in 1967. That song was called simply "Respect." Although the lyrics bespeak a woman's warning to her man about fidelity, the message of what she demands is made even clearer as she spells out the word "R-E-S-P-E-C-T" and the admonition to *find out what it means to me*. Since the demand for respect was at the heart of the women's movement, the song became a natural anthem for many of its followers. As National Public Radio noted in 2017, the song turned then gospel singer into a champion of feminism.

The 1960s began where the 1950s ended, with most popular songs featuring women swooning over men and/or begging them to come back after their man had dumped them for someone else. Songs like "My Boyfriend's Back," "He's So Fine," "Stop in the Name of Love," and "Johnny Angel" typify that genre of songs about women who are held in the emotional grip of a more dominating man they can't help but adore. In many of these songs, there is an underlying tone of reverence by women toward men. Did that change as the 1960s progressed? Yes. Like nearly every other aspect of life, the relationship of women to men was put under the microscope in the decade where the bumper sticker "Question Authority" was a ubiquitous fixture on many cars. Contrasting with the early 1960s, the latter half of the decade brought songs featuring stronger and more independent women. One of the most striking examples was "Wedlock Is a Padlock," a rhythm and blues song made successful by Laura Lee. This and other songs like it gave evidence that women were starting to assert themselves in the era of newfound sexual freedom that was ushered in both by changing attitudes and culture and by the introduction of the birth control pill. With new contraceptives came the reality that sex could be purely recreational, with minimal fear of pregnancy attached. Even country singers like Loretta Lynn spoke of this in her song "The Pill," wherein she admonished her boyfriend that she was "tearing down your brooder house, cause now I've got the pill." Other singers followed suit as Janis Joplin—far removed from country music—let it fly with "Get It While You Can" and "Women Is Losers." Contrary to what this latter title might suggest, Joplin's song questions why men "always seem to end up on top." She also criticizes men for wearing "nice shiny armor" but refusing to hang around for the battles.

Even with the inroads made by such revolutionary songs, however, women still finished the 1960s as second-class citizens in the workplace as cultural attitudes were slower to change. Keep in mind the 1960s also saw the birth of *Playboy* magazine, a hugely successful publication that extolled the pleasure of sexual freedom but that didn't exactly advance the image of women being sexual objects. And witness the accurate description of women's role in the workplace as depicted in the multi-award-winning television series, *Mad Men*, and you see the tough road that women had to travel then. But music helped them advance in that journey.

THE DRUG THEME

Music had other kinds of impact on the 1960s beyond the songs protesting the war in Vietnam, civil rights abuses, and women's inequality. Many songs either hinted at or directly addressed the recreational use of marijuana, hallucinogenic drugs like LSD and cocaine, and even more dangerous drugs like heroin, for along with the experimentations in sexual freedom in the 1960s came the experiments into widespread use of drugs, especially among followers of the counterculture movement and hippie movement in America. That culture had its own songs, often promoting the alternate realities and escapism found in drugs.

Finishing first on the list of top 10 songs about drugs, on the Ultimate Classic Rock site, was a song by the Velvet Underground. The song was called simply "Heroin," and it was something of a shock to the musical world that was accustomed, by now, to hearing lyrical references to marijuana and LSD in songs but not the harder drugs like heroin. This song bespoke not only the escapism of drugs but did so in a nihilistic context of despair where the writer wonders if he is not better off dead. It talks of feeling the rush after shoving a needle into the vein and of the decision to "nullify my life" in so doing. In escaping the problems of life—and the 1960s produced many of them for young people facing the threat of Vietnam, a war that claimed 600,000 American lives—songs like "Heroin" spoke of finding the ultimate alternative reality of death, death on one's own terms. Dire as this song was, however, most other drug songs were lighter and bespoke the pleasures of recreational drugs like marijuana and LSD. One song that became something of an anthem for the drug culture, even though not overtly endorsing the use of drugs, was the Jefferson Airplane's "White Rabbit." The lyrics mixed together references to hallucinogens with the rabbit of Lewis Carroll's *Alice in Wonderland* (Rettmann, n.d.).

Often drugs were referenced only metaphorically, seemingly implied in the lyrics of songs like the Doors' "Light My Fire," the Beatles' "Lucy in the Sky with Diamonds," and even Peter, Paul, and Mary's (PP&M's) "Puff the Magic Dragon." Often, as in the case of the latter two songs, the writers denied they were talking about drugs, and it was left for the listener to draw their own inferences. According to one reviewer speaking about "Lucy in the Sky with Diamonds," "There's always been speculation on whether [this song] is about LSD. John Lennon claimed he wrote it about a drawing his son Julian drew. But with all those lyrics about looking glass ties and kaleidoscope eyes, we're a bit skeptical, to say the least." With PP&M's "Puff the Magic Dragon," however, writers Peter Yarrow and Leonard Lipton were adamant that their song was only about the innocence of a lost childhood. Commenting on the phenomenon of inferring drug meanings from pop songs of the 1960s, Snopes.com explains:

The 1960s being what they were, however, any song based on oblique or allegorical lyrics was subject to reinterpretation as a "drug song," and so it was with "Puff." For Peter, Paul & Mary, at least, the revelation that their song was "really" about marijuana came after the song had finished its chart run; other groups were not so fortunate, and accusations of "drug lyrics" caused some radio stations to ban songs such as the Byrds' "Eight Miles High" from their playlists. "Puff" was an obvious name for a song about smoking pot; little Jackie Paper's surname referred to rolling papers; "autumn mist" was either clouds of marijuana smoke or a drug-induced state; the land of "Honali" was really the Hawaiian village of Hanalei, known for its particularly potent marijuana plants; and so on. As Peter Yarrow has demonstrated in countless concert performances, any song—even "The Star-Spangled Banner"—can be interpreted as a "drug song." (Puff the Magic Dragon and Marijuana, 2007)

OTHER MUSIC OF THE 1960s

Beyond songs of protest or songs about drugs (or not), music in the 1960s also introduced new genres of music, moving the 1950s rock and roll into a harder-edged rock and opening the door for future iterations of acid rock and metallica. About the evolution of music in the 1960s, *Rolling Stone* magazine said three decades later:

In 1960, the music of Frankie Avalon, Paul Anka, Connie Francis and Mitch Miller (an avowed enemy of rock & roll) ruled the airwaves and the record charts, giving some observers the notion that decency and order had returned to the popular mainstream. But within a few years, rock would regain its disruptive power with a joyful vengeance until, by the decade's end, it would be seen as a genuine force of cultural and political consequence. For a long and unforgettable season, it was a truism—or threat, depending on your point of view—that rock & roll could (and should) make a difference: that it was eloquent and inspiring and principled enough to change the world—maybe even to save it. . . . For a long and unforgettable season, rock & roll was a voice of liberty and unity. (Gilmore, 1990)

THE BEATLES

You can't talk about music in the 1960s without talking about the Beatles. When this British band burst on the American scene with its "British invasion" in 1964, the music world was rocked in more ways than one. Along with it, so was American culture and its fascination for what was then seen as long hair on men. It was more "mop top" for Beatles John Lennon, Paul McCartney, George Harrison, and Ringo Starr, but it would change the way men would wear their hair in America for years to come. The music of the Beatles has been described as being rooted in "skiffle" (1920s and 1930s jazz), beat, and rock and roll from the 1950s. But it was more than that. The Beatles went into their studio—more like a musical lab for them—and came out with eclectic mixtures of pop, ballads, hard rock, classical, and even Indian musical strands. The music quickly worked its ways into the pores of America and became an influential soundtrack for the counterculture generation. Arriving in America on their first tour in 1964, they became widely known by performing on the most popular variety show of the day *The Ed Sullivan Show*, performing in February, garnering 73 million viewers, and sending ratings through the roof. Their first hit, "Love Me Do," had appeared in Britain two years earlier, and it would be followed up by "I Want to Hold Your Hand," "Hard Day's Night," "Help," and a long discography of other hit songs over the decade and into the 1970s.

About the Beatles' influence, writer Liam Dempsey said in 2016:

The Beatles were many things simultaneously: the most famous celebrities of their day, the most successful songwriters of their age and, ultimately, the most beloved band of all time. And one more thing: The Beatles were also the most creative single force to ever hit popular music. The band has influenced generations, and still continues to have a profound impact. The Beatles not only changed music; they also forever altered the way music is made. Through ceaseless inventiveness, The Beatles set musical trends that are still being followed. They never rested on their achievements, constantly stretching the boundaries of pop music. There is a chartable creative progression that begins with the first Beatle album and ends with the last. (Dempsey, 2016)

I clearly remember when Beatles music made its way into the interior of America. I was a student at the University of Oklahoma from 1964 through 1968, and the Beatles starting offering a serious challenge to my world of folk music in 1968. What I remember most about the Beatles at first, however, was the sensation that their mop-top haircuts were causing in this land where conservatism was so prevalent. How outlandish and shocking for men to wear hair over the ears and in long bangs, many of my friends thought! Many music fans refused to take their music serious, in fact, because of their hairstyles. Of course, looking back, those styles appear extremely tame, especially in light of the shoulder-length hair that was already coming on the scene and would last through the 1970s.

THE MOTOWN SOUND

The 1960s also gave America the "Motown" sound and put African American groups like the Supremes, the Jackson 5 (from which

Michael Jackson would break out as a solo icon of pop music), the Temptations, Martha & the Vandellas, and individual vocalists like Diana Ross and Gladys Knight into the spotlight. In the process, it helped foster common ground between black and white America at a time when that common ground was sorely needed. The unique and upbeat sound of Motown (a concept and record label begun by Detroit's Berry Gordy in 1959 and standing for "Motor Town") crossed over racial, ethnic, and age lines as everyone seemed to embrace songs like Marvin Gaye's "I Heard It through the Grapevine" or the Supremes' "Where Did Our Love Go?" And, in the outset of a decade that would prove to divide America politically over a number of issues, it is perhaps ironic that a Motown song emerged in 1961 as one that would be a theme song for those wishing to unify. The song was made successful by soul singer Ben E. King, was called "Stand by Me," and would contain simple but powerful lyrics declaring that any danger can be handled better by handling it together. Twenty-five years later, the lasting power of that song was still being felt as it was featured in a poignant coming-of-age film of the same name *Stand by Me*.

A FOLK MUSIC REVIVAL

The 1960s also reintroduced the baby boomers to the folk music that America had grown up with and that supplied the backdrop of Appalachian culture, the era of the Great Depression, and so on. The 1960s turned folk music into a mainstream musical style with groups like the Kingston Trio ("Tom Dooley," "The MTA," "Tijuana Jail"), the Brothers Four ("Greenfields," "Green Leaves of Summer"), the Chad Mitchell Trio ("Mighty Day," "Marvelous Toy"), and Peter, Paul, and Mary ("Leaving on a Jet Plane," "Early Morning Rain," "Don't Think Twice"). Some of that music joined in protests of the day, but some of it just bespoke traditional Americana.

As for me, I got my first real guitar in 1960, and I spent the entire decade learning, playing, and singing folk songs. I still sing many of them today. Although I wasn't a 1960s activist, I loved the ballads. There seemed to be a simple profoundness and purity about them that I didn't find in other genres at the time. And the lyrics—especially from groups like the Chad Mitchell Trio and Peter, Paul, and Mary—started me thinking about some of the injustices in America and put me on a path to expand my awareness of the world. In all honesty, though, the real thing was that no other genre of music seemed to fit with the acoustic guitar like folk music did, so there was great synergy between my guitars and folk music over that decade. I don't know which I loved more actually.

I was not alone. Here is how a fellow baby boomer describes her love of folk music (Songs I Sang, 2018):

I started singing along with Joan Baez in high school. I knew all the songs on Joan Baez Volume 1. "Mary Hamilton" was my favorite. I still know the words. Google it. . . .

I sang Leonard Cohen's "Suzanne," but I learned it the way The Sandpipers sang it. I read his poetry, but I didn't own a Cohen album until I earned money at my first job after college graduation. That year I learned every song on his Greatest Hits. *From that album I still sing "Sisters of Mercy." I played that album almost every night in my little apartment in Roanoke, Virginia in 1969 and part of 1970. Then I moved in with roommates. Didn't want to drive them nuts.*

My first Dylan album was Nashville Skyland. A Roanoke, Virginia radio station played "Lay Lady Lay" every day when I drove home from work. The Joan Baez album Any Day Now *(songs by Bob Dylan) was a treasure that I did not own until a few years into the '70s, but I knew some of the songs earlier and sang "I Shall Be Released" and "Sad Eyed Lady of the Low Lands" alone in my car on long drives across Virginia or to North Carolina.*

I sang other songs [later] in the early '70s. Songs by the Beatles, Neil Diamond, Simon and Garfunkel, Fleetwood Mac, Marvin Gaye, The Temptations, Janis Joplin, but I loved/love my folk music period.

JUST FEELING GOOD

Finally, music of the 1960s did what it always does for people in every generation: it provided entertainment and gave them a soundtrack for their everyday lives. There were plenty of eclectic songs that just put people in good moods. Among the *Billboard* magazine's top 20 hits of the decade were "The Twist" (Chubby Checker), "A Summer Place" (Percy Faith Orchestra), "I Want to Hold Your Hand" and "Hey Jude" (The Beatles), "I'm a Believer" (The Monkeys), "Aquarius/Let the Sunshine In" (The 5th Dimension), "It's Now or Never" and "Are You Lonesome Tonight?" (Elvis Presley), "I Can't Stop Loving You" (Ray Charles), "I'm Sorry" (Brenda Lee), "Big Girls Don't Cry" (The Four Seasons), and "Sittin' on the Dock of the Bay" (Otis Redding) (Laight, 2014).

WOODSTOCK

The end of the 1960s—1969 to be exact—produced one of the most important and musically significant events of the decade that showcased nearly all of what music meant to that decade. That event took place on a dairy farm in the Catskills in upstate New York, lasted four days (one day longer than planned), drew a very participative audience of 400,000 people, and was called Woodstock. Originally billed as "An Aquarian Exposition: 3 Days of Peace and Music," Woodstock featured 32 different acts performing in intermittent rain to a joyful crowd undeterred by the weather. Music historians regard it as a pivotal event in the history of pop music, and *Rolling Stone* magazine has called it one of 50 moments that changed the course of rock and roll (Varga, 2014).

THE GUITAR DECADE

Finally, memories by writer John Unger Zussman illustrate the pervasiveness of music in the counterculture 1960s, and of the acoustic guitar's importance in that decade. As young people moved about, the guitar and the music went with them.

Bud and I went to college at different ends of Massachusetts. So in December of freshman year, we arranged to embark from different airports and meet up in Chicago, where we would connect up, fly to Denver together, and continue on to Aspen. But fate, or at least winter weather, had different plans. We both made it to Chicago, but our flight to Denver was delayed—by hours. We were stuck at O'Hare. What to do? Well, we both had our guitars. It seems ludicrous now—they'd never fit in the overhead racks—but in 1968, there was plenty of room on airplanes. So if you played the guitar, you brought it along. We found a free gate, sat down, unpacked our instrument cases, and started singing. It was a blast! We had plenty of repertoire, it turned out. We were both fans of Peter, Paul, & Mary, Bob Dylan, and Simon & Garfunkel—as almost everyone was in those days. And then, as musicians do, we started working out harmonies. Although we were both baritones, Bud's voice was a bit higher, so he ended up with most of the melody parts. That was fine with me. I would rather harmonize. With the close harmonies, it was like our own two-man doo-wop group. People wandered by—other stranded passengers, no doubt—and listened approvingly. What else did they have to do? Finally, our flight was called and, a few hours later, we landed in Denver. But we had missed our connection to Aspen. The airline put us up in a cheap hotel. We didn't care. We had our guitars. We kept singing. (Zussman, 2016)

BIBLIOGRAPHY

Candaele, Kerry. "The Sixties and Protest Music," an essay in *History Now*, The Journal of the Gilder-Lehrman Institute of American

History, n.d., as accessed on October 23, 2017, at https://www.gild
erlehrman.org/history-by-era/sixties/essays/protest-music-1960s

Dempsey, Liam. "How the Beatles Changed Music," Digital Media
Academy, January 21, 2016, as accessed on April 27, 2018, at
https://www.digitalmediaacademy.org/2016/01/21/how-the-
beatles-changed-music-2/

Dylan, Bob. "The Times They Are-A Changin'," Columbia Records, January 13, 1964.

"Eve of Destruction," Songfacts, n.d., as accessed on October 19, 2017, at
http://www.songfacts.com/detail.php?id=799

Gilmore, Mikal, "Bob Dylan, the Beatles, and the Rock of the Sixties,"
Rolling Stone, August 23, 1990, as accessed on May 18, 2019, at
https://www.rollingstone.com/music/music-features/bob-
dylan-the-beatles-and-the-rock-of-the-sixties-176221/#!

Hilton, Robin. "The Sound of a Generation," National Public Radio,
June 6, 2008, as accessed on October19, 2009, at http://www.npr
.org/sections/allsongs/2008/06/the_sound_of_a_generation.html

Laight, Elias. "The Top 20 Billboard Hot 100 Hits of the 1960s," October 27,
2014, as accessed on October 26, 2017, at http://www.billboard
.com/articles/news/6296373/billboard-hot-100-1960

Lewsey, Fred. "The Musical Ages of Modern Man: How Our Taste in
Music Changes over a Lifetime," Cambridge University, October 15, 2013, as accessed on October 19, 2017, at http://www.cam
.ac.uk/research/news/the-musical-ages-of-modern-man-how-
our-taste-in-music-changes-over-a-lifetime

Mattmiller, Brian. " 'We Gotta Get out of This Place': Music, Memory and
the Vietnam War," archived February 14, 2007, at the Wayback
Machine, University of Wisconsin—Madison, February 16, 2006,
accessed on October 20, 2017.

McDonald, Country Joe. "I-Feel-Like I'm Fixin'-to-Die Rag," Vanguard
Records, November 1967.

"Music in the Civil Rights Movement," n.d., Civil Rights History Project, The Library of Congress, as accessed on October 20, 2017, at
https://www.loc.gov/collections/civil-rights-history-project/
articles-and-essays/music-in-the-civil-rights-movement/

"Puff the Magic Dragon and Marijuana," Snopes, May 25, 2007, as accessed
on October 26, 2017, at https://www.snopes.com/music/songs/
puff.asp

Rettmann, Tony. "Top Ten Drug Songs," Ultimate Classic Rock, n.d., as
accessed on October 26, 2017, at http://ultimateclassicrock.com/
drug-songs/

Sloan, P. F. "The Eve of Destruction," Dunhill Records, July 15, 1965.

"Songs I Sang," Ginger Bate, *Retrospect,* December 10, 2018, as accessed on
December 18, 2018, at https://www.myretrospect.com/stories/
songs-i-sang/

"The Times They Are-A Changin," Lyric Interpretations, as accessed on October 19, 2017, at https://www.lyricinterpretations.com/bob-dylan/the-times-they-are-a-changin

Varga, George. "Woodstock Reassessed, 45 Years Later," *San Diego Union-Tribune*, August 8, 2014, as accessed on April 21, 2018, at http://www.sandiegouniontribune.com/entertainment/music/sdut-woodstock-forty-five-years-later-2014aug08-story.html

Zussman, John Unger. "Have Guitars, Will Travel," *Retrospect*, March 7, 2016, as accessed on June 6, 2019, at https://www.my retrospect.com/stories/have-guitars-will-travel/

10

MIRRORED IN MOVIES

The values and culture of any decade are influenced by the ways current issues and ideas are portrayed on the big screen in commercial films, but that was especially the case in the turbulent 1960s. Americans were facing life-and-death issues that included the threat of nuclear attack, the Vietnam War, and the violence erupting from that war's protest and the civil rights movement. Add in the popularity of recreational drug use, the "free love" movement, and the stirrings of the women's rights movement as well as the emergence of a more open gay community, and there was plenty of fodder for screenwriters. Many of these movies had a huge effect on public opinion about the issues of the era, and some raised the awareness of issues and inspired people to get involved. This chapter looks at just a sample of some of the more culturally significant films of the decade. It certainly is not a complete list, and others could be added to it very easily. It is interesting to note, however, that the Library of Congress places 25 films a year on the National Film Registry, established by the National Film Registration Act of 1988. Films selected for inclusion are deemed culturally, historically, and aesthetically significant. As of 2018, some 750 films had been selected for the list, and they date back to films made in 1891. Eighty-five of these selected films come from the 1960s alone (Complete National Film Registry Listing, 2018). All of the ones discussed in this chapter are on that list, with the exception of one (*Bob & Carol & Ted & Alice*).

THE GRADUATE

We will start with a personal memory of a film that affected so many young people in the 1960s. This film is often cited by historians as being the signature film of the changing culture wrought by the 1960s. The film is *The Graduate*. I was a senior at the University of Oklahoma when this film premiered, and I recall going to see it with a group of my friends. We were all fairly conservative in our values, but we also enjoyed watching the changes taking place all around us, and some of us—including me—would move left of center as a result of these changes. *The Graduate* was one of those coming-of-age films that was so well made, so funny—shockingly so to many—that it caused me and my friends to begin questioning some of the traditional thinking about American values. This 1967 breakthrough movie was directed by Mike Nichols (a former comedian himself) and was cowritten by the satirical Buck Henry, along with Calder Willingham. The film introduced a very young Dustin Hoffman to the world, playing a newly minted college graduate Benjamin Braddock. In brief, Benjamin is seduced by a middle-aged Mrs. Robinson (Anne Bancroft) and then winds up falling in love with her daughter, Elaine (Katharine Ross). In the end, Benjamin and Elaine defy a string of conventional values in running off together, although having no idea where they're going next. As I've thought about the ending over the years, I've realized how this last scene of their fleeing on a city bus when their expressions changed from elation to bewilderment typified many young people in the 1960s. Escaping from the "plastic" world was one thing; knowing where to go or what to do then was another.

The film comes from a 1963 book of the same title by Charles Webb, who wrote it shortly after he graduated from Williams College. The things that the 21-year-old Benjamin experiences—most notably his total confusion about what to do with his life now and his reluctant fascination with being seduced by an older woman—ring true. What resonated with me and much of young America at the time was the hypocrisy of our parents' generation that seemed to be advising us young people to live clean—yet very material—lives even while they were putting temptations in front of us and showing how corrupt that material life and its values could actually be. One thing that really stood out—and I remember thinking this clearly that night in the theater—was that none of these older people seemed to be happy. That particular goal seemed to have gotten lost in the lifestyle they were encouraging us to emulate. Or so it seemed, anyway. Certainly, this critique was a broad-brush one, and there were many exceptions to the rule among our parents and their friends. I remember trying—and failing—to cast my own parents in the personae of Mrs. Robinson and her husband (who had one of the best and most telling lines of the film when he advised Benjamin to go into "plastics" as a career). But it certainly seemed to fit other parents I knew who were pushing their kids into leading lives that might bring wealth but not happiness.

The Graduate was a critical and popular hit and is ranked as the 22nd highest-grossing film of all time in North America (Box Office Mojo, n.d.). Nichols won an Academy Award for best director, and the film was nominated for best picture. Three decades after its release, it was honored to be included in the National Film Registry for its cultural significance in America. Helping its popularity among young people was the soundtrack that was sung by the sensational duo, (Paul) Simon and (Art) Garfunkel. The breakout singles were "Mrs. Robinson," a humorous critique of the older generation, and "Sounds of Silence," an ode to young people who encounter a world silent in worthy values.

Assessing the film, film critic Eric Melin said, "The movie just zig-zags its way across their lives, alternately mocking and sympathizing with them. That's why the film is so fascinating. . . . The ending is not happy. It's messy, like real life. *The Graduate* is exciting because it captured a specific moment in time culturally. But within its three main characters, it captures timeless themes of feeling desperate, lost, and confused" (Melin, 2016).

WEST SIDE STORY

Six years before *The Graduate* hit the big screens, Americans were enthralled by another story about two young lovers facing the challenges of the day. But while Ben Braddock and Elaine Robinson were struggling in California, Maria Nunez and Tony Wyzek were struggling in New York City in the film *West Side Story*. Directed by Robert Wise and Jerome Robbins with music by Leonard Bernstein, this 1961 film was an adaptation of a 1957 Broadway musical of the same name. It starred Natalie Wood as Maria and Richard Beymer as Tony, two star-crossed lovers fighting for a life together in the tough backstreets of New York. The story was inspired by William

Shakespeare's *Romeo and Juliet*, and the plot connections are obvious and extremely well done. Like *The Graduate*, *West Side Story* was selected in 1997 for inclusion in the National Film Registry for its cultural significance to the era. Also like *The Graduate*, it resonated wildly with Americans and became the number two grossing film of the year and won 10 Academy Awards including Best Picture.

Although most who saw the film were swept up in the intense love story between Tony and Maria, they were also exposed to a cultural depiction of the juvenile delinquency theme of several 1950s films, as well as the ethnic, racial, and gender tensions that would become a part of the 1960s tapestry. The two lovers find their path to happiness blocked by two warring gangs—the Jets and the Sharks—one comprised of whites and the other of Puerto Ricans. Tony and Maria—like Romeo and Juliet—found themselves belonging to different gang-related families. Also at work in the story was the beginnings of women's rights, as depicted in a show-stopping musical dance number on a tenement rooftop where the women friends of the Puerto Rican Sharks squared off against their male counterparts and matched them barb for barb in the rousing song "America." Coming at the outset of the decade, *West Side Story* served as a kind of preamble for the civil rights and women's rights confrontations that were just beginning to take form in the country, three years before passage of the Civil Rights Act of 1964. The film also pitted the forces of love and violence against each other, just as the coming years would do in real life.

This was a film that gripped especially the young people of the 1960s in a very real and emotional way. One midwesterner said *West Side Story* was an eye-opener for him. "*West Side Story* made me more aware that discrimination was broader than just black and white," he said (Richard Cheek, telephone interview with Jim Willis, September 17, 2017). Certainly, that message was helped by the great music and dancing that, ironically, seemed to fit perfectly as a way to depict the turbulence—as well as gentleness—of the time. Although Hollywood wasn't quite ready to present the issue of racism head-on (that time was coming soon, though, and had been broached tangentially in the 1950s with *South Pacific*), *West Side Story* managed to weave it into the fabric of a musical love story. The point was not lost on many who saw it.

Sarah Fishko recalled on National Public Radio that she couldn't wait to tell others about seeing it. "I was 10 or 11 and I had just been swept off my feet: I'd just seen *West Side Story*," she said. "I practically flew downstairs to see a neighbor of ours—a filmmaker—who was an old family friend" (Fishko, 2009).

Famed *New York Times* critic Bosley Crowther called the film "a 'cinematic masterpiece'" and noted that "the moral of the tragedy comes through in the staggering sense of wastage of the energies of kids. It is screamed by the candy-store owner, played trenchantly by Ned Glass, when he flares, 'You kids make this world lousy! When will you stop?' It is a cry that should be heard by thoughtful people—sympathetic people—all over the land" (Crowther, 1961).

BOB & CAROL & TED & ALICE

A part of the free love philosophy, promoting the "liberation" of sex outside of marriage, focused on the practice of wife swapping. Willing couples would simply agree to try out each other's wives for a while, right down to sleeping with them. It was inevitable that someone would come along and make a film about it, which Paul Mazursky did in 1969 with *Bob & Carol & Ted & Alice*. The film, which some critics saw as more of a commentary on truth telling than wife swapping, fit with—and reflected—what some Americans were already experimenting with. For example, the practice of wife swapping was probably more prevalent in California than anywhere else. In one instance, San Bernardino police raided a long-running sex club on April 24, 1962. The club advertised openly and communicated with respondents about the sexual delights they could experience there, including swapping wives for the evening. Following that raid, a grand jury in San Francisco indicted the publisher of a wife-swapping magazine called *Personals*. The magazine was circulated nationally and included personal ads from men and women seeking out other like-minded husbands or wives. One such ad read, "Very broad-minded man, 36, seeks couples and others who share bizarre and unusual tastes." Another man advertised that he was interested in exploring unusual sexual arrangements. Wife-swapping clubs were springing up in many places, announcing their presence often via ads placed in local publications and inviting applications from interested parties. Club organizers would then sort through the responses, toss out the ones from people just seeking dates or platonic relationships, and respond—often in lewd and suggestive tone—to those wanting something kinky like wife swapping. The applicants would be invited to come and meet other club members and engage in the activities. One detective working the case said, "This thing has spread all over California" (Wife-Swap Clubs: A 1960s Scandal, 1962).

Bob & Carol & Ted & Alice focused on two couples who decided to experiment with wife swapping. The plot follows Bob and Carol

Sanders as they participate in a group therapy session for couples where they embrace the idea that too many people are keeping their true feelings bottled up. Their enlightenment bubbles over when they get together with close friends and chide them for not dealing with the way they really feel about each other. It's important to get these feelings out in the open and share them with others, they feel, even if it causes awkwardness for a time between friends. Two of their close friends are Ted and Alice Henderson who go along with this thinking while, in the process, expose their own sexual interest in them: Bob for Alice and Ted for Carol. The interest seems mutual among these pairs. They decide to see how the experiment will play out, all in the interest of being honest about their feelings.

One baby boomer, Judy Chrisope Porter, recalled her memory of the film this way: "I went on my first date since high school with a guy who took me to see Bob & Carol, Ted & Alice. I was thoroughly embarrassed by the opening scenes. I flipped my hair so he couldn't see my face. I married him six weeks later. Forty-eight years later, he still teases me about this movie" (Judy Chrisope Porter, Facebook comments, May 5, 2018).

Some critics believed what set this award-winning film apart from other romantic comedies was more than the obvious focus on wife swapping. The late Roger Ebert commented that the film "isn't really about wife swapping at all, but about the epidemic of moral earnestness that's sweeping our society right now. For some curious reason, we suddenly seem compelled to tell the truth in our personal relationships" (Ebert, 1969).

Ebert points out how the film reflects the "openness" debate about feelings prevalent in the 1960s. He also brings up the concept of the "in-between generation" that didn't get much press amid the headlines about the generation gap between young revolutionaries and old parents. He does this by noting, "Now this sort of honesty is all right for deep conversations over a cup of coffee in the student union, but it's dangerous when practiced by couples over 30. . . . If they start telling the truth too much, they might have to decide who keeps the kids. That's the dilemma of the in-between generation, the one we overlook in the generation gap, the couples who are too young to be the parents of the revolutionary kids, and too old to be the kids" (Ebert, 1969).

TO KILL A MOCKINGBIRD

The depiction of racial tensions in the South was on full display in the 1962 film, *To Kill a Mockingbird*, the film adaptation of Harper

Lee's famed novel of 1960. Gregory Peck plays Atticus Finch, a widowed Alabama lawyer who defends an innocent black man who is accused of raping a white woman in the small town of Maycomb in the early 1930s. While he is doing that, his two children Scout and Jem are going through coming-of-age moments and learning themselves about negative stereotypes and discrimination. They do this by watching their fair-minded father defend Tom Robinson and by suffering taunts from school friends for their father's decision to defend a black man. But they also learn by their spying on, and later interaction with, their mysterious neighbor, Arthur "Boo" Radley. He is a shadowy figure of a man who seldom leaves his home and about whom many rumors are circulating in town.

Here is how one baby boomer, Carol King, describes the impact the film had on her as a young person in Oklahoma:

> *To Kill a Mockingbird really influenced me in a number of ways. I've watched it numerous times including just a few months ago. Courtrooms and the law have always interested me. . . . The movie gave me more compassion regarding race. I believe we all had our prejudices, but I was raised to respect others. My first job was at the Borden Ice Cream store, near downtown Oklahoma City. I was 15. A black man came to the door but hesitated, unsure if he was allowed. I walked over and opened the door and invited him in. I'm not sure my boss appreciated what I did but we served him. The movie had a lasting effect on me in many good ways.* (Carol King, Facebook comments, May 5, 2018)

The film was a critical and popular success, winning Oscars for Best Adapted Screenplay (Horton Foote) and Best Actor (Peck). Well-known film critic Roger Ebert liked the film, felt it important for the times, but also had reservations about the way it focused less on the blacks in the film and instead portrayed an image of an honest white man standing up for a helpless black man. Ebert wrote: "It expresses the liberal pieties of a more innocent time, the early 1960s, and it goes very easy on the realities of small-town Alabama in the 1930s." He also felt it somewhat naive to believe that a young girl (Atticus's daughter Scout) could turn away a lynch mob by shaming them with the words and hurt expression of a child (Ebert, 2001).

Those kinds of reservations aside, the film seemed to open the eyes of many Americans to racism and inspire them to do something about racial injustice (two years before passage of the Civil Rights Act). As Oklahoman Richard Cheek said, "At the top of my list of 1960s films was *To Kill a Mockingbird*. It was largely responsible for helping to bring my incipient social consciousness out into the open" (Cheek, 2017). And critic Laure Boeder said the film "raises great questions of racism, poverty, ignorance and injustice with enormous grace and emotional power. Moral and deeply humane, the movie is a classic come-of-age story of childhood innocence lost in the segregated American South" (Boeder, 2017).

Actress Mary Badham, who was only 10 when she played Scout, said in 2012 that the film—and especially Peck's Atticus—served as a role model for her for fairness and responsibility.

> To Kill a Mockingbird *set the standard for how I want to parent. It serves as a model for how to live one's life. There are a lot of people who have done that. They've taken this book and this film and modeled their lives after it because it has all of life's lessons included in it that we just don't seem to have learned yet. It's one of the greatest books and movies in teaching about being a father, about what it is to be a family and what it is to be a community. It's just brilliant for that.* (McLaughlin, 2012)

One filmgoer described her reaction to the film in this way:

> To Kill a Mockingbird *encouraged me to go to law school in 1980 and become an attorney. I even named my cat Atticus. I have always felt the need to represent the neediest of our population.* (Lydia Lee, Facebook comment, May 5, 2018)

GUESS WHO'S COMING TO DINNER

By 1967, racial tension was not an unusual aspect of story lines in many American films. But one aspect of black–white interactions had yet to be depicted, at least in a major Hollywood commercial film. That aspect was interracial marriage, and the movie introducing it for public discourse was *Guess Who's Coming to Dinner*, directed by Stanley Kramer and written by William Rose. It is noteworthy that the film premiered in the same year that the U.S. Supreme Court overturned laws in a dozen states that banned mixed-race marriages.

The film had an A-list cast with Spencer Tracy and Katharine Hepburn as parents Matt and Christina Drayton, and starred Sidney Poitier as Dr. John Prentice, the dinner guest in question who had captured the heart of the older couple's daughter Joey, played by Katharine Houghton. Joey is just returning from a vacation in Hawaii where she had met John and fallen in love, and this was the first time the Draytons had met him and the first time they realized he was black. Adding to the drama was that John and Joey were planning to leave that evening for Geneva where he was going to work with the World Health Organization, but he insisted on first getting permission from Joey's parents to marry her. That meant the clock was ticking on the most difficult decision Matt and Christina had ever made. Far from being racist, both were liberal in their worldviews, and Matt published a highly respected daily newspaper that backed liberal causes. But the idea of their daughter marrying outside her race was something the couple had never considered before. Their liberal views were being tested mightily this day, and both were on the spot to make a decision and make it quick.

Like the film *West Side Story* did using music and dance to deliver a controversial theme, *Guess Who's Coming to Dinner* did it using humor and terrific acting from a quartet of intelligent and relatable actors. The film not only made Matt and Christina Drayton face their true beliefs but also had the audience doing the same thing. As retired school teacher Mary Clem Good Morris said, "Having grown up in a segregated community, the film was eye-opening. I was not raised with racial discrimination but was unfamiliar with other races. The film proved to me my parents' teaching that all races are equal" (Mary Clem Good Morris, Facebook comments, November 18, 2017).

On the 50th anniversary of the film, the *Los Angeles Times* placed the glossy commercial hit in an accurate cultural and historical context. "Even 50 years ago, in a nation inflamed by prejudice and civil rights marches, the interracial marriage fable, *Guess Who's Coming to Dinner* played suave and polite at a defining moment when cinema was shifting from studio conventionality to bracing realism ... the film was a mannered Hollywood take on an incendiary topic. [Director Stanley] Kramer was known for his socially conscious if orthodox movies including *Inherit the Wind,* and *Judgment at Nuremberg*. [Both of which also starred Tracy]. *Guess* fit his political and narrative instincts" (Fleishman, 2017).

As cushioned as the interracial marriage theme was, the film still offended many Americans who were not willing, ready, or able to move forward in their thinking about racial equality. That much was evidenced by some reviews in southern newspapers and by the fact that both director Kramer and star Houghton received death threats after the film was released. Apparently the scene that irritated reactionaries most was one in which this young white woman kissed a black man. No matter that he was an erudite, Yale-trained physician, they could not get past the skin-color barrier.

IN THE HEAT OF THE NIGHT

Sidney Poitier became the most visible and popular African American actor of the 1960s—among both black and white audiences. He was really the first who was given so many starring roles, although Harry Belafonte was popular as well. But Poitier also had the advantage of being chosen in several high-profile commercial successes, of which *Guess Who's Coming to Dinner* was one. But in that same year of 1967, Poitier also starred in the popular films *To Sir with Love* and *In the Heat of the Night*. The latter, like *Guess*, directed by Norman Jewison, stirred the pot in America again over the issue of racial equality. But, whereas the former focused on interracial marriage, *Heat* focused on interracial police forces and the idea that a black detective could be just as good as—maybe even better than—his white counterparts in blue. The fact that the setting was the American South in the 1960s created an even more incendiary canvas to depict the characters, action, and issues.

The plot basically revolves around black Philadelphia homicide detective Virgil Tibbs, played by Poitier, who is passing through and awaiting a change of trains in the town of Sparta, Mississippi, when he is suddenly arrested for the murder of a business executive. Bill Gillespie, the racist police chief of Sparta, is played by Rod Steiger in an Academy Award—winning performance. The Sparta chief has no evidence but concludes that since Tibbs is a transient black who has $200 in his pocket, he must be the guy who did it. A call to Tibbs's police captain in Philadelphia proves otherwise, but the captain suggests to Gillespie that Tibbs stay and help him find the killer of the well-known Chicago businessman. Reluctantly, Gillespie asks Tibbs to do it since he hasn't got a clue who the murderer is and—even more reluctantly—Tibbs agrees. This pair of opposites must learn to get along and develop respect for each other, and in the end that becomes more important to the story and the audience than who actually committed the crime. There is a key scene in the film that produced different reactions from black and white theatergoers in many cities across America. The trail of evidence leads to the Sparta estate of a wealthy white businessman, Eric Endicott, who has deeply racist feelings himself covered with a thin veneer of politeness when he meets Tibbs. In a moment of anger, however, Endicott slaps Tibbs, only to have Tibbs immediately slap him back. To many who saw the film, Tibbs's action represented black America striking back at racism and bigotry. Many whites, especially southern whites, were just startled to see a black man slap a white man. To gauge audience reaction for themselves, Steiger and Poitier would slip into the back of the Capitol Theater in New York during the film's initial run. They reported that black theatergoers would often let out a cheer in reaction to the retaliatory slap, while white audience members either gasped or let out an audible "Oh!" (Harris, 2008b).

The film fit the times, coming three years after the passage of the Civil Rights Act, which was yet to be effectively enforced in some areas of the country. Outside of the southern states, tempers were boiling in urban areas like Detroit, Los Angeles, and New York, especially during the hot summer months. During the long, hot summer of 1967 alone, the country experienced 159 race riots, including the one most often mentioned because of its heavy violence: the Detroit riot, also known as the 12th Street Riot. It was against this turbulent backdrop that *In the Heat of the Night* made its appearance and provided hope to those who saw the film that white and black America might actually be able to get along after all. To some critics, however, the movie presented too simplistic of a solution to deep-seated racism. And others felt that the South had grown beyond the kind of racism depicted in the film. In thinking about this last critique, it is interesting to look at what *Slate* had to say in revisiting the film in 2008. Judge for yourself if the movie was presenting "old news."

"When *In the Heat of the Night* began shooting in 1966, it was in Illinois, not Mississippi," writer Mark Harris said. "Poitier, worried that he'd be a target, flatly refused to shoot in the South; he had been tailed by Klansmen when he had visited Greensboro, N.C., with Harry Belafonte, and a cross had recently been burned on the lawn of his wife's home in Pleasantville, N.Y."

"He finally agreed to a few days of tense location work in Tennessee, which were cut short when trouble-hunting rednecks drove into the lot of the motel where he was staying (Poitier told Jewison he was sleeping with a gun under his pillow). Though the movie may have seemed a step behind the news to critics in New York, it was undeniably of its moment in much of the rest of the country" (Harris, 2008b).

In the Heat of the Night beat out *The Graduate* in the race for the Academy Awards Best Picture of 1967 and was the 11th highest–grossing film of the year in box office revenues (Top U.S. Grossing Films of 1967, n.d.).

DR. STRANGELOVE

Before Americans began worrying about the war in Vietnam in the 1960s, they were worried about Russia and especially the threat of nuclear war with Russia. The worry was a carryover from the 1950s, but it had advanced beyond the communist witch hunt days of McCarthyism and was a fear focused on what nuclear weapons could do to America. Schools had been conducting "duck and cover" drills for years—as if they would do any good in the face of a nuclear blast and its fallout—and the country was pretty frightened. Certainly, the Cuban Missile Crisis of 1962 didn't help matters, when America and Russia came to the brink of nuclear war before President John F. Kennedy and Soviet Premier Nikita Khrushchev found a compromise path around the crisis at the last minute.

I was a senior in high school in 1964 and just two years earlier had voluntarily attended weekly evening sessions at the school on the threat of communism. Many of my classmates did the same, along with their parents who felt the threat of a Russian takeover was very real. Add the notion of nuclear annihilation into the mix and you had a country on edge. So it was that many of us did not know what to make of a movie that was premiering in January 1964 with the odd title of *Dr. Strangelove*. The part that made us shake our heads, though, was the rest of that title: *Or: How I Learned to Stop Worrying and Love the Bomb*. It appeared, from the title and the star Peter Sellers, that this was going to be some kind of weird comedy. But laughing at the threat of a nuclear bomb would take some getting used to. I don't recall anyone I knew ever laughing at it, anyway. Still, partly because we were curious and partly because of the film's star power (Sellers in multiple roles including the mad Dr. Strangelove, George C. Scott as one crazy General Buck Turgidson, and Sterling Hayden as unhinged General Jack D. Ripper), many of us went to see it. There are two times I remember in my younger conservative years where I laughed hard at films that I shouldn't have. One was *The Graduate*, and the other was *Dr. Strangelove*. I also realized that laughter was a way of dealing with an issue that was beyond my control. I know I wasn't alone in feeling that.

Directed by Stanley Kubrick, *Dr. Strangelove* asks the question of what might happen if a deranged general who has the power to launch a nuclear strike decides to do so. That, in itself, is the kind of question many Americans are still asking themselves. It is a universal and a logical question that deserves an answer. *Dr. Strangelove* provided one, suggesting a doomsday scenario might be triggered for both Russia and the United States, but if America struck first, it might go harder on the Russians. That would not have been easy medicine for 1960s America to swallow without what another film character of the decade, Mary Poppins, might call a spoonful of sugar. In this case, the sugar in *Strangelove* was a broad kind of humor, and it came from all the central characters, including both crazed generals, an equally paranoid Russian ambassador, and Dr. Strangelove himself. Favorite scene in the film for many? Watching a heroic B52 bomber pilot from Texas, played by Slim Pickens, free a trapped nuclear warhead from the plane and ride the reluctant bomb down through the clouds, waving his cowboy hat and shouting, "Yeehaw!!"

The film drew critical praise and was one of the movies from the 1960s selected by the National Film Registry Board for inclusion in the National Film Registry for cultural, historical, and aesthetic significance. The American Film Institute listed it as third on its list of 100 funniest films of all time. Still, many critics were worried about the film and even thought it could be dangerous. America in the 1960s was not as used to such universal satire as 21st-century America is.

That much is obvious from reading what famed *New York Times* film critic Bosley Crowther wrote when he said,

> My reaction to it is quite divided, because there is so much about it that is grand, so much that is brilliant and amusing, and must that is grave and dangerous. On the one hand, it cuts right to the soft pulp of the kind of military mind that is lost from all sense of reality in a maze of technical talk, and it shows up this type of mentality for the foolish and frightening thing it is. . . . On the other hand, I am troubled by the feeling, which runs all through the film, of discredit and even contempt for our whole defense establishment, up to and including the hypothetical Commander in Chief. . . . When virtually everybody turns up stupid or insane—or, what is worse, psychopathic—I want to know what this picture proves. (Crowther, 1964)

PLANET OF THE APES

What could a sci-fi movie about a distant planet where apes capture and enslave a human visitor have to say about the culture of the 1960s? Here is how California author Diana Gyler answers that question: "Simply put, it's that if we continue to devote our lives to power and greed, we are no better than animals; in face, we are worse than animals. Unthinking progress and an unbridled commitment to technology will not save us. It would sure lead to ruin. [This film] convinced me that we had to find a way to commit ourselves to compassionate care for the earth and each other" (Diana Glyer, Facebook comment, November 19, 2017).

Planet of Apes premiered in 1968 at a time when concern over the health of the environment, coupled with the worry over nuclear war, was on the minds of a lot of people. The film, directed by Franklin J. Schaffner, would give birth to several sequels that would run over the next several decades and into the 21st century. The film starred Charlton Heston who played George Taylor, an American astronaut who awakens from a sleep-induced state above a spacecraft that crashes onto an unknown planet. His light-speed voyage began on Earth in 1972, but now it is the year 3978. Still, he has aged only 18 months. When Taylor emerges from his craft, he sees the plant is controlled by intelligent apes who walk upright, talk, and have organized themselves into a caste system. They ruled over a population of primitive and mute human beings, and he is captured while the apes try to figure out who he is, where he came from, and what to do with him. The tribe is composed of sympathetic ones like Zira and Cornelius, and villains like Dr. Zaius. One of the primitive humans on the planet, Nova, becomes romantically involved with Taylor. Taylor knows he is in peril but learns to understand the apes and their civilization, still realizing he must flee to survive. Nova escapes with him and, while they are traveling along the East Coast, they come upon an ancient statue that turns out to be the devastated Statue of Liberty. That's when Taylor realizes he has been on Earth all along. Only it's an earth that was long ago destroyed by nuclear holocaust.

The film received critical and box office success as both an adventure film and a message film about what could happen to a people that refuse to follow a path of peace or lose sight of their environmental caretaking function. Commenting on the film's relevance to the times, the *Hollywood Reporter* said when it was released, "By its appeal to both the imagination and the intellect within a context of action and elemental adventure, in its relevance to the consuming issues of its time, and by the means with which it provides maximum entertainment topped with a sobering prediction of the future of human folly. . . . Planet of the Apes is that rare film which will transcend all age and social groupings, its multiple levels of appeal and meaning winning response in similar kind if not degree. At different moments, Planet of the Apes is Swiftian social satire, allegory, straight-faced science-fiction, and spoof." (THR Staff, 2017).

EASY RIDER

As the decade wore on, more and more young Americans went in search of America and of a set of values that seemed more constituent with what they had learned about the country's founding principles. Therefore, when a well-made movie came out in 1969 about two bikers who hit the road looking for that freer America, it's no wonder it was a hit. Such was the story of *Easy Rider*, a film by Dennis Hopper and starring him and Peter Fonda, the son of legendary movie star Henry Fonda. Fonda played Wyatt and Hopper was his biking pal Billy who peddle some drugs in Southern California, hide their cash in their motorcycle gas tanks, and turn their bikes east for a cross-country ride. Along the way the pair find the beauty of American landscape but also the ugliness of hatred among many who still aren't ready to acknowledge the value in hippies or their culture. Along with these, however, Wyatt and Billy find a fair number of people like themselves who are attempting alternative lifestyles, sometimes in hippie communes and sometimes alone or in pairs living off the land. Although the journey ends tragically for them, Wyatt and Billy resonated with audiences who saw the film and found kindred spirits in the two nonconformists.

Easy Rider affected viewers in many different ways, as most films do. Who one is when one goes into the theater will usually affect what one reads into—and gets out of—the film. But there were many theatergoers who did not identify with the hippie culture in the 1960s who still found the film to be a life-changing experience. For example, one such man from Great Britain wrote the following:

> *I cannot overstate the importance of this movie in my personal development. In 1969 I was eighteen and a freshman at Cambridge University. I was also a near-fundamentalist and a member of the Christian Union. Its officials decreed that* Easy Rider *was unsuitable for Christian viewing. I'd seem some enthusiastic reviews which made me curious. . . . So I went and it blew me away. I thought then and think now, that this is a magnificently perceptive commentary on hippie culture and one that only the medium of film*

can deliver. Naïve idealism is weighed against the squalid reality of drugs and indeed alcohol. Freedom is portrayed as often aimless, self-indulgent and downright boring. The underlying morality could be seen as puritanical: a celebration of the free-lovin' drop-out sixties, it aint. It's more of a wary, end-of-decade critique thereof. I would have thought there was much to commend it to the Christian Union moralisers, yet as ever, they couldn't see past the surface of drug abuse and loose women. . . . No one's ever going to tell me what I can or can't watch again. (Rjbrad, 2005)

Reflecting on the film, one younger critic wrote in 2004,

This film should be shown in every American history class in the United States. It not only showed the beauty of the country . . . but it also spoke about the people who reside in it. . . . We are afraid of what is different. We are a culture afraid of change, yet seek it so badly. . . . We thrive on the fact that we are the best country in the world, yet somebody shows any disassociation of routine, we are the first to question and get angry. I would dare say that we have moved so far from the '60s that I cannot see why our parents do not cry every day. Their generation was a free-spirited, mind-challenging culture that explored all possibilities no matter the cost. The experience was all they needed as a reward. (Andy, 2005)

BREAKFAST AT TIFFANY'S

The modern-day struggle for women's rights was just beginning in the 1960s, and it was slow going as can be seen by 21st-century depictions of the 1960s male-dominated business world in the acclaimed television series *Mad Men*. Sexual harassment and discrimination in the workplace were quite common, and women often seemed valued more for their looks than their abilities. The image of a strong, independent woman was beginning to take shape, however, and some films presented that image on screen. One doesn't have to read too much between the lines to see that image in the character of Holly Golightly, played by Audrey Hepburn, in the 1961 film version of author Truman Capote's book, *Breakfast at Tiffany's*, directed by Blake Edwards and written by George Axelrod. Also Holly was free-spirited to the point of seeming zany; here was definitely a young woman who was fully capable of handling life on her own and making her own decisions, bad as some of them were. Many other theatergoers, however, just reveled in the film as a great romantic comedy with a great musical score by the legendary Henry Mancini. The hit song, "Moon River," coming from the film didn't hurt either. The fact that Holly let men pay to help support her Manhattan lifestyle and the fact that her new best friend was a male prostitute were tolerated or overlooked because of the charm Audrey Hepburn injected into Holly. Here is how one writer, Suzy Underwood, reflected on the influence on her life of this film and of Holly Golightly:

> *My favorite actress of all time was Audrey Hepburn, and over the years I saw all of her movies. The one I liked best was* Breakfast at Tiffany's, *because she was so glamorous in that one, although I'm sure when I first saw it as a sixth-grader in 1962 I didn't understand most of the salient plot points. Still, she had that long cigarette holder, those great sunglasses, a cat called Cat, and she sat out on the fire escape of her New York apartment playing her guitar and singing "Moon River." As a result of the scene where she and George Peppard get a Crackerjacks ring engraved at Tiffany's, my friend Amy and I tried to have a silver cigarette lighter engraved there in 1968, but they wouldn't do it, stating that they only engraved items that were purchased there. I suppose after the movie came out, Tiffany's was inundated with people bringing things in that they wanted engraved.* (Underwood, 2017)

Underwood was certainly not alone in finding a kindred spirit in Holly Golightly or *Breakfast at Tiffany's*. The Library of Congress selected the film for inclusion in its National Film Registry for its cultural significance to its time period. A main theme of the film is the tension a young woman wrestles with between her desire for freedom and her need for security and stability. On the one hand, Holly is obsessed with the need to escape from places and people before they come to depend on her too much. This she did when she left her husband in Texas and fled to New York where she assumed a new identity. On the other hand, once there, she schemes to marry a wealthy man from Brazil although she doesn't love him. Her New York friend Paul, who falls in love with her, finds Holly exasperating as she seems to be in a never-ending state of flux, avoiding commitment and instead treating her life like she is on a constant holiday. Commitment, to her, endangers her prized freedom and individuality. She sees these as paramount and expresses love for her cat by granting the animal the same freedom and independence that she herself wants. She refuses to actually name the cat because she feels she doesn't "own" the cat that should be allowed to remain a wild thing. Still, despite the fear of being needed and of needing someone else, there is that dream about being financially secure and there is the fantasy that Holly will indeed one day have breakfast at Tiffany's.

OTHER SIGNIFICANT FILMS

These 10 films represent only a small sample of the culturally and historically significant films that depicted life, attitudes, and issues in the 1960s. Others were equally significant, and some drew equal or greater critical and popular praise. As noted earlier, the Library of Congress selected 84 films from this decade for its list of movies important in mirroring and influencing America. There are remaining 75 films on that list, including documentaries. A few of them are the following (Complete National Film Registry Listing, 2017):

- *In Cold Blood*
- *Who's Afraid of Virginia Woolf*
- *Flower Drum Song*
- *Bullitt*
- *Cool Hand Luke*
- *A Raisin in the Sun*
- *The Sound of Music*
- *The Wild Bunch*
- *Mary Poppins*
- *The Apartment*
- *Midnight Cowboy*
- *Bonnie and Clyde*
- *2001: A Space Odyssey*
- *Lawrence of Arabia*
- *Judgment at Nuremberg*
- *The Manchurian Candidate*
- *The Zapruder Film*
- *The Hustler*
- *Funny Girl*
- *Rosemary's Baby*
- *The Magnificent Seven*
- *The Pink Panther*
- *Once upon a Time in the West*
- *The Pawnbroker*
- *The Music Man*
- *Butch Cassidy and the Sundance Kid*
- *The Producers*
- *Ride the High Country*
- *The Birds*

AN ENLIGHTENING INSPIRATION

To many Americans, myself included, good films not only serve as entertainment but also have the added values of enlightenment and inspiration. Long after the film has ended, these are using the aspects that stick with us, cause us to reflect on scenes from those films, and maybe even help guide us through real-life challenges we are facing. Good films can cause us to do three things, generally in sequence as one builds on the previous. They can cause us to stop whatever else we're doing or thinking and *perceive* what's going on in the story among the characters. That's where the initial entertainment quality of the film and its plot come into play. Then, having gotten our attention, a good film invites us to *identify* with the characters; we can come to find parts of ourselves in them, even if some parts are only in our imagined self. Having identified with them, we come to care about them and that brings us deeper into the experience. Finally, we find ourselves so wrapped up in the story and the characters that we start the process of *discernment*: asking ourselves (a) what we think and feel about the way these characters make decisions and how they act in response and (b) whether we might handle the challenge in the same way and whether we feel we're even capable of doing so. There is a moral dimension associated with this discernment effect, and that may be the deepest impact the film has on us. In the end, it is these effects of identification and discernment that may well cause this film to become a kind of road map for us when we face similar real-life challenges.

This was certainly true for filmgoers in the turbulent 1960s who saw several of the films like the ones just listed. Many of the films caused us to probe social issues and concerns that we were reluctant to address for ourselves, even though we often had found ourselves wondering about them. If you grew up in a segregated town like I did, for example, how could films like *To Kill a Mockingbird*, *In the Heat of the Night*, and *Guess Who's Coming to Dinner* not be enlightening? If you couldn't relate in your hometown to African Americans, at least you could do it in a virtual sense by imagining yourself as a protagonist or antagonist in one of these films that focused on racial tensions. And you could see how the characters resolved their differences or at least came to a different understanding of each other.

The instruction about life came through for young people in films like *The Graduate*, *Easy Rider*, and even *Midnight Cowboy*. How many of us college students who wondered about what lay beyond graduation and questioned how we would navigate a world dominated by what we called "the establishment" didn't love the lead character of Benjamin Braddock in *The Graduate*? As he was finding answers to these life questions, so were we as we joined him vicariously in responding to the challenge.

From these and other films of the decade, we learned things we didn't know about love, heroism, justice, civil rights, war, the drug culture, and navigating a society increasingly characterized by the derisive term "plastic."

And for inspiration? How many of us found role models in Atticus Finch from *To Kill a Mockingbird*, Virgil Tibbs from *In the Heat of the Night*, Maria and Tony from *West Side Story*, or even Chris and Vin from *The Magnificent Seven*? I recall vividly Steve McQueen's character of Jake Holman in *The Sand Pebbles* and how he inspired me to join the navy as a young 20-year-old college student.

When you lived through a decade with so much tension, so many fears, so much frustration, and so many unanswered questions, good films were there to help guide you through the maze.

BIBLIOGRAPHY

Boeder, Laurie. "The Film Version of 'To Kill a Mockingbird,'" ThoughtCo .com, updated June 21, 2017, as accessed on November 18, 2017, at https://www.thoughtco.com/to-kill-a-mockingbird-728541

Box Office Mojo, n.d., as accessed on November 17, 2017, at http://www .boxofficemojo.com/movies/?id=graduate.htm

"Complete National Film Registry Listing," Library of Congress, as accessed on November 18, 2017, at https://www.loc.gov/programs/ national-film-preservation-board/film-registry/complete- national-film-registry-listing/

Crowther, Bosley. Movie Review: *West Side Story, New York Times*, October 19, 1961, as accessed on November 17, 2017, at http://www .nytimes.com/movie/review?res=EE05E7DF1739E774BC4152DFB 667838A679EDE

Crowther, Bosley. Movie Review: *Dr. Strangelove . . . Or How I Learned to Stop Worrying and Love the Bomb, New York Times*, January 31, 1964, as accessed on November 20, 2017, at http://www.nytimes .com/movie/review?res=EE05E7DF173DE367BC4950DFB766838F 679EDEhttp://www.nytimes.com/movie/review?res=EE05E7DF 173DE367BC4950DFB766838F679EDE

Ebert, Roger. *"Bob & Carol & Ted & Alice,"* Roger Ebert.com, December 22, 1969, as accessed on November 18, 2017, at https://www.rogere bert.com/reviews/bob-and-carol-and-ted-and-alice-1969

Ebert, Roger. *"To Kill a Mockingbird,"* Rogerebert.com, November 11, 2001, as accessed on April 23, 2018, at https://www.rogerebert .com/reviews/to-kill-a-mockingbird-2001

Fishko, Sarah. "The Real-Life Drama behind *West Side Story*," NPR, January 7, 2009, as accessed on November 17, 2017, at https://www .npr.org/2011/02/24/97274711/the-real-life-drama-behind-west-side-story

Fleishman, Jeffrey. "*Guess Who's Coming to Dinner* Is 50 and Racial Tension Is Still a Problem in America," *Los Angeles Times*, February 2, 2017, as accessed on November 19, 2017, at http://www .latimes.com/entertainment/movies/la-ca-guess-dinner-anniver sary-20170131-story.html

Harris, Mark. *Pictures at a Revolution: Five Films and the Birth of a New Hollywood*. New York: Penguin Press, 2008a, pp. 335–36.

Harris, Mark. "Guess Who's Coming to Solve Your Murder," *Slate*, February 5, 2008b, as accessed on November 20, 2017, at http://www .slate.com/articles/arts/dvdextras/2008/02/guess_whos_com-ing_to_solve_your_murder.html

McLaughlin, Katie. "'Mockingbird' Film at 50: Lessons on Tolerance, Justice, Fatherhood Hold True," CNN, February 3, 2012, as accessed on November 19, 2017, at http://www.cnn.com/2012/02/03/show biz/to-kill-a-mockingbird-50/index.html

Melin, Eric. "*The Graduate* Criterion Blu-Ray Packed with Insight into a Classic," Scene Stealers, February 27, 2016, as accessed on November 17, 2017, at http://www.scene-stealers.com/reviews/ the-graduate-criterion-blu-ray-packed-with-insight-into-a-classic/

"Rjbrad." "*Easy Rider:* Review and Ratings," Internet Movie Data Base (IMDB), September 25, 2005, as accessed on November 22, 2017, at http://www.imdb.com/title/tt0064276/reviews?=tt_ov_rt

THR Staff. "*Planet of the Apes:* THR's 1968 Review," March 27, 2017, *Hollywood Reporter*, as accessed on November 22, 2017, at https:// www.hollywoodreporter.com/review/planet-apes-1968-review-i-original-movie-973869

"Top U.S. Grossing Films of 1967," IMDB, n.d., as accessed on November 20, 2017, at http://www.imdb.com/search/title?sort=box office_gross_us&title_type=feature&year=1967,1967

Underwood, Suzy. "Hooray for Hollywood," *Retrospect*, August 17, 2017, as accessed on April 23, 2018, at https://www.myretrospect .com/?s=hooray+for+hollywood

"Wife-Swap Clubs: A 1960s Scandal," True Love Magazine, October, 1962, as reprinted on TruLove Stories, n.d., as accessed on November 18, 2017, at http://trulovestories.com/1960s-love-stories/ wife-swap-clubs-how-they-work/

BIBLIOGRAPHY

Anderson, Erika. "What Life Is Like When You're Born on a Commune," *Vanity Fair*, August 28, 2014, as accessed on March 28, 2018, at https://www.vanityfair.com/news/daily-news/2014/08/the-farm-born-on-a-commune

Bell, Janet Dewart. *Lighting the Fires of Freedom: African-American Women in the Civil Rights Movement.* New York: New Press, 2018.

Blauner, Andrew. *In Their Lives: Great Writers on Great Beatles Songs.* New York: Blue Rider Press, 2017.

Braine, Bruce, and Braine, Maryanne. *I've Got the Music in Me: A Fan's View of 1960s and 1970s Pop Music.* Seattle, WA: Amazon Digital Services, 2017.

Brooks, Allen. "Remembering the 1960s: Racism, Prison, and What Went Wrong?" July 24, 2012, as accessed on January 11, 2018, at https://ieet.org/index.php/IEET2/more/brooks20120724

Buckley, William F. *Miles Gone By: A Literary Autobiography.* Washington, DC: Regnery Publishers, 2004.

Callan, Jim. *America in the 1960s.* New York: Facts on File, 2009.

Carter, David. *Stonewall: The Riots That Sparked the Gay Revolution.* New York: St. Martin's, 2010.

Chambers, John Whiteclay. *The Oxford Companion to American Military History.* New York: Oxford University Press, 1999.

Chomsky, Noam. *American Power and the New Mandarins.* New York: Pantheon Books, 1969.

Chomsky, Noam. *The Responsibility of Intellectuals.* New York: The New Press, 2017.

Cox, Harvey. *The Secular City*. New York: MacMillan, 1965.

Degelman, Charles. "Digger Bread," *Retrospect*, December 14, 2015, as accessed on April 16, 2018, at https://www.myretrospect.com/?s=digger+bread

Degelman, Charles. "Rosewood, Petwer, Oak, Resistance, and a Friend," *Retrospect*, May 15, 2016, as accessed on April 16, 2018, at https://www.myretrospect.com/?s=rosewood+pewter

Dempsey, Liam. "How the Beatles Changed Music," Digital Media Academy, January 21, 2016, as accessed on April 27, 2018, at https://www.digitalmediaacademy.org/2016/01/21/how-the-beatles-changed-music-2/

Didion, Joan. *Slouching towards Bethlehem*. New York: Farrar, Straus, and Giroux, 1968.

Ebert, Roger. *The Great Movies*. New York: Three Rivers Press, 2003.

Farber, David. *The Age of Great Dreams: America in the 1960s*. New York: Hill and Wang, 1994.

Finder, Harry, and *The New Yorker*. *The 60s: The Story of a Decade*. New York: Random House, 2016.

Fishko, Sarah. "The Real-Life Drama behind West Side Story," National Public Radio, January 7, 2009, as accessed on November 17, 2017, at https://www.npr.org/2011/02/24/97274711/the-real-life-drama-behind-west-side-story

Fleishman, Jeffrey. "*Guess Who's Coming to Dinner* Is 50 and Racial Tension Is Still a Problem in America," *Los Angeles Times*, February 2, 2017, as accessed on November 19, 2017, at http://www.latimes.com/entertainment/movies/la-ca-guess-dinner-anniversary-20170131-story.html

Freeman, Tyson. "The 1960s: Prosperity Spurs Malls, Hotels, in Technicolor Dream," National Real Estate Investor, September 30, 1999, as accessed on January 19, 2018, at http://www.nreionline.com/mag/1960s-prosperity-spurs-malls-hotels-technicolor-dream

Friedman, Milton. *Capitalism and Freedom*. Chicago: University of Chicago Press, 2002.

Galbraith, John Kenneth. *The Affluent Society*. New York: Mariner Books, 1998.

Goldstein, Richard. "Drugs on Campus: Why Marijuana Use Soared in the 1960s," *Saturday Evening Post*, July/August 2017, as accessed on March 27, 2018, at http://www.saturdayeveningpost.com/2017/06/22/in-the-magazine/marijuana-use-surged-1960s.html

Grant, Tobin. "The Great Decline: 60 Years of Religion in One Graph," *Religion News Service*, January 27, 2014, as accessed on January 8, 2018, at https://religionnews.com/2014/01/27/great-decline-religion-united-states-one-graph/

Halberstam, David. *The Best and the Brightest*. New York: Ballantine, 1993.

Harris, Mark. *Pictures at a Revolution: Five Films and the Birth of a New Hollywood*. New York: Penguin Press, 2008.

Hart, Amy. "Religious Communities of 1960s America," as accessed on January 5, 2018, at http://digitalcommons.calpoly.edu/cgi/view content.cgi?article=1113&context=forum

Harvey, Paul. "Civil Rights Movements and Religion in America," Oxford Research Encyclopedias, August 2016, as accessed on January 8, 2018, at https://oxfordre.com/religion/view/10.1093/acrefore/9780199340378.001.0001/acrefore-9780199340378-e-492

Hilton, Robin. "The Sound of a Generation," National Public Radio, June 6, 2008, as accessed on October 19, 2009, at http://www.npr.org/sections/allsongs/2008/06/the_sound_of_a_generation.html

Hoskyns, Barney. *Beneath the Diamond Sky: Haight-Ashbury 1965–1970*. New York: Simon & Schuster, 1997.

Hughes, John. *Invisible Now: Bob Dylan in the 1960s*. Abingdon: Routledge, 2016.

Isserman, Maurice, and Kazin, Michael. *America Divided: The Civil War of the 1960s*. New York: Oxford University Press, 2008, 251.

Johnson, Haynes. "1968 Democratic Convention: The Bosses Strike Back," *Smithsonian* magazine, August 2008, as accessed on March 27, 2018, at https://www.smithsonianmag.com/history/1968-democratic-convention-931079/

Kahre, Ken. "Did the Vietnam War Make Profits for the US Economy in Any Way?" November 11, 2017, Quora, as accessed on April 24, 2018, at https://www.quora.com/Did-the-Vietnam-War-make-profits-for-the-US-economy-in-any-way

Kamienski, Lucasz. "The Drugs That Built a Super Soldier," *Atlantic*, April 18, 2016, as accessed on March 23, 2018, at https://www.theatlantic.com/health/archive/2016/04/the-drugs-that-built-a-super-soldier/477183/

Karnow, Stanley. *Vietnam: A History*. New York: Penguin, 1997.

Killens, John Oliver. *And Then We Heard the Thunder*. Washington, DC: Howard University Press, 1984.

Killens, John Oliver. *Youngblood*. Athens: University of Georgia Press, 1982.

Landsperger, A. David "Should I Stay or Should I Go?" October 3, 2017, *Retrospect*, as accessed on April 16, 2018, at https://www.myretrospect.com/?s=should+i+stay+or+should+i+go

Leonard, Hal Corporation. *Songs of the 1960s*. New York: Hal Leonard, 2015.

Levy, Peter B. *The Great Uprising: Race Riots in Urban America during the 1960s*. Cambridge: Cambridge University Press, 2018.

Lewsey, Fred. "The Musical Ages of Modern Man: How Our Taste in Music Changes over a Lifetime," Cambridge University, October 15, 2013, as accessed on October 19, 2017, at http://www.cam.ac.uk/research/news/the-musical-ages-of-modern-man-how-our-taste-in-music-changes-over-a-lifetime

MacLean, Nancy. *The Women's Movement: 1945–2000*. New York: Bedford/ St. Martin's, 2008.

Marcuse, Herbert, and Leiss, William. *The Essential Marcuse: Selected Writings of Philosopher and Social Critic Herbert Marcuse*. Boston: Beacon Press, 2007.

Matthews, Chris. "Americans Think the Economy Was Better in the 1960s," *Forbes*, May 15, 2016, as accessed on February 20, 2018, at http://fortune.com/2016/05/13/americans-economists-1960s/

Matthews, Dylan. "Americans Think John F. Kennedy Was One of Our Greatest Presidents. He Wasn't," *Washington Post*, November 22, 1963, as accessed on May 19, 2019, at https://www.washington post.com/news/wonk/wp/2013/11/22/americans-think-john-f-kennedy-was-one-of-our-greatest-presidents-he-wasnt/

McLaughlin, Katie. "'Mockingbird' Film at 50: Lessons on Tolerance, Justice, Fatherhood Hold True," CNN, February 3, 2012, as accessed on November 19, 2017, at http://www.cnn.com/2012/02/03/show biz/to-kill-a-mockingbird-50/index.html

Menand, Louis. "Out of Bethlehem: The Radicalization of Joan Didion," *New Yorker*, August 24, 2015, as accessed on April 1, 2018, at https:// www.newyorker.com/magazine/2015/08/24/out-of-bethlehem

Moretta, John Anthony. *The Hippies: A 1960s History*. Jefferson, NC: McFarland, 2017.

Nelson, Laura J. "Digital Projection Has Drive-In Theaters Reeling," *Los Angeles Times*, January 19, 2013, as accessed on May 19, 2019, at https://www.latimes.com/entertainment/la-xpm-2013-jan-19-la-et-ct-drive-ins-digital-20130120-story.html

Nourman, Tony, Hurn, David, and Doggett, Peter. *The 1960s Photographed by David Hurn*. London: Reel Art Press, 2015.

O'Brien, Tim. *The Things They Carried*. New York: Mariner Books, 2009.

Pitney, David Howard. *Martin Luther King Jr., Malcolm X, and the Civil Rights Struggle of the 1950s and 1960s*. New York: Bedford/St. Martin's, 2004.

Rielly, Edward J. *The 1960s: American Popular Culture through History*. Westport, CT: Greenwood, 2003.

Roach, John. "Apollo Anniversary: Moon Landing Inspired World," National Geographic News, July 16, 2004, as accessed on March 24, 2018, https://byjohnroach.com/writings/space/apollo-anniversary-moon-landing-inspired-world.html

Romney, Kat. "Women in the Workforce in the Mid-1960s," December 20, 2016, Letterpile.com, as accessed on April 17, 2018, at https:// letterpile.com/memoirs/Women-in-the-Workforce-in-the-mid-1960s

Shutkin, John. "Mustang Katy," *Retrospect*, November 14, 2017, as accessed on April 24, 2018, at https://www.myretrospect.com/stories/ mustang-katy/

Siemaszko, Corky. "Birmingham Erupted into Chaos in 1963 as Battle for Civil Rights Exploded in the South," *New York Daily News*, May 5, 2012, as accessed on February 21, 2018, at https://www.nydaily news.com/news/national/birmingham-erupted-chaos-1963-battle-civil-rights-exploded-south-article-1.1071793

Sontag, Susan. *Essays of the 1960s and 70s*. New York: Library of America, 2013.

St. John, Rick. *Tiger Bravo's War*. New York: Currahee Press, 2017.

Stars, Laurie. *She's So Fine: Reflections on Whiteness, Femininity, Adolescence, and Class in 1960s Music*. Abingdon: Routledge, 2010.

Teicher, Jordan G. "Why Is Vatican II So Important?" National Public Radio, October 10, 2012, as accessed on January 5, 2018, at https://www .npr.org/2012/10/10/162573716/why-is-vatican-ii-so-important

Thompson, Hunter S., and Steadman, Ralph. *Fear and Loathing in Las Vegas*. New York: Vintage, 1998.

Thoreau, Henry David. *Walden*. Princeton, NJ: Princeton University Press, 2014.

Tucker, Carol. "The 1950s—Powerful Years for Religion," USC News, June 16, 1997, as accessed on March 27, 2018, at https://news.usc .edu/25835/The-1950s-Powerful-Years-for-Religion/

Underwood, Suzy. "Hooray for Hollywood," *Retrospect*, August 17, 2017, as accessed on April 23, 2018, at https://www.myretrospect.com/ stories/hooray-for-hollywood/

Underwood, Suzy. "Teach Your Children," *Retrospect*, November 7, 2017, as accessed on May 9, 2018, at https://www.myretrospect.com/ stories/teach-your-children/

Underwood, Suzy. "The Universe Is Ablaze with Changes," *Retrospect*, August 10, 2016, as accessed on May 9, 2018, at https://www .myretrospect.com/?s=the+universe+is+ablaze

Varga, George. "Woodstock Reassessed, 45 Years Later," August 8, 2014, *San Diego Union-Tribune*, August 8, 2014, as accessed on January 28, 2018, at https://www.sandiegouniontribune.com/entertainment/ music/sdut-woodstock-forty-five-years-later-2014aug08-story.html

Walker, Daniel. "Rights in Conflict," Report to the National Commission on the Causes and Prevention of Violence, December 1, 1968, as accessed on January 1, 2018, at http://chicago68.com/ricsumm.html

Willis, Jim. *Daily Life behind the Iron Curtain*. Santa Barbara, CA: Greenwood Press, 2013.

Wolfe, Tom. *The Electric Kool-Aid Acid Test*. New York: Picador, 2008.

Wolfe, Tom. *The Right Stuff*. New York: Bantam Books, 1984.

Zussman, John Unger "Secret Sauce," *Retrospect*, August 10, 2017, as accessed on April 18, 2018, at https://www.myretrospect.com/?s= secret+sauce

Zussman, Patricia. "Forbidden Fruit," *Retrospect*, December 14, 2015, as accessed on April 16, 2018, at https://www.myretrospect.com/ stories/forbidden-fruit/

INDEX

About the Author

JIM WILLIS is a veteran journalist and professor emeritus at California's Azusa Pacific University. He has authored or coauthored 16 books covering the fields of journalism and the news media, history, and football. Willis holds the PhD in journalism from the University of Missouri, is a former reporter and editor with *The Oklahoman* and *The Dallas Morning News*, and divides his time between Southern California and Kentucky. As a journalist he has covered the Oklahoma City bombing in 1995, the major anniversaries of the fall of the Berlin Wall, the Syrian refugee crisis in Germany, and the 500th anniversary of the Reformation in Germany. He currently contributes to *Christianity Today* magazine. Willis has conducted numerous lecture tours in Europe for the U.S. State Department, speaking about American media coverage of issues. He is married to a gifted musician, Anne Kindred Willis, and has two sons, three stepdaughters, and six grandchildren.